LONDON YOUTH, RELIGION, AND POLITICS

London Youth, Religion, and Politics

*Engagement and Activism from
Brixton to Brick Lane*

DANIEL NILSSON DEHANAS

UNIVERSITY PRESS

Great Clarendon Street, Oxford, OX2 6DP,
United Kingdom

Oxford University Press is a department of the University of Oxford.
It furthers the University's objective of excellence in research, scholarship,
and education by publishing worldwide. Oxford is a registered trade mark of
Oxford University Press in the UK and in certain other countries

© Daniel Nilsson DeHanas 2016

The moral rights of the author have been asserted

First Edition published in 2016

All rights reserved. No part of this publication may be reproduced, stored in
a retrieval system, or transmitted, in any form or by any means, without the
prior permission in writing of Oxford University Press, or as expressly permitted
by law, by licence or under terms agreed with the appropriate reprographics
rights organization. Enquiries concerning reproduction outside the scope of the
above should be sent to the Rights Department, Oxford University Press, at the
address above

You must not circulate this work in any other form
and you must impose this same condition on any acquirer

Published in the United States of America by Oxford University Press
198 Madison Avenue, New York, NY 10016, United States of America

British Library Cataloguing in Publication Data
Data available

Library of Congress Control Number: 2015958675

ISBN 978-0-19-874367-5

Links to third party websites are provided by Oxford in good faith and
for information only. Oxford disclaims any responsibility for the materials
contained in any third party website referenced in this work.

Acknowledgments

I would not have been able to write this book without the generous support of various colleagues and friends who deserve my thanks and acknowledgment. The first mention must go to my academic mentors Christian Smith, Grace Davie, and Tariq Modood. This project began its life as a PhD thesis I completed at the University of North Carolina at Chapel Hill. I am grateful to my supervisor Christian Smith, whose crystal clear prose in his many books serves as an inspiration for my own writing. From the beginning Chris encouraged me to take on an ambitious doctoral project rather than just "filling a gap." I was fortunate that at the time I was developing my PhD proposal, Chris had invited the eminent British sociologist of religion Grace Davie to UNC to give two lectures. Grace's lectures introduced me to paradoxes of religion in Britain that I had never considered. She was kind enough to spend much of the evening over dinner offering advice on my research and on the prospect of moving to Britain. In the time before the move I also became well acquainted with the books of Tariq Modood in the UNC library. These gave me my first real insight into the social disadvantages and political prospects of British South Asian and British Caribbean people, and led to my interest in comparing these two groups. I was fortunate to later come to know Tariq in the very fruitful postdoctoral years I spent at the Centre for the Study of Ethnicity and Citizenship at Bristol University. I am greatly indebted to Chris, Grace, and Tariq for their formative influences and continued support over the years.

I am grateful to the members of my UNC PhD thesis committee for their guidance and their trust in letting me loose on a "risky" thesis. Lisa Pearce tutored me in research methods and gave me a first foray into ethnography in Carrboro, North Carolina. Jackie Hagan alerted me to the need for research on second-generation youth and introduced me to central ideas in migration studies. Margarita Mooney provided extensive feedback that helped shape my overall narrative. And Krishan Kumar, a Londoner himself, bolstered my confidence that this research could make valuable contributions to British debates. I am also grateful to many other American professors, mentors, and friends who have helped shape my thinking over the years. To name only a few: Michael Emerson, Jane Gullickson, Mikki Hebl, Charlie Kurzman, Ijlal Naqvi, Andy Perrin, and Steve Vaisey.

Moving to London in the summer of 2007 was an exhilarating experience, largely because of the ready support of friends and colleagues. I owe much to Fiona Adamson, Ed Bacon, Gordon Lynch, Tariq Modood, Therese O'Toole, and Natasha Warikoo who so warmly welcomed me in my early years in British academia, and to my many friends at the BSA Sociology of Religion Study Group (SocRel) which would quickly become my disciplinary hearth and home.

Thank you to all of the young men and women in Brixton and Tower Hamlets who contributed with an interview or otherwise helped me with this research, giving of their time and making this such an enjoyable experience. I have kept up with some of you, but if you are reading this and we have lost touch please feel free to contact me again. Thank you also to church and mosque leaders Jamie Gittens, Ehsan Abdullah Hannan, Mark Liburd, and Sajjad Miah (mentioned in Chapters 4 and 5) who graciously agreed to be interviewed and quoted, and who helped me access their congregations.

In this book I have chosen to retain the American English spellings that I used in my original field notes and writing. I hope that these spellings will subtly yet consistently convey the outsider status I felt while conducting this research as a newcomer to Britain. By now I have lived nearly a decade in London, and my sense of "outsider" status has faded over time.

The research expenses for this study were generously funded by the US National Science Foundation (SES-0902878), a UNC Smith Graduate Research Grant, and the National Study of Youth and Religion. Over the years I have presented versions of this research for various invited talks, conferences, and workshops. I am grateful to my hosts at these events and to all who asked questions that helped take my thinking further. Thank you also to my students at King's College London in the 2014/15 academic year for offering such helpful feedback on the book's title or on sections of the text.

Many people have read all or part of this book in different forms or have otherwise provided significant feedback as critical friends. I would like to thank: Humayun Ansari, Rebecca Catto, Grace Davie, Abby Day, John Eade, Jon Fox, David Garbin, Mathew Guest, Jacqueline Maria Hagan, Sadek Hamid, Warwick Hawkins, Keith Hayward, Titus Hjelm, Damian Howard SJ, David Jacobson,

Acknowledgments

Stephen Howard Jones, Krishan Kumar, Stuart Long, Sam Longair, Gordon Lynch, Seán McLoughlin, Tariq Modood, Margarita Mooney, Jørgen Nielsen, Sara Nilsson DeHanas, Alex Oldfield, Therese O'Toole, Lisa Pearce, Christian Smith, Jonathan D. Smith, Miri Song, Tim Strangleman, Anna Strhan, Manuel Vásquez, Natasha Warikoo, Matthew Wilkinson, and Linda Woodhead.

I am especially grateful to Sam Longair who read all of the original text and spurred me on to complete it, and to John Eade who read the full book more than once, offering extensive suggestions which have improved it significantly. Thank you to my editors Tom Perridge and Karen Raith and to the staff of OUP for their efforts and guidance. Thank you also to my parents Steve and Sinikka whose own adventures in London, the Middle East, and elsewhere set in motion my interests in the topics covered in this book. Finally, an acknowledgments page cannot adequately express my deep gratitude to my wife Sara for all she has contributed to my work and life over the years. Without your steadfast love and support, completing this would never have been possible.

Contents

List of Figures   xi
List of Tables   xiii

   Introduction   1
1. Losing Faith in the State?   20
2. Muslim First   54
3. Looking for Black in the Union Jack   81
4. Rooted Religion   109
5. New Religion   138
6. The Building Blocks of Social Change   165
7. Believing Citizens   188

References   207
Index   225

List of Figures

0.1.	Passengers on the *Empire Windrush*, 1948	8
0.2.	Brixton Market on Electric Avenue	11
0.3.	Whitechapel Road Market in the East End	13
1.1.	A "Boycott Israeli Goods" campaign sticker at a pedestrian crossing on Whitechapel Road	45
2.1.	The self-identification ranking exercise	55
3.1.	A young man walking along Atlantic Road, Brixton	94
4.1.	The Universal Pentecostal Church on Acre Lane, Brixton	111
4.2.	The Brick Lane Mosque and Christ Church Spitalfields	112
4.3.	The Brixton Seventh Day Adventist Church, Santley Street	122
4.4.	The Brick Lane Mosque	129
4.5.	The Altab Ali protest on Brick Lane, 1978	133
5.1.	Ruach Ministries	144
5.2.	The East London Mosque and London Muslim Centre after Friday prayers	150
5.3.	Relationships between subjective experience, objective reality, and action	161
6.1.	The Seventh Day Adventist LIVE march	166
6.2.	Personal faith as a causal mechanism of individual and social change	173
6.3.	The Big IFtar charity event	177
6.4.	Solidarity through ritual as a causal mechanism of individual and social change	179
7.1.	Two young men on Electric Avenue, Brixton	191

List of Tables

1.1.	Hypotheses of youth civic engagement	28
1.2.	Political literacy measure	32
1.3.	Political participation measure	33
1.4.	Jamaican and Bengali youth political literacy, by religiosity	35
1.5.	Jamaican and Bengali youth political participation, by religiosity	38
1.6.	Brands that Bengali youth boycott	43
1.7.	Brands that Jamaican youth boycott	44
2.1.	Theorized styles of second-generation youth self-identification	60
2.2.	Labels used in the self-identification ranking exercise	63
3.1.	Self-identifications chosen "first"	102
4.1.	Religious organizations visited for participant observation	118
4.2.	Mega-churches in Britain, with estimated weekly attendance (2005)	119
7.1.	"What is the biggest problem in your local area?"	189

Introduction

"Can Europe be the same with different people in it?" This question is the subtitle of a book by Christopher Caldwell in which he writes on the cultural implications of Muslim immigration in Europe.[1] Caldwell sees Muslims in Europe as a characteristically different people who are beginning to replace Europe's populations and institutions with their own. As they become citizens in European states, he believes, these states will gradually but irrevocably shift beyond recognition as European.

The "Muslim question"—on Muslim cultural practices, integration, or extremism—tends to dominate European debates on religion in public life. Caldwell's book provides just one version of this question, posed in many different guises since September 11, 2001. Questions on Muslims are asked in earnest by a broad range of journalists. They are raised by public intellectuals across a wide ideological spectrum, from Samuel Huntington to Michael Walzer.[2] In an ever-growing list of local and national political debates, such as on headscarves in France, minarets in Switzerland, or extremism in Britain, issues involving Muslims have precisely defined the borders of what can or cannot be deemed acceptable. These domestic

---

[1] Caldwell's (2009) European edition of the book is *Reflections on a Revolution in Europe: Can Europe Be the Same with Different People in It?* which is published by Allen Lane. In North America the subtitle is simply "Immigration, Islam, and the West" and the book is published by Doubleday.

[2] The late Samuel P. Huntington was a conservative political scientist, well known for his "clash of civilizations" (1993) thesis in which he, among other things, postulated that deep cultural fault lines lie at the root of violent conflicts between an Islamic "civilization" and its neighbors. Michael Walzer is a left-leaning political theorist who after the *Charlie Hebdo* affair has called for greater courage from the left to oppose what he terms "Islamist zealotry" (2015).

concerns seem further exacerbated by geopolitical threats, including the recruitment by ISIS of Europe's most "vulnerable." Considering all of these possible dimensions to the Muslim question, perhaps political scientist Anne Norton is right to argue that it is the definitive contemporary test of our humanity. "The Jewish question was fundamental for politics and philosophy in the Enlightenment," she writes. "In our time, as the Enlightenment fades, the Muslim question has taken its place."³

Norton's phrase "as the Enlightenment fades" is a perceptive one. In post-Enlightenment times, Europe's supposed secular settlements can seem threatened not only by immigrant Muslims but also by other fervent new arrivals, such as Pentecostal Christians. The appeal of assertive "new atheist" thinkers such as Richard Dawkins and Sam Harris reveals a growing constituency that has become uneasy with any and all forms of public religion.

I began my work on this book with the intuition that the Muslim question, or any religious question, as weighty as these may seem, will not get us far in understanding the place of immigrants and their descendants in Europe. Religion certainly is important. Indeed it is a central focus of this book. But asking if Islam (or public religion) can be reconciled with Europe is a rhetorical question. It is bound to highlight differences rather than build understanding.

In this book one of my main aims is to take us beyond the Muslim question to questions that can be more tangibly answered. I have built the book on extensive comparative research that sets Muslims in context with others. I focus on a group at the center of many European public debates: the children of immigrants. This group is often called the second generation, meaning that they follow on from their immigrant parents who were the first generation in Europe. I spent about two years coming to know second-generation 18- to 25-year-olds in one city, London, UK. I attended their places of worship, walked the streets where they have grown up, and sat down with many for interviews and informal conversations. I was able to study in an in-depth and qualitative way how sixty of these young second-generation Londoners are emerging into adulthood and becoming engaged or disengaged as British citizens.

³ Norton (2013).

Introduction

I broaden the lens beyond Muslims in this book to also look at second-generation Christians and non-religious young people. Even a decade ago, there were probably more than one thousand research publications and popular books written about Muslims in Europe[4] and the steady growth of this literature continues. This book contributes to that important field. Yet the European research tradition on Christianity among immigrants and subsequent generations is much thinner and less well developed. This research disparity is unfortunate because it results in lopsided accounts of European religion and migration. The number of Christian migrants in the European Union (26 million) is double the number of Muslim migrants (13 million), if we include those moving across intra-European borders, such as Poles and Romanians. Even when only migrants who have come to Europe from outside the continent are considered, Christians slightly outnumber Muslims: 13 million to 12 million, respectively.[5]

By conducting research with Christians, Muslims, and some non-religious youth, I have been able to compare them across religious traditions, showing how they are (or are not) influenced differently by particular strains of Islam or Christianity. I can also discern general influences of religiosity, or broader trends that are not related to religion at all. Perhaps most importantly, in taking a comparative approach I can more accurately represent the varieties of religious experience among Europe's second-generation youth.

Only by opening our view beyond Muslims alone can we judge whether Muslim youth really are an exceptional case that requires urgent attention. It may be, instead, that some young Muslims' struggles and reactions are common to the wider experience of migrant communities and their religions. Or perhaps the answer is somewhere in between—there could be aspects of the situation of second-generation young Muslims that are unique (as there could be for second-generation young Christians), but these do not constitute an unreasonable or unbridgeable gulf of difference with the rest of Britain and Europe.

In this book I put forward an alternative question about second-generation London youth, which I call the "civic question": *"What kinds of citizens are they becoming?"* This new question gets to the

---

[4] Bujis and Rath (2003).
[5] Pew Research Center (2012: 17). These proportions are changing to some extent with the current refugee crisis (since 2015) in which most of the new refugees and migrants are Muslims.

heart of legitimate concerns about civic integration and political participation that can sometimes underlie the Muslim question. The civic question improves our understanding because it is not merely abstract but can be addressed through empirical research, without expecting one group to be outliers from the outset.

To address the civic question I compare British second-generation youth of two different immigrant origins, British Bangladeshis (predominantly Muslim) and British Jamaicans (largely Christian). These two immigrant groups have had important roles in Britain's imperial and post-imperial history. With these two groups as touchstones, I can capture something of (though not fully address) common concerns about the broader ethnic populations they represent. The most recent Census, in 2011, found that 11.3 percent of the population of England and Wales are of non-White or mixed ethnicities. The largest non-White ethnic populations are South Asians[6] (Pakistani, Indian, and Bangladeshi) who together compose 5.9 percent of the population, Blacks (Caribbean and African) who compose 2.8 percent, and mixed race at 1.8 percent. Bangladeshis and Jamaicans are large and historically important ethnic minority populations in London. These two groups provide us with leverage for understanding issues faced by Britain's South Asian, Black, and mixed-race populations more broadly.

The problems that Black British and British South Asians face are legion. As ethnic sub-populations, they are the most economically deprived in Britain and have the lowest levels of educational achievement.[7] Most relevant to this book on the civic question, research studies have found that Black Caribbeans have the lowest levels of participation in British elections.[8] The effect appears to be particularly acute among Black youth.[9] Initiatives such as Operation Black Vote are attempting to respond to this democratic deficit and to mobilize young Black voters. It is also possible that religion could

---

[6] In Britain, historic immigration from Asia has predominantly been from the Indian subcontinent due to colonial ties. For this reason, the general term "Asian" is typically used instead of "South Asian." I choose to use "South Asian" in this book to provide clarity, because the term "Asian" in the North American experience of immigration most often connotes ethnic origins in East Asia.

[7] CoDE (2014); Modood (2005).   [8] Sanders et al. (2014).

[9] The Sanders et al. (2014) study mentions "exploratory evidence" of this age effect. The lower levels of electoral participation among British ethnic minority young people have been a consistent theme in previous studies (e.g. Purdam et al. 2002; Saggar 1998).

Introduction 5

help address this issue—particularly Christianity, which is widespread in the Black British population. Can religion motivate and structure the civic engagement of Black British youth? Or does religion more often influence Black youth into otherworldliness, alienation, or simply apathy? These are questions for which we need better answers.

Questions are also frequently asked about citizenship among British South Asian Muslims.[10] Worries about their participation in British civic life first became nationally widespread during the protests and book burnings of the 1989 Rushdie Affair.[11] In the wake of the civil disturbances in Oldham, Burnley, and Bradford in summer 2001, Ted Cantle led a government-commissioned review team which argued that South Asians seem to be living "parallel lives" set apart from the rest of Britain.[12] The London bombings of July 7, 2005 then raised new fears of a "home-grown" terrorist threat from youth in insular Pakistani and Bangladeshi enclaves. Trevor Phillips, then Chair of the Equality and Human Rights Commission, stated that in Britain "we are sleepwalking our way towards segregation."[13] After the 2007 introduction of the CONTEST counterterrorism strategy and its controversial Prevent "hearts and minds" approach (revised in 2011), concerns about Muslim "extremism" continue to remain a fixture of British public debates. Recent episodes highlighting this concern include the murder of army drummer Lee Rigby in Woolwich in 2013, investigations into alleged Islamist "Trojan Horse" plots to wrest control of schools in Birmingham and Tower Hamlets, and ISIS' recruitment of young Britons as foreign fighters in Syria and Iraq.

These issues about South Asian youth, like those about Black African and Caribbean youth, can be framed as issues of disengagement from the nation of citizenship. Some questions that highlight commonly raised concerns are: Does religion (particularly Islam) contribute to the ghettoizing and separation of communities from

---

[10] Because such a large proportion of South Asians in Britain have their origins in Pakistan or Bangladesh, a slight majority of the British South Asian population is Muslim. Many British Indians and other British South Asians practice other faiths such as Hinduism, Sikhism, or Christianity.
[11] Weller (2009); Werbner (2002).   [12] Cantle (2001).
[13] Phillips renamed the Commission for Racial Equality as the Equality and Human Rights Commission, partly reflecting a change in philosophy to more classically liberal notions of equality.

British national life and culture? Is religion leading youth to take on radical and violent ideologies? Or can religious influence be more benign, more varied, or perhaps more positive when it promotes stable identities and practices?

To address these questions of everyday citizenship, I conducted sixty in-depth interviews with young people along with dozens of interviews with local leaders and community observers. All of the youth were aged 18 to 25 at the time of interview, placing them in a period in their lives that can be called *emerging adulthood*.[14] As such, many of them were working through the issues of education, employment, and long-term relationships that are common to people of this life stage. Emerging adulthood is the time period in which youth are first able to vote (age 18 in Britain). The political attitudes and preferences that are formed in these relatively early years of political enfranchisement can solidify and last a lifetime. In this book I will tend to refer to the young people I interviewed as "youth," simply for ease of expression. Yet it is important to remember that they are in a transitional period of life, a period that falls somewhere between youth and adulthood. The term "emerging adulthood" captures this well.

Along with being in a certain age cohort, the youth in this study are members of the *second generation*. With very few exceptions, all sixty youth that I interviewed in-depth were born in Britain to immigrant parents and are legal British citizens.[15] Second-generation youth have been a focal point for much contemporary social scientific research, partly because their integration and citizenship activities can be read as a barometer of the future outcomes for their ethnic groups. While

---

[14] Arnett (2000).

[15] In defining the second generation as the children of immigrants, born in Britain, I follow an extensive research literature (e.g. Crul and Vermeulen 2003; Kasinitz et al. 2009; Portes and Rumbaut 2001). The youth I interviewed also most often thought of the second generation in this way, perhaps because they have internalized media and policy language. For example, without my own mention of the term, a Bangladeshi youth named Yasmin (introduced in Chapter 2) offered her own description: "Being a second generation, my connection to my ancestors has my parents between the two." The exceptions (those who were not in the second generation) in my research were: one Jamaican female and one Bangladeshi female in the third generation, and a Jamaican female, Jamaican male, and Bangladeshi male who are in the 1.5 generation because they came to the UK during childhood. These five exceptional cases were generally more similar than different when compared to their second-generation peers.

many immigrants of the first generation naturally retain their closest feelings of cultural and family connection with their country of origin, their second-generation children are socialized in Britain and are educated in British schools. Thus the second generation, more than the first, might be expected to have a cultural affinity with Britain and to contribute to it as a nation. Some scholars are concerned that second-generation failings in integration and citizenship could herald problems that will last for generations to come.[16]

WHY STUDY JAMAICANS AND BANGLADESHIS? WHY IN BRIXTON AND THE EAST END?

I chose to focus this book on Jamaicans and Bangladeshis primarily because these two groups provide for a well-matched political and sociological comparison. Both have played important roles in London's immigration history. The Bangladeshi Muslims of Tower Hamlets constitute the highest proportion of Muslims of any local area in Britain, and have played a major role in the public face of British Islam.[17] The Jamaicans of Brixton, while not as ethnically concentrated, have also been highly influential in British religious and cultural arenas. Both ethnic populations are at comparable points in their migration histories. Both have large populations of second-generation youth. Jamaican and Bangladeshi youth each face problems that are typical to inner cities, including drugs, violent crime, socio-economic deprivation, and educational disadvantage. Next I briefly profile the histories of both groups in these particular areas of London.

Jamaican immigration to Britain was symbolically inaugurated with the "Windrush generation." The story of their arrival has become a defining episode for modern Britain.[18] In 1948, the British

---

[16] Leiken (2012).

[17] Tower Hamlets is 34.5 percent Muslim according to the 2011 Census, which is the highest percentage of any local authority in England and Wales. Bangladeshis are 32 percent of the population of Tower Hamlets and, because they are predominantly Muslim, they account for a significant majority of Muslims in the borough.

[18] On the *Windrush* arrival and its legacy, see Phillips and Phillips (1998). For a critical historiography that brings further nuance to our understanding of the event, see Mead (2009).

Nationality Act made the first legal distinction between citizens in Britain and those who lived in Britain's colonies, who became Citizens of the United Kingdom and Colonies (CUKC).[19] In the same year Britain was suffering from a post-war labor shortage. Royal Mail placed an advertisement in a Jamaican daily newspaper for the *Empire Windrush* steamship, which would carry passengers and commercial goods from Jamaica to Britain. A total of 490 men and two women bought tickets and undertook the journey from Jamaica. The *Windrush* voyage was highly publicized in Britain—even as it sailed, it provoked vigorous debate about immigration in Parliament. When the *Windrush* arrived at Tilbury Docks on June 22, 1948, the image of scores of Black Caribbean passengers aboard became a symbol of Britain's transition into a multi-ethnic society (Figure 0.1).

Figure 0.1. Passengers on the *Empire Windrush*, 1948. © Thurrock Museum. Used by permission of Thurrock Museum and Black Cultural Archives

---

[19] Until 1948, all members of British colonies were in practice entitled to the same citizenship rights and participation as "native" Britons. In fact, the first MP from the Indian subcontinent was Dadabhai Naoroji, elected by a London constituency to the House of Commons in 1892 (Anwar 2001). The British Nationality Act did not actually institute substantive changes to this citizenship arrangement, but was instead a precursor to the more significant Commonwealth Immigrants Act of 1962.

The Windrush generation arrived in a society largely unwilling to welcome them. In the years following 1948, accommodation notices began to include a phrase that captured xenophobic feelings that were widespread at the time: "No dogs, blacks, or Irish." Such were the difficulties of finding accommodation that 200 *Windrush* passengers were compelled to live in the Clapham South air raid shelter and to seek work from the nearest Labour Exchange, which happened to be in Brixton.[20] It was from this initial point of connection that Brixton became the heartland for British Jamaicans and a wellspring of Black British culture. The area has long been noted for Brixton Market that stocks Caribbean and African foods, its classic 1911 Ritzy Cinema building, and its dynamic live music scene.

In the post-Windrush decades, the experiences of these Jamaicans and subsequent Blacks in Britain would be marred by racist confrontations and institutional discrimination. Racial tensions came to a head in the Brixton riot of 1981. Police had been scouring the streets in Operation Swamp, using a surge of "stop and search" methods to root out local crime. A struggle between police and a crowd involving a stabbed youth led to different interpretations of the incident on both sides. Five hours of violence erupted, involving hundreds of injuries, destroyed vehicles, and dozens of burning buildings, in what was called a "fireball of anger."[21] The Scarman Report, published in the aftermath of the riot, confirmed that some police were at fault for discrimination and overreaching their authority.[22] Brixton has seen more riots of a smaller scale since then, in 1985 and 1995, which also pitted Black residents against mostly White police, as well as a minor disturbance in 2011.[23]

Over the years, Jamaicans in Brixton have responded to racialized British society in various ways. In a seminal article, Stuart Hall outlined a history of Black British self-definition that moved from "West Indian migrant," to "black identity," to "new ethnicities."[24] Hall's historical account is exemplified by Jamaicans in Brixton. Their

---

[20] Reddie (2009: 62).   [21] *The Guardian* (1981).   [22] Scarman (1981).
[23] In early August 2011 riots spread across urban areas of England, following the police shooting of Mark Duggan in Tottenham, North London. Brixton at first seemed above the fray, but on the night of 8 August groups looted various stores on the Brixton high street and at a nearby Currys electronics store, clashing with police (Taylor 2011). These Brixton "riots" seem to have been more opportunistic, and less race-based, than the local riots of previous decades.
[24] Hall (1992).

first years of settlement were marked by strong identification as West Indian migrants. The 1970s and 1980s saw a cresting of "black identity" as Rastafarianism, Pan-Africanism, and race-based political movements provided different Black responses to racism. It was in this period that minorities developed a strong political consciousness, and "Black" political activism included South Asians alongside Caribbeans and Africans.[25] According to Hall, the 1990s and onwards have signaled a period of "new ethnicities," in which mixed-race identities and hybrid ethnic allegiances have become more common. New ethnicities are expected to be especially prevalent in second and further generations, as youth have more freedom from their parents' origins and take part in multicultural peer groups. In Hall's model of identity transitions, vestiges of each previous period continue. Thus, in Brixton today, Jamaicans may have many interweaving options along the spectrum from relatively fixed West Indian ethnicities to fluid new ethnicities.

Contemporary Brixton is gentrifying as young professionals are attracted to its arts, nightlife, and generous stock of Victorian properties. The area has also diversified in terms of immigration. Numbers of African migrants have grown and Portuguese now constitute a sizable community, among several others. Brixton struggles with poverty, hard drugs, knife crime, and criminal group violence. Cannabis use is widespread, provoking a range of opinions (cannabis is legal in Jamaica). Brixton is also the setting of variegated spiritualities, from many modest storefront churches to a well-known megachurch, from spiritual practices loosely based in West African Vodun to a staunchly Salafi mosque. Brixton has been and continues to be a place of many and diverse influences. It has a busy and vibrant street life that Jamaican second-generation youth described to me as "loud" or a place of "hustle and bustle." Brixton is much more a place of movement than stability (Figure 0.2).

The East End of London, now home to Britain's largest Bangladeshi population, has also played stage to migratory movements. Yet these movements have taken a somewhat different form than in Brixton. East End immigration has generally resembled a succession of "waves" rather than a mix of simultaneous currents. East End immigrant communities have each retained a relatively solid character in their

---

[25] Solomos and Back (1995).

Introduction 11

Figure 0.2. Brixton Market on Electric Avenue

first generation or even first several, with low rates of intermarriage. The less permeable nature of these communities can be attributed, at least in part, to religion.

Immigration history in the East End began with French Huguenot Protestants fleeing persecution from the Catholic monarchy in the middle of the eighteenth century. Many of these Huguenots took occupations as weavers: the upper windows that allowed light for their looms can still be seen on Fournier Street. Although an enclave community at first, the French Huguenots assimilated within a few generations. They are now remembered largely in names: for example, the actor Laurence Olivier. After the Huguenots, there was a migration of Irish to London, escaping the potato famine of the mid-1800s. A sizable number settled in the East End. The East End borough of Tower Hamlets still retains the most Catholic schools per head of any London borough.[26] It was next that Jews, fleeing Russian pogroms or seeking economic improvement, arrived in the late nineteenth century. In this same period Jack the Ripper murdered his

---

[26] Back et al. (2009).

hapless female victims in overcrowded East End slums, and William Booth, touched by the area's poverty, founded the Salvation Army. The Jewish population of the East End swelled to over 100,000 by the turn of the twentieth century, and the area took on the informal designation of "Little Jerusalem." Anne Kershen notes that for these successive waves of immigrants it was religion (though not necessarily religiosity) that provided cultural stability and the institutions of community life.[27]

Bangladeshis can trace their history in the East End to *lascars* who worked on ships that landed at the London docks.[28] Many of these sailors came from the Sylhet region, an area with good river links down to Bengal's main ports.[29] However, it was the fateful combination of the Commonwealth Immigrants Act of 1962 and East Pakistan's independence as Bangladesh in 1971 that led to a substantial wave of Bangladeshi immigration. The 1962 Act restricted what had been a very generous British policy of admitting all members of Commonwealth lands, as it instead required immigrants to prove employment, economic independence, or armed forces service. A rush of Bangladeshis entered Britain under the more generous policy before the bill was passed. The largest numbers came from the Sylhet region of Bangladesh, due to lineage and patronage connections with the earlier generations of *lascars*.[30] It is because of a process of chain migration—Sylhetis progressively bringing family members and others to join them—that the composition of the East End Bangladeshi population today is predominantly Sylheti (Figure 0.3).[31]

The Bangladeshis had arrived for economic opportunities, and many began by working in textiles. Others started restaurants or small shops. Bangladeshis would over time come to account for the majority of "Indian" restaurant owners in Britain. Brick Lane in the East End became the heartland of settlement, with many businesses and organizations beginning there. The Brick Lane area gained such a visible Bangladeshi character that, with the support of local entrepreneurs, it was dubbed Banglatown in the late 1990s. In 1997 an arch reminiscent of those in many Chinatowns (but in a more Bengali

---

[27] Kershen (2005).
[28] *Lascar*: a sailor. The term, originally Persian, was used by the British for the South Asian seamen who manned the ships of the Empire.
[29] Eade and Garbin (2006).   [30] Gardner (1995).   [31] Gardner (2002).

Introduction

Figure 0.3. Whitechapel Road Market in the East End

style) was erected at the entrance of Brick Lane, which has earned the reputation of Britain's heartland of curry houses. The area has been portrayed frequently in literature, most notably in Monica Ali's acclaimed *Brick Lane* and in Salman Rushdie's highly contentious *The Satanic Verses*.[32]

Like Jamaicans and other Blacks in Brixton, the Bangladeshis of the East End have been targets of racism and discrimination. Street violence reached its height in the 1970s when Brick Lane became a regular target of the National Front. In 1978, White racists murdered the 25-year-old textile worker, Altab Ali. A demonstration of thousands of Bangladeshis and others carrying the young man's coffin made a powerful statement against racism. Today, a sculpted gate at Altab Ali Park stands in memory of the incident. As virulent racism

---

[32] Ali (2003); Rushdie (1988). Although at a much smaller scale than the Rushdie Affair, the book *Brick Lane* also generated controversy. In 2006, when filming for a movie-version of the novel was taking place, a group of local traders and businessmen organized protests that received national press coverage. The protesters argued that Monica Ali had unfairly stereotyped Bengalis as illiterate and closed-minded (see Alexander 2011).

continued to threaten the Bangladeshi community, young men formed groups to oppose racist violence. Young Bangladeshi males in the area took on tougher personas and formed petty gangs to defend their areas. Some of these "gangs" may have taken on lives of their own, becoming involved in the local drug trade.[33] Bangladeshi youth have been influenced by broader British and global youth culture. Many listen to the hip hop of 50 Cent or Lil Wayne as much as their Jamaican peers.

The other common Bangladeshi response to British racial exclusion has been to take on strong identities as Muslims. Indeed, while Bangladeshi and Sylheti identities are important for the first generation, and a form of Black politics may have had unifying potential in the 1980s, today among this population Muslim identity is the most widespread and valued.[34] In the East End area, the East London Mosque is the largest and most well known mosque propagating strong Muslim identities. Ed Husain, author of *The Islamist*, argues that in his younger years this mosque primed him for the development of an aggressive Islamist identity, which he has since abandoned.[35] Others situate Husain's biography in religious developments of the 1990s that have become less relevant[36] or critique him for too readily adopting the government's stance on Muslims.[37] Yet whether benign, dangerous, or positive, it is clear that globally oriented, revivalist streams of Islam have been growing in their influence in the East End.[38] These forms of Islam are finding traction among the young, both male and female.

The East End, like Brixton, is a relatively impoverished area that struggles with issues of crime and delinquency. Yet both are gentrifying as well. In the East End, the Canary Wharf development transformed acres of abandoned dockland warehouses into a business complex with some of the sleekest skyscrapers in Britain. The City of London has also been expanding into the area, with a set of major towers now planned for the Shoreditch Goodsyard.[39] The startups of Silicon Roundabout and the thriving artistic scene in Bethnal Green are additional drivers of urban renewal projects. The 2012 Olympic Games in East London contributed another chapter to the East End's

---

[33] See Dench et al. (2006); but compare to Alexander (2000).
[34] On these transitions among British South Asian Muslims see Modood (2005).
[35] Husain (2007).   [36] Birt (2007).   [37] Bunting (2007).
[38] Riaz (2013); Glynn (2015).   [39] Wong (2014).

long history of cultures, conflict, and competition for resources. The potential influences of corporate local investment and the Olympic "legacy" on the wellbeing of the second and further generations of Bangladeshis is, for the moment, difficult to discern.

HOW I STUDIED SECOND-GENERATION YOUTH

The sixty young people I interviewed for this book are from inner city areas of London. I met and interviewed all of the Jamaican youth in Brixton, South London, and all of the Bangladeshi youth in Tower Hamlets in East London. Tower Hamlets is ranked as the third most deprived borough out of 354 in England, while Lambeth (where Brixton is located) is ranked the nineteenth most deprived.[40] My youth interviewees were born into immigrant families, and typically come from humble socio-economic backgrounds. The average Bangladeshi youth I met was living in cramped social housing conditions with parents, siblings, and perhaps extended family. Many Bangladeshis told me that their parents were currently unemployed or suffer from serious health conditions or work injuries. Most of the Jamaican youth I interviewed had been raised in single-parent households. Some were estranged from one or both of their parents. Jamaicans and Bangladeshis both spoke of the ravages of drugs and delinquency among friends and schoolmates in their generation.

The aspirations and likely life outcomes of my interviewees varied widely. Some were attending university. Mike, a Jamaican mixed-race youth, was about to enter a prestigious law program at the London School of Economics. For others, university or even a stable career was impossible to imagine. Some of the young men I interviewed were "hustling" to make ends meet. Others had chosen to live on modest means to devote themselves to intensive religious study and prayer. Yet others were putting careers on hold to plan and start families. Rubina, a 19-year-old Bangladeshi woman, is a university student who has ambitions to become a well-known Muslim writer. Samia, of the same age and ethnic background, attends a basic work

---

[40] Government Office for London (2010).

skills center in the hope of shedding alcoholism and scraping her life back together.

My research in these inner city areas of Brixton and the East End (specifically Spitalfields, Whitechapel, and Shadwell) began when I explored each area on foot. I spoke with shopkeepers and community contacts to gain a better orientation in the two research sites. I read academic studies of both places and kept up with British news media. Through these initial months of research I was able to identify the religious and community institutions in each site that are the most influential with local young people. These institutions would be key to my analysis of whether and how religion can motivate second-generation youth into civic engagement or perpetuate disengagement.

I then began visiting the local institutions I had identified, focusing on churches and mosques. I chose two Jamaican-led churches in Brixton, which I attended for in-depth case studies: the large Brixton Seventh Day Adventist Church and a Neo-Pentecostal megachurch called Ruach Ministries. In the East End, I chose two case-study mosques: the traditional Bengali Jamme Masjid on Brick Lane and the prominent East London Mosque on Whitechapel Road, where I attended many mosque congregational prayers and special events. From all religious institutions I built a network of contacts with congregants and leaders, observed events carefully, and took in-depth field notes to which I would refer later.

I found my sixty youth interviewees in two ways. Twenty of them were young people whom I met naturally through attending their churches and mosques. For example, Mike, mentioned earlier, is someone I met as we stood in the foyer of Ruach Ministries waiting for the youth service to begin. These twenty youth from "religious contexts" gave me a detailed view into how particular religious institutions influence the young people who regularly attend them for worship.

I recruited the other forty youth interviewees from "secular contexts." To do this, I simply wandered the streets, markets, libraries, and other public places of Brixton and the East End, meeting young people who might fit my research demographic, and recruiting those who did to join the study. I met Mahmoud while I was shopping at the large Sainsbury's grocery store in Whitechapel. I met Chanel simply by introducing myself to her on the streets of Brixton. The strategy for the forty interviews from "secular contexts" was to continually develop fresh contacts from a carefully varied set of places. By doing this, I built a sample that more accurately represents the full Bangladeshi and Jamaican youth populations than could have been possible by following referrals through social networks. The sample from secular contexts is a diverse cross-section of "ordinary" youth. I developed it for a different purpose than the religious contexts sample, which places sharper focus on youth actively involved in religion. By using the two samples in tandem, I achieve more depth to analyze religious influences and breadth to contextualize these within the overall population.

I conducted most of the interviews in public places such as coffee shops, libraries, or park benches. I paid each youth £10 as a participation incentive.[41] Each interview lasted one or two hours and was recorded on a digital recorder. I designed the interviews to be semistructured, meaning that I tended to ask the same questions in the same order yet had flexibility to let the conversation flow more naturally and to continue with follow-up questions. In many cases, I kept in touch with interviewees over time. I use some of my later conversations with these key informants to refine my analysis. Overall, the youth interviews provide the main basis for my findings about religion and its role in second-generation youth civic engagement. My ethnographic observations in churches and mosques contribute the institutional side to my analysis and help to put the interviews in broader social context.

The final component of my research process was a set of about twenty "perspective interviews" with religious and community leaders and other key observers. These included interviews with at least one pastor, imam, or youth worker directly involved with the young people in each of the religious institutions I studied. I also conducted interviews with a select group of local and national level figures. Some of the perspective interviews I conducted were with "ordinary" locals, such as shopkeepers and teachers. Although these interviewees are not well known on the British national stage, a number of them—such as Brixton CD sellers Reggie and Vernon introduced in Chapter 4—are astute observers of their local areas and offered insights that would drive my thinking further.

---

[41] Funding for this participation incentive was generously provided by a Smith Graduate Research Grant from the University of North Carolina at Chapel Hill (where I was completing my PhD: DeHanas 2010b) and by the National Study of Youth and Religion.

PLAN OF THE BOOK

In the next chapter, in response to the civic question, I provide a baseline comparison of the kinds of British citizens Jamaican and Bangladeshi second-generation youth are becoming. I find that both groups have similar levels of political knowledge which compare positively to the British population overall. Both groups have relatively low levels of identification with Britishness and British citizenship. In these first two dimensions of citizenship—knowledge and identification—the ethnicity and religiosity of youth seem to make not much, if any, difference. However, both religion and ethnicity do appear to have an influence on political participation (the active practice of citizenship). Bangladeshis are much more active than Jamaicans in several aspects of participation, with Bangladeshis who are highly religious being the most active of all. The chapters that follow each unfold part of a progressing explanation for this surprisingly large participation gap.

Chapters 2 and 3 consider the identity options of second-generation young people.[42] I focus on how young people tactically choose and use self-identification for their own purposes. Among British Bangladeshis, I find the most prevalent phenomenon is "deculturation," in which the apparently "impure" influences of Bangladeshi culture are brushed away in favor of a more totalizing vision of Islam. Muslim identity is nearly always valued first and foremost. I do not find the same sort of comprehensive cultural or identity patterns among British Jamaicans in Brixton. Instead there is a fragmentation of cultural influences acting in various directions. Jamaican youth more often take situational and hybrid approaches to identity, enabling them to better navigate their diverse environments. Common self-identifications as Muslim and the reactions against traditional culture, then, provide fertile ground for political mobilizations in the East End, whereas the various forces at work in Brixton do not consolidate into a single position or trend.

---

[42] Some of the material from Chapter 2 appeared in my chapter in the book *Everyday Lived Islam* (DeHanas 2013c) and some of it appeared in my article in *Ethnicities* (DeHanas 2013b). The raps and some of the description of the young rappers in Chapter 3 appeared in my article in the *Journal of Contemporary Religion* (DeHanas 2013a). Some of the material from this Introduction appeared in my article on Tower Hamlets in *Public Spirit* (DeHanas 2014). In all cases the material has been reprinted with permission of the respective publisher or publication.

In Chapters 4 and 5, I investigate how churches in Brixton and mosques in the East End contribute to the socialization of young people into citizens. In these chapters I present case studies of two churches and two mosques, varied enough to capture a significant amount of the religious diversity in each of the two local contexts. Through observing religious practices, studying the language used in sermons, and speaking with youth and religious leaders, I am able to compare how religious institutions help shape the civic imaginations of young people. I find that generational differences between youth and their parents are often strengthened by patterns of practice in religious institutions. I also find that young people are encouraged into different understandings of the religious self in the East End compared to Brixton, with a much more communally oriented self presented in the mosques and a more individualistic, subjective self in the churches. These differences in religious imagination have implications for the ability of community-level political efforts to be mobilized (or even conceived of in the first place) in the two contexts.

In Chapter 6, I investigate actual religious mobilizations for civic and political change. I profile a rally against youth violence led by Black Majority Church leaders and a Bangladeshi Muslim event during Ramadan that raised funds to combat hunger and poverty. The chapter uncovers specific social mechanisms that are building blocks for Jamaican Christian and Bangladeshi Muslim efforts to effect political change.

Chapter 7 brings the various strands of explanation together into a conclusion. I reflect briefly on how Black British political participation may have the potential to increase, and why when Bangladeshis are highly mobilized around Muslim-related political issues this can in fact be a mixed blessing. I consider how the findings contribute to academic work on the sociology of religion, comparative politics, and multiculturalism.

1

Losing Faith in the State?

At 6 feet 4 inches, 18-year-old Mike Williams is a striking fellow.[1] Mike is mixed race, with a light brown complexion. When I first walked into Ruach Ministries, a predominantly Black church in Brixton with Jamaican leadership, I almost immediately noticed Mike's towering presence. We stood in the crowded atrium as we waited for the doors of the youth service to open. With an unhesitant smile, Mike reached out his hand to introduce himself to me. I soon learned that he is half Jamaican and half Greek Cypriot. It was a fortunate coincidence—I had lived in Cyprus myself as a child. We started to talk about the beaches of Cyprus and the warmer weather there ("Seems a million miles from London!"). As the doors opened, we found seats together in the youth service.

My interview recruitment often worked in this way. I would visit a religious service or public place to observe and learn from it, meet someone informally, and then arrange an interview to take place afterwards. In this case, after the youth service Mike and I went across the street to have our conversation over a meal at a Jamaican restaurant. We both ordered the spicy jerk chicken and settled into a relaxed interview that would last almost two hours.

Mike is a charming person who describes himself as a bit shy, but comes across with natural confidence and sincerity. He thinks of himself as mixed race: "I don't really 'act Black' like Black people do or 'act White' like White people do. I'm definitely mixed race. And people can tell that," he said. "I'm interested in other people's cultures, and I think that really comes by being mixed race." His Jamaican and Greek Cypriot sides are both significant to him, mainly

---

[1] All of the names of the young people in this book have been changed to protect their anonymity.

through the influence of his parents. He can see something of both sides of his family in his personality. Mike thinks of himself, racially, as both Black and White. But Black is more prominent "because in this country, people cast you as Black."

However, Mike's first and foremost identity is as a Christian. He says this means "having a personal relationship with God, in Jesus." In fact, Mike had gone through major changes in his faith in the year before our interview. A friend had invited him to the Ruach Ministries youth service. Since attending Ruach and regularly reading the Bible for himself, Mike had grown much more serious about his faith. He now goes to the Ruach youth service each week and says that the preaching gives him something to change or apply to his life "every single time." He spoke with amazement at the spiritual atmosphere of the youth service: "I have felt the power of God more in that place than anywhere else."

Mike is very thoughtful and articulate when talking about religious, ethnic, and racial identities. I found it most interesting, however, to talk about the aspect of his identity he was *least* passionate about: his national identification with Britain. Mike does not think of himself as British. "I'm not going to say I'm British," he told me, "I'm not a very patriotic person." I knew that Mike was born in Britain, that he grew up in London, and that he has British citizenship. So I asked what this citizenship means to him: "Not much," he told me, "Only the fact that I live here." Mike went on to explain that if he lived in the United States he might think of himself as an American. "But British culture is a weird one."

Mike did choose to describe himself as "English" (rather than British). He ranked this in last place out of nine components of his personal identity.[2] In explaining why Englishness was relatively low in his affections, Mike told me:

> As I said, I'm not very patriotic. I support England, I guess, in the soccer[3] and stuff like that. But I'm not very English. I'm not a very English person. I see what English people do in general. They go out to

---

[2] I will describe the identity-ranking portion of the interviews in depth in Chapters 2 and 3. Mike's choices to describe his self-identification, beginning with his highest ranked, were: Christian, mixed race, Londoner, Greek Cypriot, Jamaican, Black, White, Caribbean, West Indian, and English.

[3] Mike used the word "soccer" rather than the usual British word "football," almost certainly because he was speaking to an American interviewer.

the pub and stuff. I don't really do that. There is definitely like a distinct polar opposite between what I'm influenced by in this top part [the core of my identity] and being English.

At times during the interview, Mike seemed to feel indifferent towards Britishness and Englishness. At other points—as seen here—he distanced himself significantly from the cultural content of these identities, speaking of them as the "distinct polar opposite" to how he understands himself.

Some of the same themes emerged in my interview with Hamid Majid, a 22-year-old Bangladeshi. I first met him on the Queen Mary University of London campus. Hamid has a thin build, a gentle face, and a very easy smile. He is quite intentional about his Muslim appearance. He keeps a beard and wears a prayer cap, attempting to dress "Islamically." Hamid arrived at the campus by bike. Seeing him other times in the subsequent months, I would learn that Hamid always keeps his bike close at hand. He likes to be ready to cycle in response to meetings, events, and text messages sent from friends all around London.

We met for our interview in late December, the time of year in England when darkness falls early. Hamid and I chose to talk at the Queen Mary University physics building because it was near the campus prayer room. The early darkness meant that the *maghrib* and *isha'a* prayers came very near each other.[4] We went first to the prayer room where Hamid and five of his fellow students joined together in the *maghrib* prayer. He and I then walked to the physics building to begin recording our interview. About halfway through the conversation, we took a brief intermission to allow Hamid to leave for the *isha'a* prayer, returning later to finish the interview.

Hamid, like Mike, thinks of faith as an integral part of his life. He told me that "Islam is a complete way of life, and being Muslim is something that I really hold on to daily." Also much like Mike, Hamid went through a significant religious change during his young adult years. He says that as a teenager he constantly got into trouble and was expelled from school. "I used to get away with murder," he told me—and then quickly added: "I don't mean [murder] literally! You know how the media can twist things." As he said this to me he

---

[4] *Maghrib* and *isha'a* prayers are the fourth and fifth in the day. These prayers are determined by sunset and by nightfall, meaning that they fluctuate with time of year. For male Muslims, prayers are ideally performed together in congregation.

laughed. Yet his comment resonated in my mind. It was a gut reaction from someone who knows media distortion to be a commonplace danger for those of his faith.

Hamid says his life began to turn around when he listened to a tape from Black American convert Sheikh Khalid Yasin about the purpose of life.[5] He reflected on the preacher's message and then "it was during Ramadan that I really started to get rid of some bad habits and take Islam more seriously."

Hamid had an interesting way of thinking about how Britishness and Islam fit together in his identity. He says he is inspired to "be like a bee and to take in the good from all the flowers" (see Surah 16 of the Qur'an).[6] By this he means that he can take the best of both worlds. Hamid says that being British is a good thing for him "because I'm allowed to pray, I'm allowed to keep my beard, and at the same time I'm allowed to do certain things that I probably wouldn't have the chance to do otherwise." Yet he also sees some aspects of British culture that are in conflict with his own views and actions. "British culture and Muslim culture are very different in a lot of aspects," he told me. The differences that came to his mind were "drinking alcohol... the dress sense, and some of the foreign policy." Although he was very generous and diplomatic in our conversation, it was clear that Hamid also saw certain aspects of British culture as the "distinct polar opposite" (in Mike's phrase) of his own Islamic way of life.

Hamid, like Mike, was willing to identify himself as English (in addition to British). Yet in this case he was not referring to symbols particular to the English nation, such as the national football team. When Hamid identifies with the English he simply means the English language. He told me: "[I relate to] English because I speak the English language most of the time. English is my first language. I actually speak more fluently in English than I am in Bengali, having been born here. So yes, English, in the books I read. Everything's, like,

---

[5] Sheikh Khalid Yasin can be considered a radical sheikh, particularly due to his preaching on topics relating to non-Muslims and homosexuality. Yet Hamid should not necessarily be viewed as guilty by association from listening to this sheikh. A large number of the Muslim youth I interviewed respect figures such as Sayyid Qutb and Abul Ala Maududi—major ideologues of Islamism—for their pious writings. Yet these youth would not necessarily be willing to take forward the full implications of these intellectuals' programs of thought. In this case, it was the religious revivalist message of Sheikh Khalid Yasin that struck a chord with Hamid.

[6] *The Qur'an*, An-Nahl 16:68–9.

English." Elsewhere in the interview Hamid contrasted his own native English with the struggles his parents have with the language. His identity as an English speaker is something in which he takes pride.

We have established that cultural identification with England or Britain was mixed at best for Hamid and Mike. Hamid values British legal freedoms and communicating in the English language. Mike supports England in football. But neither of them, it seems, articulate ideals, cultural traits, or a history that would serve as an indicator of "British values." In fact there are cultural or value-laden aspects of Britain that both young men find personally objectionable—such as foreign policy (for Hamid) and pub-going (for Mike). At most, a cultural Britishness or Englishness can be accepted in a piecemeal fashion, just as a bee would pick and choose the best pollen from a variety of flowers.

If Mike and Hamid's engagement with cultural Britishness is a bit lukewarm, then the views they express on political participation in Britain are icy cold. When we reached the section of our interview about politics, Hamid told me several times that he does not trust British politicians, nor does he think or act very politically himself. "I find [politics] a dirty game. The amount of lies, the amount of spin, the amount of stuff that happens in politics—it's not something I enjoy," he said. Later he expressed this view in visceral terms: "There's not a political bone in my body." Hamid believes that his distaste for politics is characteristic of Muslims in general: "Muslims tend to be apathetic when it comes to politics," he said. Similarly, Mike has a negative stance on British politics. He thinks that any potential he has for political involvement "doesn't make that much of a difference."

One possible interpretation of Mike and Hamid's words is that they demonstrate a generalized apathy—an apathy inclusive of national identity and political participation. After all, Hamid's own self-diagnosis is that he is "apathetic when it comes to politics." It will now be worthwhile to consider if, and in what ways, these young people may be losing faith in the state.

APATHY, ALIENATION, OR ATOMISM?

It is commonly acknowledged that, at least on some dimensions, a large proportion of British youth today are *disengaged* from civic matters. Difficulties and disagreements arise when attempting to specify the problems, why these are problems, and how youth disengagement should actually be understood. Is it apathy, alienation, or atomism?

If voting in government elections is considered the bread and butter of British political participation, as it traditionally has been, then evidence suggests that British youth have an ascetic political diet. The overall adult turnout for the 1997 British national elections reached a post-war low, at 71 percent. Yet participation from the segment of youth (age 18 to 24) in that election was far lower, at 51 percent. Youth turnout took a further nosedive in the 2001 election, to 39 percent. It continued to dip in 2005 to 37 percent and then to modestly upturn to 44 percent in 2010 and 43 percent in 2015, while remaining well below figures for other adult age groups.[7]

The low election turnout results for young people are in some cases compounded for ethnic minority youth. Several studies have found that people of Black African and Caribbean origin have the lowest levels of reported voting in Britain, at 60 percent and 65 percent respectively in the 2010 general election.[8] These groups also have the lowest rates of voter registration.[9] Because young people are less likely to be registered or vote than other adults, the youthful age profile of Black ethnic minorities in Britain produces a particularly low rate of electoral participation in this population segment.[10]

In contrast, national election studies have actually found robust involvement from South Asians in Britain.[11] Research from David Sanders and colleagues shows that Bangladeshis had the highest reported voting rate in the 2010 general election among all UK ethnic minority groups, at 78 percent. This Bangladeshi figure nearly reaches the White British rate of 79 percent, and is higher than the respective voting rates for Indians (74 percent) and Pakistanis (72 percent).[12]

Even if these results bolster confidence in South Asian electoral participation, other research and policy work has raised concerns about the citizenship practices of Muslim South Asians in particular. The Cantle Report on the summer 2001 civil disturbances in

---

[7] All of the voter turnout figures in this paragraph are exit poll estimates from Ipsos MORI (1997, 2001, 2005, 2010, 2015).
[8] Sanders et al. (2014); see also earlier studies by Purdam et al. (2002); Saggar (1998); Anwar (1998b).
[9] Saggar (1998).   [10] Purdam et al. (2002).
[11] Fieldhouse and Cutts (2007); Purdam et al. (2002); Saggar (1998); Anwar (1998b).
[12] Sanders et al. (2014).

Northern English industrial towns questioned whether Muslims have been leading "parallel lives" that separate them from British civic life. In the years following this influential report, government officials frequently singled out Muslim citizens as a cause for concern. For example, in 2004 Permanent Secretary to the Home Office John Gieve wrote pessimistically on Muslim civic engagement:

> Muslim communities appear to have low levels of civic participation and volunteering, mixed attitudes towards integration and (fairly small) minorities who do not feel loyal or patriotic towards Britain . . . but this may reflect demographic rather than faith-specific factors.[13]

If these observations are correct, British Muslims in the aggregate can be expected to score poorly on the three dimensions of civic engagement that I will investigate in this chapter: civic identification, political literacy, and political participation.

Taking youth civic disengagement in Britain as a problem, several possible descriptions of the situation have been offered. The most common among politicians and media in Britain is the view that youth are *apathetic* towards politics. The late Sir Bernard Crick, a British educationalist and policy advisor to the Blair administration, understood the problem as generalized youth apathy. Crick sought to address this apathy by spearheading policy interventions aimed at active citizenship, civic education, and his own concept of "political literacy."[14] The problem, as researchers Heath and Park once succinctly put it, is that young people "don't know, don't care and don't vote."[15]

Pirie and Worcester also believe that British youth are apathetic, and understand this in generational terms, arguing that Millennials are the first "apolitical generation."[16] Pippa Norris memorably characterized the 2001 election turnout as an "apathetic landslide."[17] She does not necessarily see apathy as a problem inherent to age or to a certain generation. The poor voter turnout was "less a dramatic crisis of British democracy . . . nor even widespread public cynicism,"[18] and more the inevitable consequence of a media which, during the run-up to the 2001 election, focused on the election result being a "foregone conclusion."

---

[13] Gieve (2004).
[14] On policy, see the Crick (1998) report on citizenship education. For Crick's thinking on political literacy and other themes, see Crick (2000).
[15] Heath and Park (1997: 6).   [16] Pirie and Worcester (1998).
[17] Norris (2001).   [18] Norris (2001: 570).

Youth political apathy might have any of various causes, such as media influence, age, or generation. Regardless of its causes, there are logical manifestations of apathy that we should expect to observe. The *hypothesis of youth apathy* is that youth will show low levels of civic identity, low levels of political literacy and interest, and low levels of actual practices of political participation. Youth who are truly apathetic are disengaged from and uninterested in citizenship at all levels.

Researchers David Marsh, Therese O'Toole, and Su Jones have criticized the youth apathy perspective.[19] They conducted their own inductive study of how British young people, aged 16 to 25, define the political. Based on open-ended focus groups and interviews, they conclude that youth consider a very broad set of actions and themes to be political, with many of these themes not well captured by traditional ballot-box politics. In their initial study and in subsequent ones, researchers from this team have argued that youth do have opinions about government policies, yet at the same time do not believe their voices will be taken seriously.[20] Far from being apathetic, youth are increasingly *alienated* from British political institutions and processes. In this youth alienation perspective, the onus is placed on politicians and policy-makers to listen more closely to youth and to re-enfranchise them, because "political literacy cuts both ways."[21] The causal mechanisms for disengagement are most often sited in institutions, historic processes, and the political system, rather than in the content of youth culture or the character of young people themselves.[22] Academic consensus in Britain has moved towards the alienation perspective. With particular reference to Bengali Muslims in East London, Justin Gest writes that UK foreign policy has attenuated the relationship of Muslims to the state, leading to a kind of political seclusion he calls "apartism."[23] Several studies of various groups in Britain support the alienation position along similar lines, with policy-makers also increasingly taking this view.[24] The report of the Power Inquiry, chaired by Baroness Helena Kennedy QC, declares

---

[19] Marsh et al. (2007).
[20] For overviews of these research studies see Marsh et al. (2007); O'Toole and Gale (2013).
[21] O'Toole et al. (2003).   [22] Griffin (2005).   [23] Gest (2010).
[24] For research studies, see Henn et al. (2002); Sloam (2007); Purdam et al. (2002); Fahmy (2006).

Table 1.1. Hypotheses of youth civic engagement

	Civic identity	Political literacy	Political participation
Apathy	Low	Low	Low
Alienation	Any level	Any level	Low
Atomism	Any level	Any level	Any level; primarily individualistic practice

that distrust of politicians and alienation from the political process are the key issues in Britain and that there is simply a "myth of apathy."[25]

If youth are alienated from conventional politics, then they will not necessarily have low levels of civic identification or of political literacy. Instead, a lack of faith in the political system and political actors will lead to low levels of political participation regardless of their political literacy and identity. In other words, the *hypothesis of youth alienation* predicts low political participation, but does not have specific predictions of the other two dimensions of civic engagement. This hypothesis, along with others, is listed in Table 1.1.

A third and final perspective on youth civic engagement can be found in Pattie, Seyd, and Whiteley's book *Citizenship in Britain: Values, Participation and Democracy*.[26] This book is based on the Citizen Audit, a large nationally representative survey of Great Britain carried out in two waves, one before and one after the 2001 general election. The co-authors studied British citizens of all adult ages (not only young adults). Like other researchers, they find relatively low levels of participation in the 18 to 25 age group.

Pattie and colleagues' most intriguing argument is that British citizens have become more *atomized* in their engagement with politics over the past few decades. They measure seventeen civic behaviors, including voting and campaign activities, along with less "conventional" forms of politics such as boycotting products or organizing a group of "like-minded people" around a common cause. Their list of seventeen civic behaviors clusters into three categories: communal, individual, and communicative. Pattie and co-authors state in the conclusion that: "This book could have been entitled 'The Atomised Citizen' since this reflects many of the trends we are observing in contemporary Britain. The rise of individualistic forms of participation

[25] Power Inquiry (2006).   [26] Pattie et al. (2004).

at the expense of collectivistic forms characterises this process."[27] For example, the authors note the rising popularity of "cheque-book participation" through boycotting products, purchasing products, and financially supporting charities with good brand recognition, such as Oxfam or Christian Aid. This style of participation, based on individual ethics and convenience, contrasts with more collective participatory actions in labor unions or political parties, which have seen sharp declines in membership.

Although Pattie and colleagues' observations about the atomized citizen are meant to apply to British adults as a whole, they may have particular relevance to youth. Their observations mirror other work from Anthony Giddens that emphasizes the rise of a life politics that contrasts with emancipatory politics,[28] from Charles Taylor on the deepening of contemporary ethics of authenticity in political and life choices,[29] and from Kevin McDonald on the greater individualization of young people's connections with the state, especially in terms of the labor market.[30]

If youth are indeed atomized in their civic engagement, we should not necessarily expect low levels of engagement, but rather a particular pattern in engagement styles. The *hypothesis of youth atomism* posits that youth will primarily participate in individual-level activities, while their engagement in collective forms of participation will be minimal.

MEASURING RELIGIOSITY AND CIVIC ENGAGEMENT

In order to consider the three rival hypotheses of second-generation youth civic engagement, I asked questions in the interviews that allowed me to measure several factors and then analyze them. My main goal in analysis is to determine whether religion has an influence on civic engagement and, if so, to specify which ways it does. To determine this, I compare youth who have "high religiosity" with those who do not. I am interested in whether there are any causal

[27] Pattie et al. (2004: 275). [28] Giddens (1991).
[29] Taylor (1992). [30] McDonald (1999).

relationships—if being religious (or becoming religious) tends to cause youth to have different citizenship outcomes than the youth who are not religious. The logic here is simple: youth will most often develop their levels of religiosity *before* they express themselves as citizens, because religious development typically progresses throughout childhood and adolescence, while the practice of citizenship develops most significantly after reaching legal voting age (age 18 in Britain). Therefore if relationships between religiosity and citizenship are found, they are very likely to work in the direction of religiosity influencing civic engagement.[31]

My research sample is composed of the sixty young people I interviewed, twenty-four of whom are Jamaican and thirty-six of whom are Bangladeshi. As described in the Introduction, I recruited about one-third of these youth in religious institutions and two-thirds from systematic recruitment in secular contexts. Because I used religious institutions for some of my recruiting, the sample that results has a greater proportion of religiously active youth than could be expected in the Bangladeshi and Jamaican youth populations overall. Even though this is the case, the youth from secular contexts (sixteen Jamaicans, twenty-one Bangladeshis) should approximate a representative picture of the overall populations. Sometimes in my analysis that follows I will refer to the complete sample (from both religious institutions and streets) and sometimes to the systematic sample of youth that I recruited from varied secular contexts. I will now explain, in turn, how I measured religiosity and the three component parts of civic engagement.

Religiosity: My measurement of religiosity is important to the way that I conceive and carry out the analysis. I attempted to define high religiosity in the same way that my youth interviewees did. To do this, I needed to discern the symbolic boundaries in my two fieldwork sites

---

[31] The US nationally representative National Study of Youth and Religion finds a strong level of continuity in religion from parents to teenage children (Smith with Denton 2005). It in turn finds substantial continuity from teenage years into the emerging adulthood years of 18 to 25 that I am studying here (Smith with Snell 2009). Religious tastes are usually established early, though religious practice may fall off to some degree in the teenage years. The age of political consciousness, in contrast, typically begins in the years before youth are able to vote (age 18 in Britain) and develops most significantly in the emerging adult years. The sequence of religious development followed by political development is not static nor is it universal, but it is reasonable to expect that youth religious development will more often shape youth civic development, rather than the other way around.

that separate religious people from others. This distinction was extremely easy to make among the Bangladeshi Muslim youth of the East End. When youth admitted to me that they were *not* very religious, they almost always used the term "not practicing." The main standard of Muslim practice in the East End (virtually unanimous among my interviewees) is praying five times a day. Those who did not pray five times a day knew that they were on the deficient side of an acknowledged common standard among local Muslims.

Discerning the boundary that marks high religiosity among Jamaicans was considerably more difficult. Some youth I interviewed could speak in powerful flights of Christian oratory, yet had not been to church in a long while. Others attended religious services every week, but had very little to say about religious matters. I settled on weekly attendance as the standard for high religiosity among Jamaican youth. I did so because (1) the measurement of this is considerably clearer than making gradations of theology or of the importance of faith and (2) as a measure of religious practice, it is more comparable with the Muslim five daily prayer standard. One might argue that attendance once per week is hardly as much evidence of high religiosity as five daily prayers. However, because religious norms are not as strong in Brixton as they are in the East End, regular church attendance is a significant and relatively demanding step. For most of the Jamaican youth attendees I interviewed, weekly attendance meant a substantial time commitment each weekend in church activities that might, for example, include a morning service, community lunch, and then a later youth service.

After defining high religiosity as five daily prayers for Bangladeshi Muslims and weekly church attendance for Jamaican Christians, I was able to classify the complete sample of youth as high, medium, or low religiosity. In total, the proportion of high religiosity to medium/low religiosity was the same for Jamaicans (14 to 10) as it was for Bangladeshis (21 to 15). Therefore the complete (non-representative) sample had enough cases for viable qualitative analysis.[32] In order to divide the

---

[32] Low religiosity youth were those who showed little or no interest in matters of religion. These ranged from atheists and agnostics (three Jamaicans) to those who may have some cultural or family connection to religion but are not practicing it now (three Jamaicans, one Bangladeshi). Medium religiosity was the residual category between low and high: all youth who pray sometimes, attend church or mosque sometimes, and talk with some connection to faith, but do not show the consistency to be classified as high religiosity (four Jamaicans, fourteen Bangladeshis).

sample into these categories, of course, I was relying on the self-reports of young people about religious practices I had not witnessed directly. Previous research indicates that people who are asked about religious practices may exaggerate these when it seems socially desirable.[33] Indeed, because urban life is complex and potentially contradictory there will always be limitations to a study based on self-reports as compared to a more intimate ethnography focused on a smaller group of people.

Along with religiosity, the other key measure in my research is civic engagement. I conceptualize civic engagement as having three component parts: civic identification, political literacy, and political participation. I separately compare high religiosity youth and other youth across all three of these components.

Civic identification: This component of youth citizenship was the most qualitative and subjective. I used two sections of the interview to investigate the civic identifications of youth. The first was an identity section in which I had youth rank and compare various components with which they self-identify. The second was a section at the end of the interview when I asked all youth "What does British citizenship mean to you?" In this chapter I will only report the essentials of the analysis of these components of civic identity, expanding considerably on the analysis in Chapters 2 and 3.

Political literacy: To measure political literacy, I replicated a measure from Pattie, Seyd, and Whiteley (2004) in their Citizen Audit. Their measure is a seven-question true/false quiz on British politics, shown in Table 1.2. All of the answers on the quiz have remained consistent since it was devised by Pattie and his colleagues, except for

Table 1.2. Political literacy measure

Political quiz (true or false)
1. The minimum voting age is 21.
2. Britain has separate elections for European Parliament and British Parliament.
3. The number of Members of Parliament is about 100.
4. Britain's electoral system for Westminster is based on proportional representation.
5. No one may stand for Parliament unless they pay a deposit.
6. The House of Lords has equal powers to the House of Commons.
7. The European Union (the EU) is composed of 15 states.

---

[33] Hadaway et al. (1993).

Table 1.3. Political participation measure

During the last 12 months have you done any of the following to influence rules, laws, or policies?

1. Contacted a politician (for example, a Member of Parliament or a local councilor).
2. Contacted an organization (for example, Shelter or Oxfam).
3. Contacted a public official (for example, a person from housing or social security offices).
4. Contacted the media.
5. Contacted a solicitor or judicial body.
6. Worn or displayed a campaign badge or sticker.
7. Signed a petition.
8. Taken part in a public demonstration.
9. Taken part in a strike.
10. Boycotted products.
11. Bought certain products for political, ethical, or environmental reasons.
12. Donated money to an organization.
13. Raised funds for an organization.
14. Attended a political meeting or rally.
15. Voted in a local government election.
16. Participated in illegal protest activities.
17. Formed a group of like-minded people.

question 7, which states "There are 15 countries in the European Union" (true or false). The answer to this question was true at the time that Pattie and colleagues asked. But due to accession of several countries to the EU including Romania, Latvia, and Bulgaria, the question was false when I interviewed youth in 2008–9.[34]

Political participation: I also replicated Pattie, Seyd, and Whiteley's (2004) measurement of political participation. They include seventeen questions on different ways in which citizens might get involved, shown in Table 1.3. These questions can be grouped into three main clusters of civic actions: Contact (1 to 5), Collective (8, 9, 14, 16, 17), and Individual (the remaining questions).[35]

---

[34] This is a valid question, of course, both when asked by Pattie and colleagues and when I asked it. However, if a respondent did not know the answer, the logic of guessing may be somewhat different in both cases. It might seem better to guess "false" because the question asks about an exact number of nations—this would lead to being incorrect in Pattie and colleagues' research, but correct in mine. The chances of guessing correctly on question 7, then, appear to have increased in my research, meaning that the comparability of results for question 7 should be treated with some caution.

[35] While this is a fairly extensive list of political activities to discuss in an interview situation, it is certainly not exhaustive of all potential ways youth could approach the

I made one change to the usage of Pattie, Seyd, and Whiteley's questions on civic engagement. They had prefaced the questions with the statement: "Which of these have you done to influence rules, laws, or policies in the last 12 months?" This introductory question could be helpful for emphasizing only actions that are motivated by a civic/political purpose. Unfortunately, some of my pilot interviewees found this language confusing. I made the decision in these early interviews to de-emphasize the starting text. I would still read it to my interviewees, but I would say "It is okay to include any time you have done this in the last twelve months." Because I asked a more generous and open-ended version of this question, it should be expected that the resulting levels of civic engagement will be inflated in comparison to the levels found by Pattie, Seyd, and Whiteley.[36] However, I maintain that because of the potential confusion of their introductory question, Pattie and co-authors' respondents likely underestimated their own involvement in actions that are civic or political.

RESEARCH FINDINGS

Civic identity: When I asked second-generation youth about being British or about what their British citizenship means to them, the responses were quite consistent. By far the most common response to these questions was "I was born here"—locating Britain as the place of birth and thus justification for membership in British society. Very often, youth would also speak of British citizenship as a source of legal rights or life opportunities. Rare was the young person who spoke of Britain as a source of their cultural identity or common history. The responses of second-generation youth to these questions of civic identity tend to resemble those of Mike and Hamid, as they contain a certain ambivalence to the cultural and political markers associated with Britishness and with the British state. I will examine these issues of loyalty and identity in more depth in Chapters 2 and 3.

---

political. For research with young British Muslims that considered a larger range of "borderline" political actions, such as discussing political cartoons or creating political graffiti, see Mustafa (2015).

[36] Pattie et al. (2004).

Table 1.4. Jamaican and Bengali youth political literacy, by religiosity

	British national sample[a] % correct	2nd-gen. youth average % correct	Jamaican low/med religiosity % correct	Jamaican high religiosity % correct	Bengali low/med religiosity % correct	Bengali high religiosity % correct
Minimum voting age 21? FALSE	91	94.5	67	100	100	100
British and EU elections separate? TRUE	75	66	78	75	47	79
Number of MPs is about 100? FALSE	60	72	67	73	85	65
Proportional representation? FALSE	43	47	11	54	69	45
Deposit for Parliament? TRUE	59	27	22	36	31	20
Commons and Lords equal? FALSE	62	72	56	62	62	95
EU is 15 States? FALSE	35	70	67	57	85	70
Average correct (of 7)	4.25	4.29	3.67	4.51	4.69	4.69

[a] The 2000 British national sample data are derived from Table 3.6 of Pattie et al. (2004: 89). Used with permission of Cambridge University Press.

Political literacy: Are second-generation youth knowledgeable and articulate citizens? Table 1.4 shows how well second-generation youth scored on each question and in total on the seven-question political knowledge quiz. The results are given for youth as a whole and are broken down by ethnicity, and then by religiosity within ethnicity. As one can see from the table, second-generation youth in my sample did remarkably well compared with citizens in Britain at large. The youth outscored the average British citizen on most questions and overall, demonstrating a level of political knowledge that is close to the group Pattie, Seyd, and Whiteley highlighted as most politically knowledgeable in Britain: high income middle-aged men who are highly educated and in professional or managerial positions. Nearly one-half of the youth in the complete sample for which I have full results (twenty-six of fifty-six) would be considered "politically knowledgeable" by Pattie and colleagues because they answered at least five questions correctly.

Why do these second-generation youth perform so well in a quiz of political knowledge? One overall factor may simply be their proximity to the British government, due to living in London. News on political issues may seem directly relevant, or more understandable, because Westminster is not far away. Another factor may simply be age and education. These youth were closer in age to a time when they learned political facts in school, making these easier to remember than they would be for many older adults. Some of the 18- to 25-year-olds I interviewed had taken A-Level exams or university courses in politics, and unsurprisingly these young people usually scored well on the political knowledge test.

There is reason to treat these results with caution. The sample size of youth is small and thus cannot be seen as a wholly reliable indicator of political knowledge. However, taking this objection seriously, it is nonetheless clear that second-generation youth score rather well in terms of political literacy.

Table 1.4 breaks down youth into subgroups. Overall Bengalis score better on the political quiz than Jamaicans, though not remarkably so. To understand the basis of this ethnic difference, we should first determine if there are religious effects.

As youth have been broken down further into categories of religiosity, we can see that, for Bengalis, religiosity appears to have absolutely no relationship with political knowledge. Someone who prays five times a day has no more likelihood of being knowledgeable in politics than someone who does not. In contrast, for Jamaicans high religiosity does seem to match with higher levels of political knowledge.

There are at least two possible explanations for this difference. First, maybe there is something different in terms of the religious environment of church in comparison to a mosque that boosts political knowledge—perhaps a greater emphasis on politics in sermons, for example. Or, to take this in the opposite way, there may be influences with a greater power to *dis*engage youth from political knowledge if they spend time on the streets of Brixton and away from religious institutions. Levels of violent crime and drug use are higher in Brixton than in the East End, for example.

A second explanation, which I find more compelling in this case, is that church attendance for Jamaicans is partly a proxy for social class.

The young people that I met at the two churches I studied, such as Mike, were most often either middle class or had middle-class aspirations. The Jamaican youth I recruited from the streets tended to be from lower income and class backgrounds. The class disparity can partly be explained in this way: the well-known churches of Brixton (e.g. Ruach Ministries and Brixton Seventh Day Adventist) attract attendees from across London, who come for the preaching or for the connection with a larger Jamaican or Black community. While most Jamaicans living in Brixton have lower incomes and social class, a much greater proportion of the Jamaicans in church each week are of relatively high class and income. Social class can be highly related to political knowledge. In the case of these young people, religion may simply be a proxy for class.[37]

The relationship of religion and class in the East End is not the same as it is in Brixton. The Bengali youth I came to know through interviews were, almost without exception, from families that are considered poor or working class by UK standards. The typical Bengali youth I met in an East End mosque was local from a modest socio-economic background; the typical Jamaican youth I met in a Brixton church was upwardly mobile and not local. The class effect, then, was not clearly evident for Bengali youth.[38] Instead, the overall strong scores for Bengali youth on political knowledge may have something to do with the civic culture of the East End. It is an issue we will examine more in the pages ahead.

In summary, second-generation youth as a whole are not disengaged from news and information on government. They have relatively high levels of political knowledge, which may in part be the result of proximity to Westminster, student age, or in some cases social class. Regardless, there is no clear indication that religion or

---

[37] This is not to say that there is no religious effect present. For example, religious services may help to shape working-class youth to have middle-class aspirations, due to the peers they encounter or the messages of hope and life success that some churches propagate.

[38] In making these comments, I am by no means suggesting that Bengalis in the East End are somehow removed from class distinctions. John Eade (e.g. 1994a, 1994b) has written since the early 1990s on educated and upwardly mobile East End Bangladeshis; Sarah Glynn (2005, 2015) has documented Bengali involvement in housing and class struggles; and others (e.g. Gardner 1993, 2008; DeHanas 2013b) have explored uneven class relations between London and Sylhet. Instead I am arguing that I observed a strong correlation between social class and religious attendance in the institutions I studied in Brixton that was not evident in the East End mosques.

Table 1.5. Jamaican and Bengali youth political participation, by religiosity[a]

	British national sample[b] % yes	Jamaican low/med religiosity % yes	Jamaican high religiosity % yes	Bengali low/med religiosity % yes	Bengali high religiosity % yes
Individual					
Voted locally	74	0	18	57	47
Signed petition	47	<u>55</u>	25	64	80
Campaign badge/sticker	24	22	8	31	<u>58</u>
Donated money to org.	64	55	<u>77</u>	77	<u>100</u>
Raised funds for org.	30	22	<u>36</u>	31	<u>74</u>
Boycotted products	34	11	<u>36</u>	31	<u>63</u>
Bought products	33	33	15	31	<u>53</u>
Contact					
Contacted politician	17	22	8	31	42
Contacted organization	12	11	<u>39</u>	39	<u>68</u>
Contacted public official	31	33	15	85	<u>68</u>
Contacted media	9	11	15	31	<u>53</u>
Contacted legal profess.	20	<u>22</u>	0	39	21
Collective					
Public demonstration	4	22	38	21	15
Strike	3	0	0	8	0
Political meeting/rally	6	0	17	0	<u>28</u>
Protested illegally	2	0	0	0	0
Like-minded group	5	22	9	15	16
n (# of respondents)	809	9	14	13	20

[a] Differences between the high and low/medium religiosity groups of 20 points or more are shown in bold underline.
[b] The 2001 British national sample data are derived from Table 8.3 of Pattie et al. (2004: 233). Used with permission of Cambridge University Press.

religiosity has a substantial role in political knowledge, except perhaps as a mediator of some other primary cause.

Political participation: Thus far, we have seen that London second-generation youth have low levels of identification with Britain, but that their levels of political knowledge about the nation are near those of the average citizen, if not higher. This moderate to high level of political knowledge may be reason for optimism.

Yet with political participation, we begin to see a different story. Results of political participation are shown in Table 1.5. The table compares Jamaican and Bengali youth, and breaks them down by religiosity. There is also a comparison to the British population overall.

As will be clear from a quick glance at the table, the levels of political participation among Bengali second-generation youth are

Losing Faith in the State? 39

consistently higher than those of Jamaican youth. There could be many possible explanations for this disparity. Because this book focuses on religious explanations, I will primarily address the possibilities of religious causes in this chapter.

First, we should look at a key civic indicator in any democratic nation: voting. A full 74 percent of the British population in the Citizen Audit Survey said that they had voted in a local government election within the past year (in their case this was 2001). Second-generation youth do not compare well to this national figure. About 51 percent of Bengali youth who were of eligible age claimed to have voted in a local election in the last year. Remarkably, only 11 percent of eligible age Jamaican youth also claimed to have voted.

The low percentages of voting among the youth I interviewed are further accentuated because, for most youth interviewees, the past twelve months had included a significant and very high profile election: the election of the Mayor of London. The Mayor of London is the most powerful directly elected figure in Britain (because the Prime Minister is selected through an indirect democratic process).[39] The Mayor of London election in April 2008 looked to be a tight race between Labour incumbent Ken Livingstone and Conservative Boris Johnson, who was the eventual winner. In fact, I spoke with the Youth Pastor of Ruach Ministries, Mark Liburd, at length about the Mayor of London election in our interview. In a youth service that I attended, I heard Pastor Mark encourage his young people to vote in the election, as he talked about the platforms of the major candidates succinctly without showing favoritism. Yet Pastor Mark's appeal for voting did not have observable results: none of the six youth I interviewed from his congregation had voted in the Mayoral election. I happened to schedule my interview with one of these youth, Rhona, for the evening of the actual day of the election. Rhona is one of the young leaders of the congregation, and was always connecting with people or helping run the youth service at Ruach when I saw her there. I asked if she had been able to vote. "No," she said, a bit embarrassed, "because I've been at college *the whole day* and

---

[39] The Prime Minister is not directly elected. Rather, Members of Parliament (MPs) are elected by their constituents, usually on the basis of the party they represent. If a party achieves the majority of MPs, its party leader is able to form a government and become Prime Minister. In the event that no single party achieves a majority, a coalition government may be formed from parties that together amount to a majority (as in 2010–15), or a new election may be called.

I couldn't get out." She was not really sure where to go to vote, "Where is it though?"—unaware that her designated polling location is in the ward in which she lives.

From talking with other non-voting youth about why they did not vote, the reasons of being busy, finding voting inconvenient, or not having enough information were often mentioned. These results confirm the earlier work of Kingsley Purdam and his colleagues, who found inconvenience to be a major reason for missing an election.[40] Other reasons I heard from interviewees for not voting included not being interested in politics or not thinking that voting makes a difference. These views were somewhat more widespread among Jamaican youth than Bangladeshis, a likely contribution to the large differential in voting numbers. I found it interesting, though, in the specific case of Rhona, that the youth pastor's example and encouragement to vote had not been enough to motivate a young leader in his congregation. Voting rates are clearly a problem for Jamaican youth in Brixton. It seems that if churches are trying to encourage this element of political participation the results have been muted at best.

But voting, however important, is only one of many ways to engage as a citizen and in politics. Some of the other measures of political participation are quite obviously connected to mosque or church attendance. When I asked youth about whether they had contacted an organization, the religious attendees were more likely to do so, especially mosque-goers. This is unsurprising, due to the close ties many organizations have with mosques, or in the cases that youth interpreted contacting an organization to include their religious organization itself. Likewise, a full 100 percent of high religiosity Muslim youth reported that they have given to charity in the last year. Plastic charity boxes are ubiquitous around East End mosques, and *zakat*, a form of regular charitable giving, is one of the Pillars of Islam. High religiosity Jamaican Christians also gave money to organizations at much higher levels than their less religious peers, as they had both more opportunity and inclination to do so in their churches.

Beyond contacting organizations or giving money to them, however, there were many civic engagement activities in the questionnaire that are less obviously related to attendance at a religious institution.

[40] Purdam et al. (2002).

Addressing these, first among Jamaican youth, the religiosity pattern is not initially clear. In some cases, youth who are highly religious were more active (e.g. boycotting products, taking part in demonstrations, attending political rallies). In other cases, youth who did not show a regular religious commitment were more active (e.g. signing a petition, purchasing products for ethical reasons, contacting an official). We are working with very small sample sizes here—only fourteen Jamaican youth who are highly religious, and nine who are not—so there are not enough cases to make a clear judgment on any item. However, it can be said that in the aggregate there is no general trend, and no overall basis to argue for a positive or a negative effect of religiosity on the civic engagement of young Jamaicans.[41]

For Bangladeshis, in contrast, the influence of religiosity on civic engagement is positive, strong, and fairly consistent. The data set for Bangladeshis is larger than for Jamaicans, though still too small for statistical tests of significance. Instead of statistical tests, I use a guideline of 20 percentage points in difference as a rough indicator of substantial effects in the data. All 20-point differences are labeled in the table in bold and underline. For almost half of all political behaviors (eight of seventeen), the proportion of high religiosity Bangladeshi youth involved is at least 20 points higher than for those who are not as religious: contacting an organization, contacting the media, wearing a badge or sticker, signing a petition, boycotting products, purchasing products, fundraising, or taking part in a political rally. In some of these cases—such as boycotting products or wearing campaign badges—the effects are dramatic.

Also significant is the fact that high religiosity was negatively associated with voting behavior, even if this effect was modest. Seen in the light of many other positive citizenship behaviors—such as wearing campaign badges or raising funds—it seems strange that voting would not also share in the positive religiosity effect. In a few cases, youth may have abstained from voting out of Islamic principle.[42] Much more

---

[41] One possible exception here may be taking part in a demonstration. Of the Jamaican interviewees I spoke with who had taken part in demonstrations, all five who were highly religious had been involved in demonstrations that were directly church sponsored. Two had been part of the 2008 Seventh Day Adventist LIVE March against gun and knife crime. I profile the LIVE March from the following year, 2009, in Chapter 6.

[42] Hizb ut-Tahrir (HT), for example, is an Islamic social movement active in the East End of London and elsewhere that advocates total separation from the

common, however, is a simple alienation or apathy regarding voting. Yet the fact that highly religious Bangladeshi youth engage so frequently in campaigning activities but not in voting appears, for the moment, to be in tension.

To summarize the results to this point: (1) second-generation London youth have low levels of cultural identification with Britain, yet (2) reasonably high levels of political knowledge. (3) Bangladeshis have higher levels of political participation than Jamaicans and (4) among Bangladeshis higher religiosity appears to influence youth into greater participation still. Religiosity does not have an observable relationship with political participation among Jamaicans. Finally, (5) the positive effect of Muslim religiosity on political participation does not extend to the most crucial conventional political activity: voting.

Having reviewed these findings, it is now possible to begin a consideration of the three hypotheses of youth civic engagement introduced earlier in the chapter. The first hypothesis was youth *apathy*. The evidence does not provide a basis for arguing that second-generation youth as a whole are apathetic towards citizenship and politics, as they have a relatively strong performance on measures of political literacy. Certainly some second-generation youth are apathetic towards public affairs. Yet it seems that youth in general are fairly well informed about the British political system and how it works. This indicates there is a widespread interest in issues that are political, even among some youth who do not directly speak about this interest or translate it into participation.

Are youth instead *alienated* from politics? For most youth I spoke with, satisfaction with the British political process and trust of politicians was low. This was often true of youth who demonstrated significant political knowledge. Alienation from British politics, then, remains a viable explanation for at least some youth who show low levels of political participation.

The third hypothesis was that although some youth will engage in substantial civic behaviors, they will largely confine these to more *atomistic* activities. A first glance at the evidence does seem to

mainstream political process, because the process is not Islamic. HT specifically discourages voting in British elections. The proscribed organization Islam4UK, formerly known as al-Muhajiroun, also argued that voting in British elections is prohibited in Islam.

confirm this hypothesis. For all subcategories of youth in Table 1.5, the strongest levels of participation were on individual measures. The weakest were collective. The particularly strong individual measures were those relating to personal financing of a cause, which Pattie and colleagues have called "cheque-book participation."

Yet a closer look at youth civic behaviors is necessary before concluding that they are indeed primarily atomistic. A useful way to address this issue is to investigate in greater depth a particular behavior that may seem to epitomize atomism: the consumer behavior of boycotting products. In the interviews, I asked youth to tell me specifically which products they choose to boycott. I summarize their self-reports of boycotting in Tables 1.6 and 1.7, marking the frequencies that each product was mentioned with Xs.

Jamaican and Bangladeshi youth each mentioned a substantial number of different products that they boycott. The fact that Bangladeshis listed more is in large part simply an artifact of sample size, as there were about one-third more Bangladeshis in the sample for which I have complete data on this question (thirty-two) than there were Jamaicans (twenty-three). More important than the number of listed products are the frequencies that products are repeatedly listed. Seven Bangladeshi youth separately told me that they boycott Starbucks. Bangladeshis also clustered around boycotts for Danone, Coca Cola, and, to a lesser degree, the department store Marks & Spencer

Table 1.6. Brands that Bengali youth boycott

Company or item	Frequency	Reason given
Starbucks	XXXXXXX	Israel link
Coca Cola	XXXX	Israel link
Danone	XXXX	Denmark link
Marks & Spencer	XX	Israel link; child labor
McDonald's	XX	Israel link
Primark clothes	XX	Unethical labor
Animal-tested prod.	X	Unethical practice
AOL	X	Israel link
Bangladeshi shrimp	X	Unethical labor
DKNY clothes	X	Israel link
Nandos restaurants	X	False claim to be *halal*
Nestlé	X	Denmark link
Next clothing	X	Israel link
Sky Television	X	Israel link
Tesco groceries	X	Israel link
Waitrose groceries	X	Israel link
$n = 32$		

Table 1.7. Brands that Jamaican youth boycott

Company or item	Frequency	Reason given
Animal-tested prod.	X	Unethical practice
Calvin Klein	X	Blurred gender ads
Genetically modif.	X	Unethical practice
Name brand clothes	X	Unethical labor
Rowntree candies	X	Racism
Selfridges	X	Blurred gender ads
Tate & Lyle sugar	X	Racism
Timberland	X	Racism
Tommy Hilfiger	X	Racism
Top Shop/Top Man	X	Blurred gender ads
Von Dutch clothes	X	Racism
$n = 23$		

and the clothing store Primark. What appears at first to be an individualistic behavior—one's shopping choices—in fact seems to have an underlying collective nature.

When I asked Bangladeshi youth the reasons for boycotting these particular products, the collective organization of boycotting became more apparent. Easily the most common reason Bangladeshis chose to boycott products was the alleged connection of these products to financing Israel (Figure 1.1), and more particularly to what they consider to be Zionist activities against Palestinians. Second in frequency was boycotting products connected to Denmark because of the Danish Cartoons Affair.[43] My conversation with Hamid, the young man introduced at the beginning of this chapter, provides a good example:

> HAMID: I've boycotted certain Israeli products. I don't know what your view is on Israel, but certain products. I mean, Israel—I see so much injustice there, a lot that's happening and while it's not being portrayed in the media, [Palestinians are] not even getting support. Things like they're not even being allowed to get medicine because of the blockades. And I think the least we could do is boycott the funds because the Israelis, they do get a lot of funds from big businesses. And I think even companies like Coca Cola. So I try and boycott these things. One person said to me, it's like

---

[43] The Danish daily paper *Jyllands-Posten* published a set of controversial cartoons portraying the Prophet Muhammad, which led to anger and protest in many parts of the world. For a thorough analysis of the Danish Cartoons Affair, see Klausen (2009).

Losing Faith in the State?

Figure 1.1. A "Boycott Israeli Goods" campaign sticker at a pedestrian crossing on Whitechapel Road

you're paying a penny for an Israeli product, that penny will eventually turn into a bullet and that bullet will actually kill a person... Also other things, like the Danish—what happened with the cartoons. I decided to boycott Danish products.

DND: How do you know which products to boycott?

HAMID: Research on the Internet. But Israel uses certain barcodes a lot of the times. So you see—there's a website on there, it's called InMinds.com about Israeli products or companies that fund Israel.

Similarly, Rubina is one of many young Bangladeshis who boycott Starbucks due to its alleged ties to Israel. She told me "a lot of [Starbucks'] money goes to the Jewish people to kill the Palestinians." I wondered why she thought this to be true. She said: "Even though I don't know for sure if, you know, it does, there's a lot of Muslim websites I've gone on... Because the Internet anyone could throw anything on it, you know, so you don't know what to trust. But I say if I'm doubting it, I'd stay away from it." In addition to Internet sources in general, other youth told me that they knew products to boycott because friends had sent them a text, an email forward, or had notified them through Facebook.

Bangladeshis' predominant reasons for boycotting products—due to ties to Israel or Denmark—are collective in two ways. First, the behaviors are collectively organized through information and communication technologies. And second, they are collectively motivated, because youth who think of themselves as members of the Muslim *ummah* are resisting threats to a sense of collective identity.

The highly collective response of Bangladeshi Muslim boycotting can lead to strange results at times. For example, I had the following exchange with Zarena, who spoke first about the clothing company DKNY and then about Nestlé, the food company based in Switzerland:

DND: Have you boycotted certain products?
ZARENA: Yes—DKNY because they support the Israelite country in war and a percentage of their profit goes to Israel, and they're at war with Palestinians who are Muslims. So I don't want to support that. Nestlé's for a while because of the Denmark...
DND: Oh okay. How are they connected to that?
ZARENA: Yes, I heard that Nestlé's were.
DND: Because Nestlé's is—Are they Danish? Are they from Denmark?
ZARENA: I have no idea. But I just got texts!

This exchange demonstrates the highly collective nature of these boycotts. Far from being an educated individual consumer choice, boycotting Denmark and Israel is a collective effort that sometimes involves conforming to unsubstantiated claims.[44]

Salma, another young Bangladeshi woman, told me that boycotting is quite often based on "rumors." She said "everyone will just email you. Like all my friends, they'll hear it from other friends and it just gets passed through email really." For example "there was a thing about Walkers Crisps having alcohol in them." It turned out to just be a rumor: "I went on their website and they tell you all the ingredients!" Yet, the high level of sensitivity to collective Muslim issues can lead youth to take a cautious stance to products. In Rubina's words: "If I'm doubting it, I'd stay away from it."

As seen in Table 1.6, not all second-generation Bangladeshi youth boycotting is a collective response to a political issue like the boycotts of Israel and Denmark. In some cases, youth choose to boycott

---

[44] Similar to the case of Nestlé, the food company Danone was boycotted by several youth in relation to the Danish Cartoons Affair despite being headquartered in France (see Table 1.6).

companies that allegedly engage in unethical practices such as the use of child labor or the misrepresentation of their products. The overall structure of Bangladeshi youth boycotting, however, is predominantly collective in nature.

Jamaican youth also boycott a wide range of products. These boycotting behaviors do not cluster around any single product more than once. Jamaican youth apparently choose products to boycott out of their individual decisions of conscience rather than in response to collective mobilization efforts.

At times Jamaican youth boycotting decisions can be highly personal, even idiosyncratic. For example, Clarise told me about several brands she boycotts in reaction to a recent trend in "blurred gender" advertising:

> Well like Calvin Klein, right now they're promoting this whole line. It's like they've blurred gender. So it's like when they have their male models, they look very feminine and then when they have their female models they look very masculine. And I notice Selfridges is doing the same thing. I don't believe in that because to me that means that you, you're not identifying that a woman is a woman and a man is a man. And so you also promote homosexuality which I... it's not that I'm against the [homosexual] person, I just don't believe in that act. So that's why I don't buy from certain shops, like Top Shop and Top Man—they're also carrying that whole thing as well.

Clarise's reason for boycotting Calvin Klein, Selfridges, Top Shop, and Top Man is one she developed out of her convictions on appropriate representations of gender. Like most Bangladeshi Muslims, her decision to boycott is rooted in religion. Yet the fact that other Jamaican youth did not cite blurred gender as a reason indicates that Clarise's choice to boycott is an individual one.

Similarly, Michelle told me that she boycotts a significant range of products as a response to the racist policies of their companies. She spoke about Tate & Lyle, the British sugar brand: "In South Africa, they were supporting Apartheid, so I'm thinking I need to get away from these people!" Michelle also boycotts Timberland, Tommy Hilfiger, and Rowntree candies due to their alleged racism. It might seem that racism is a significantly collective reason for boycotting. Yet Michelle is virtually alone in citing it as a reason for boycotts—only one other Jamaican youth, Thaddeus, mentioned racism as a reason for boycotting. Thaddeus named a different company that he boycotts as racist, Von Dutch Jeans.

In comparing Bangladeshi and Jamaican youth, I am not making a statement on the relative weight of racism or Zionism as collective issues. Instead, the examples illustrate that the political action of boycotting is organized in a collective manner among Bangladeshis while it is an individually developed choice for Jamaicans. I am convinced by Pattie, Seyd, and Whiteley's analysis that the overall British population's political behavior has been shifting towards atomism. Such atomism appears to be mirrored in Brixton Jamaican young people's political actions. Yet atomism is not a viable description of how East End Bangladeshi youth participate in these political behaviors, as collective mobilizations so obviously underlie their actions.

REVISITING MIKE AND HAMID

Early in this chapter I profiled Mike and Hamid and the attitudes they express towards British culture and politics. Both showed relatively low levels of cultural identification with Britain and, at least on the surface, seemed to be uninterested in taking political action themselves. Now that we have reviewed general figures on political activity among Jamaican and Bangladeshi youth, we can return to Mike and Hamid to see if they will help us to put flesh on those numbers.

Mike, the Jamaican youth introduced early in this chapter, had told me that any political action he might take "doesn't make that much of a difference." When I asked him about specific political actions that he has taken over the past year his reasons for this attitude became more apparent. He said he would not contact a local politician because "my local politician is Labour, and I'm more Tory for some reason." He went on to elaborate why he thought his difference of party affiliation rendered any local political contact ineffectual:

> You know the recent fight on the embryo rule?... They're mixing like embryos, human embryos, with cow things. For Labour, that was the only party, Gordon Brown said, that is going to whip. Which basically means you have to follow the Labour position. So, because my local MP is Labour, will [contacting him] make a difference?

Mike's question was a pointed one. His explanation of British politics revealed considerable sophistication, as he was keeping current with parliamentary debates on laws regarding human embryo use in science and he had strong political (and religious) convictions to bring into these debates. Yet the political system, as he understands it, stymies any potential for his influence because the unified Labour whip position is seemingly unchangeable. Mike's description of the British political system is a far cry from the optimism that political scientists Almond and Verba observed among Britons in the 1960s, who expressed "general system pride as well as satisfaction with specific government performance."[45] Mike continued to explain his grievances with the British political system [emphasis original]:

> The thing is, when you're living in this country, the laws that will affect you are already going through and will be implemented. So it's kind of weird like. You have to vote based on a manifesto that they have beforehand, and then you *experience it during their term*. And because their term starts here [uses a hand gesture to motion the start], it's not going to make that much difference. I mean, maybe local councils are more, there's more of a place where you can have your opinion expressed in a more effectual way. But I wouldn't do that myself.

Mike's disaffection with the British political system stretched beyond relationships with political representatives to encompass other forms of conventional politics. His level of political participation is low across almost all measures. He does not claim to sign petitions, wear campaign badges, boycott products, or purchase products for political or ethical reasons, for example. Mike's only forms of "political" participation were those that took place firmly within the bounds of his church. He gives money to the church, fundraises for it, and says that he has "organized a group of like-minded people" to attend the church regularly. In fact, his church, Ruach Ministries, is the only voluntary organization in which Mike is involved. Mike did say that he would be interested in voting, but, as he had just turned 18 recently, there was no way to evaluate whether this desire would transfer into practice.

---

[45] In the early 1960s, American researchers Almond and Verba (1963: 315) praised Britain for its political culture: "Exposure to politics, interest, involvement, and a sense of competence are relatively high. There are norms supporting political activity, as well as emotional involvement in elections, and system affect. And the attachment to the system is a balanced one: there is general system pride as well as satisfaction with specific government performance" (quoted in Whiteley 2003).

Overall, Mike has no discernible involvement in politics outside church because he feels alienated from the British political system. Interestingly, as quoted earlier, he demonstrates a high level of political literacy when he expresses this alienation. In fact, on the British political knowledge quiz, Mike correctly answered five out of seven questions. His performance on this measure put him in the category Pattie and co-authors define as "politically knowledgeable." As someone entering the London School of Economics to study law, Mike's ability to reason and argue in political terms is likely to increase. He has strong convictions on issues like the embryo bill in Parliament.[46] Yet he seems unlikely to express his political concerns outside of his own Christian circles.

Hamid, the Bangladeshi youth introduced earlier, also expressed a highly negative view of politics. He had gone as far as to say: "There is not a political bone in my body." As we began to talk through potential forms of political participation, I realized that Hamid was much more involved and knowledgeable of politics than I could have expected.

Hamid's political literacy is quite high. On the political knowledge quiz he correctly answered six of seven questions, placing him in the "politically knowledgeable" category. He told me that he regularly watches the politics television show *Question Time*. Although he primarily spoke negatively about British politicians and media (using words such as "spin" and "politics [is] a dirty game"), it was clear from our conversation that he keeps abreast of current affairs and the workings of the political system.

Most of Hamid's civic and political actions arise out of his involvement in voluntary organizations. Hamid takes an active role in so many organizations that he had trouble listing them all: he is a leader in FOSIS (campus Islamic societies) for the London region, volunteers at Ummah Welfare Trust and InterPalestine (two Islamic humanitarian aid NGOs), helps arrange Islamic courses with a local organization, assists at an educational trust, helps produce a Muslim children's magazine, and is active in his locality with a Bangladeshi neighborhood association. From listening to Hamid's wide range of

---

[46] The Human Fertilisation and Embryology Act became law in 2008. Mike had noted his objection to hybrid human and animal embryos, an objection shared by many Christian MPs at the time including cabinet minister Ruth Kelly. See *BBC News* (2008).

involvements, I could understand why he needs a bike to rush from meeting to meeting. The contrast could hardly be greater with the singularity of Mike's voluntary involvement, set exclusively within his church.

Hamid's many voluntary engagements form the bulk of the context and motivation for his political participation, which has been extensive. He had recently contacted politicians, including local councilors, to involve them in events sponsored by organizations with which he volunteers. He regularly gives to charities and fundraises, wears campaign badges, signs petitions, boycotts products, and purchases products for ethical reasons. When he is angered by a portrayal of Muslims in a media source, Hamid writes a letter or email to the editor. "It probably seems like it's gone to deaf ears a lot of the time," he said, "because a lot of times we get media which is very negative and very unfair."

Hamid had recently become involved in a charged political issue at Queen Mary University. A prayer room controversy had emerged between the university and some of its Muslim students. Hamid told me that the room where I had witnessed him and fellow students praying, just minutes earlier, had been designated a Muslim prayer room for the entire previous academic year. Hamid said that this decision made good sense, because Queen Mary has the largest number of Muslim students of any British university. The Muslim students who prayed in the room appreciated the freedom to keep Qur'ans and other religious books available there. But, Hamid told me, in the current academic year:

> Funnily enough, some of us come back and find it's been made into a multi-faith room. We can't keep our books there. We can't have it after six, and stuff. So now, that's really affected the work of the Islam Society.

The Queen Mary Islamic Society was at that time campaigning to re-designate the prayer room as Muslim-only. Across the Queen Mary campus I had seen prayer room campaign posters (the posters featured Spiderman in an Islamic prayer position). Hamid described the campaign's strategy and its challenges thus far:

> HAMID: We tried all the political avenues, all the legal avenues. Like over a hundred letters were written by different [Islamic Society] members. We tried many things which are in our power, but it seems like it's not working.

DND: Okay, so you tried writing letters...
HAMID: Petitions, meetings, emails to [the new university principal].
DND: Okay. Did you do things like protest?
HAMID: Not yet, we wanted to avoid that...
DND: Or how about going on strike and saying, I'm not going to class...
HAMID: We wanted to avoid this because we thought, you know, there's peaceful methods of doing it and don't want to have a hindrance on the relationship we have. Our pressure's not working so we might have to think of Plan B... To maybe take it into protest and stuff. Let's see.

Hamid had recently contacted a legal representative to discuss the legal ramifications of some of these further alternatives.

The two cases of Mike and Hamid certainly cannot represent the diversity of civic attitudes and practices among Jamaican and Bangladeshi second-generation youth. Yet, as some of the more articulate young people I interviewed, these two young men help to illustrate some of the broader trends that are observable in the overall data. Both Mike and Hamid express relatively low levels of identification with "Britishness" as a cultural or civic category. Yet this apparent weakness in civic identity does not translate into political apathy, as both young men maintain a strong working knowledge of current affairs and the political system.

Mike and Hamid both express negative attitudes towards British politics. For Mike, this appears to be out of feeling alienated from a system in which he has little faith. For Hamid, the disaffection with politics seems instead to be an effort to avoid being tainted by the corruption he perceives.

Hamid participates in political activities in an alternative, perhaps purer, sphere of Muslim organizations such as his university Islamic Society and Islamic humanitarian NGOs. He is not taking part in what have traditionally been the major organizations in British politics, such as political parties or unions. When Hamid engages with a secular organization, his motives are expressly Islamic—such as writing a letter to a newspaper about the representation of Muslims or sending a petition about the prayer room to the Queen Mary University administration. This emphasis on an alternative politics, exemplified by Hamid, was more broadly characteristic of Bangladeshis as a group. It is perhaps unsurprising, then, that while religious involvement motivates East End Bangladeshi youth to participate in the dynamic local scene of Islamic institutions and activist networks, my findings do not indicate that it makes them more likely to vote.

Mike has not found many outlets for political participation, as he is not involved in civil society organizations beyond his church. This was more generally true of the Jamaican youth I interviewed. Some Jamaicans were apathetic towards politics and some (like Mike) alienated from it. Others, like Clarise who boycotts "blurred gender" products, are engaged in political activities. Yet each person's political activities are not widely shared, meaning that these youth largely mirror a British trend towards atomism and individual "cheque-book" participation.

The trend of atomism was not very frequently observed among Bangladeshis, most of whom are involved in collective political efforts. Some Bangladeshi youth were apathetic and some were alienated. Yet, overall, Bangladeshi political participation is much higher than that of Jamaicans. And the level of participation is higher still among highly religious Muslims. In other words, young East End Bangladeshis and young Brixton Jamaicans are qualitatively different in political terms. There is a substantial participation gap—a gap that only widens among more religiously active young Muslims and Christians. Now that we have identified this participation gap, over the chapters that follow we will progressively uncover its causes and, I hope, build towards an understanding of ways it can be narrowed.

2

Muslim First

"Many British Muslims have divided loyalties" narrates Jeremy Vine on an episode of *Panorama*, the BBC investigative journalism show.[1] The episode opens with segments of documentary footage: police in riot gear confront an angry mob of Muslim protesters, radical preachers speak out against democracy, and a troubled White Muslim convert attempts to bomb a restaurant in Exeter. Further into the episode are various street scenes from British cities, including Brick Lane in East London, where bearded Muslim men, women in *hijab*, and urban mosques are accompanied by ominous music. The overall message of the program is that radicalism lies just under the surface of British Islam. The trustworthiness of British Muslims must be questioned. The title of the episode captures these fears of divided loyalties: "Muslim First, British Second."

Although the *Panorama* episode is sensationalist, it is important not to dismiss outright the concerns it raises. Loyalties to extremist causes *are* a problem in Britain, however small the number of cases may be. The 2013 murder of Lee Rigby in broad daylight on a Woolwich street confirms this. Timothy Garton Ash, in a measured article for *The Guardian* written after the 7/7 2005 London bombings, argues that young British Muslims' loyalties are a widespread problem.[2] Ash writes: "For anyone who has hoped and believed, as I have, that the British way of integrating Muslim citizens is more promising than the French one, the last year has been discouraging." He cites a Pew Global Attitudes Survey of Muslims, which found that 81 percent of young British Muslims identified as Muslim "first," above being British. In contrast, only 46 percent of the youth surveyed in France

---

[1] Vine and Watson (2009).   [2] Ash (2006).

Figure 2.1. The self-identification ranking exercise

chose Muslim above their nation of citizenship. In the entire global survey, which included several Muslim majority countries, Pakistan was the only state in which the levels of "Muslim first" identity (87 percent) exceeded those of Britain.[3] For Ash, these figures are a worrying sign of large-scale Muslim youth alienation from British citizenship.

What do young people mean when they choose "Muslim first"? In this chapter I attempt to understand the patterns among the Bengali Muslim youth I interviewed in London's East End. I asked youth during the interview to choose between cards labeled with identity options and rank these in order of strength (see Figure 2.1).[4] This

---

[3] Pakistan's high percentage of "Muslim first" was probably at least as much due to weaknesses in the provisions of Pakistani citizenship as it was to a resurgence of Islam (see Naqvi 2011). Unfortunately Bangladesh was not included in the Pew Survey. The full list of Arab or Muslim majority nations included is: Morocco, Jordan, the Palestinian Authority, Lebanon, Kuwait, Pakistan, Indonesia, and Turkey.

[4] The term "identity" can be inadequate if it implies inheriting something that is fixed and unchangeable. In this book I tend to use the terms "identification" or "self-identification" to emphasize that identification is a process of prioritization rather than being set at a fixed point. However, because "identity" is such a widespread

exercise allowed me to explore the dynamic nature of self-identification, as they worked out which options to choose and rank, sometimes changing their minds during our conversation.

The work of French theorist Michel de Certeau can be helpful for understanding why people may choose some identity options and not others. De Certeau writes that everyday life is filled with "tactics" and "strategies." Institutions develop strategies for reproducing their power, while ordinary people try to outmaneuver these institutions by using tactics.[5] In the East End, such relationships are fairly complex. There is no single strategic influence on young people, but instead various strategies of parents, media, the state, and Islamic institutions play against each other. It is often "strategic" institutions themselves (in this context the East London Mosque and Darul Ummah Mosque) that provide young people with resources they can use, tactically, to loosen the grip of other institutions.

Therefore, as we shall see, young people in the East End have tactical motivations for choosing to identify themselves as "Muslim first." Their choice is not evidence of mindlessly stepping onto a conveyor belt towards extremism or violence. In fact, it is usually the opposite: an attempt to gain greater control over their own lives. Before these East End tactics of identity can be fully explained, however, it will be helpful to briefly consider some of the previous research on second-generation identities, which can be grouped into four styles.

FOUR TACTICAL STYLES OF SELF-IDENTIFICATION

Continuity

Much previous research on the second generation in Britain, particularly South Asians, demonstrates the high importance of generational and family influences. First-generation Bangladeshis tend to maintain

---

concept (and is a word used by young people themselves), I use this term also with the understanding that it refers to a dynamic process. For an excellent discussion of these issues, see Brubaker and Cooper (2000).

[5] Certeau (2011 [1984]). The interpretation of Michel de Certeau that I employ here builds on Linda Woodhead's (2013) lucid essay "Tactical and Strategic Religion."

strong ties with their home village, communicating frequently, sending remittances, and maintaining the illusion of eventual return.[6] Members of this first generation usually bring a traditional Sufi-infused Barelwi form of Islam. Some may become more conservative in practices (such as adopting a stricter interpretation of *hijab*) as they become aware of their distinctiveness from British society.[7] Several researchers have shown strong links between the second generation and their first-generation migrant parents. These researchers argue that there is a substantial amount of *continuity* between generations. Danièle Joly, for example, describes the critical role of families in the development of the Pakistani second generation in Birmingham, in which traditional Islam can be a medium for maintaining intergenerational family ties, communication, and understanding.[8] Jessica Jacobson finds that second-generation Pakistani youth in London may have any of a diverse set of reactions to parents' religious and cultural backgrounds—from positive acceptance to complete rejection—but that parental influence is almost always important.[9] Childhood years are typically characterized by continuity with parents' cultural traditions, and thus this identity style will initially be pre-tactical (in de Certeau's terms). As youth develop agency and enter adolescence, however, continuity is more likely to emerge as one tactical choice among others.

Between Cultures

Social scientists studying second-generation youth often recognize adolescence and early adulthood as unsettled years in which family, religious, and ethnic self-identification are all open to question.[10] In contrast with perspectives that emphasize continuity, some scholars—including Muhammad Anwar and the various authors in a book edited by James L. Watson—argue the second generation finds itself caught *between cultures*.[11] Youth may experience an identity crisis as they are torn between strong parental, community, and religious norms and the usually more "Western" and liberal perspectives of peers, schooling, and media.

---

[6] Gardner (2002); Adams (1994).   [7] Ahmed (2005).
[8] Joly (1988).   [9] Jacobson (1998).
[10] See, for example, Lewis (2007).   [11] Anwar (1998a); Watson (1977).

There are two solutions often mentioned to a between cultures situation. Some youth will supplant the religio-cultural identities of their parents with a more "Western," or perhaps "White," identity espoused in school and by broader society. Other youth will resist the "host" culture and respond with a strengthened identification based in race, ethnicity, or religion. This second solution is variously termed the development of an "oppositional culture" or of an "adversarial subculture."[12] Researchers Katy Gardner and Abdus Shukur have argued, consistent with this view, that the affirmation Bangladeshi youth fail to receive from British society they may find instead in a strengthened, and possibly resistant, Muslim identity.[13]

Hybridity

While the "between cultures" approach emphasizes the disjuncture between discrete ethnic and national identities, other researchers have argued that second-generation identities have become blurred and multiple. Christine Sheikh argues that while Muslim American youth may identify "the West" and "Islam" as discrete cultural worlds, they are most often inclined to "take the best of both worlds."[14] Gerd Baumann studied second-generation youth of several ethnic backgrounds in the multicultural Southall area of London. He concludes that most youth are skilled in a multiplicity of cultural discourses, often creatively combining cultural influences, such as in *bhangra*, a fusion of Black hip hop and South Asian musical styles.[15] John Eade's work with young Bangladeshis in the East End and Claire Alexander's work with young Black Londoners also conclude that youth self-identifications are hybrid, situational, and should not be essentialized as fixed choices.[16] Les Back studied South London youth of many ethnic origins, including mixed-race youth. He argues that their syncretic and situational uses of identity cast doubt on whether—in the South London context—discussion of "British identity" is of any use at all.[17]

---

[12] On "oppositional culture" see Ogbu (1995). On "adversarial subculture" see Portes and Zhou (1993).
[13] Gardner and Shukur (1994).   [14] Sheikh (forthcoming).
[15] Baumann (1996).   [16] Eade (1994b); Alexander (1996).
[17] Back (1996).

The *hybridity* perspective represented by these researchers usually emphasizes the influence of peers in the social construction of identity. The theoretical underpinnings of hybridity can be found in the cultural studies and post-colonial writings of Stuart Hall, Paul Gilroy, Homi Bhabha, Gayatri Spivak, and others. It has rapidly grown to be an important, if not the dominant, view of ethnicity and identity within British social science.

Deculturation

Although hybridity perspectives are highly influential, especially in Britain, they have not gone unquestioned. Jessica Jacobson studied British Pakistani Muslims in East London in the 1990s. In *Islam in Transition* she writes that a "recurring theme throughout this book has been that theorists should be careful not to overestimate the extent to which aspects of identity are malleable and subject to interpretation." Jacobson continues:

> It seems to me vitally important to recognize that there are certain limits to the extent to which individuals can redefine themselves and the groups to which they belong; or that, at the very least, even if theoretically it is possible to challenge in countless ways such limits, they are very often accepted and hence, in practice, they exist.[18]

Jacobson found certain consistencies in the identities of her young Pakistani informants that belie what she considers to be an overemphasis on hybridity. In particular, while British, Pakistani, and other sources of self-identification can be questioned and redefined, for Jacobson's informants Islam was very commonly perceived to be a central source of orientation and stability. Many of Jacobson's informants appear to be attracted to the comprehensive answers of a culturally purified Islam, and have taken this all-encompassing, "universal" Islam as their seemingly immutable core identity marker. Similar observations of starkly purified Muslim identities have been noted by researchers of Bengalis in London, including Gardner and Shukur as well as Kibria, among others.[19]

---

[18] Jacobson (1998: 137).
[19] Gardner and Shukur (1994); Kibria (2008).

Table 2.1. Theorized styles of second-generation youth self-identification

	Primary ID	Polarization	Theorized language
Continuity	Parents' cultural/religious	Low. Insulated from conflict	"My mum always says..." "We have this tradition every year..."
Between cultures	Parents' cultural/religious OR British/English	High. Polarization of culture/religion against British/English	"It's hard to be a Bengali here..." "I had to get away from Bengalis to fit in..."
Hybrid or situational	Changes with the situation, context	Low. Ease in code-switching	"There's a bit of everything in me..." "It just depends on the situation..."
Deculturation	Religious	High. Polarization of "born again" religion and parents' culture/religion	"That's cultural. Religion is different..." "My parents don't know *real* Islam..."

Olivier Roy provides perhaps the most influential statement of this position in his work on the globalization of Islam.[20] Roy argues that the forms of Islam that have gained most ground among second-generation youth are "deculturated." Charismatic sheikhs, often in a Salafi tradition, claim to preach a universal and pure form of Islam that is unencumbered by the traditionalist cultures of the first generation. Youth who feel distanced or alienated from Western society and from the older generation find this narrative of an all-encompassing Islam very attractive. The *deculturation* perspective differs from a "between cultures" perspective because it locates the greater share of identity conflict as occurring between generations rather than between the culture of origin and the "host" society. Indeed Roy argues that even in cases when deculturation is rhetorically counterposed to Western modernity, its forms and methods are largely Western and intrinsically modern.

The four styles of self-identification (summarized in Table 2.1) span a wide range from seemingly fixed and stable identities to highly fluid and adaptable ones. Can de Certeau's idea of tactics help us understand such a range? The relevance of tactics to studying more hybrid or situational styles is obvious (for example, the tactics of code-switching).

[20] Roy (2004).

But tactics seem, at least initially, to be of less importance when there are firmer identity boundaries (as in deculturation) or when identities need not be chosen at all (in continuity). In any case, it is necessary to remember that tactics must be understood in reference to the strategies to which they respond. As Richard Jenkins has argued, self-identification is at the ongoing intersection of what is ascribed (strategies from the outside) and what is achieved (tactics from within).[21] The relative influence of each of these will vary.

BASIC YOUTH VALUES

How do youth in the East End talk about identity? I quickly learned some basic ground-rules. I was interviewing Tariq, an 18-year-old Bangladeshi, and we had just started to speak about being Muslim. I asked him to tell me more precisely what kind of Muslim he is. I was prepared to hear about Islamic schools of jurisprudence such as Hanafi and Shafi'i, or at least the broader division in Islam between Sunni and Shi'i. His response defied my expectations:

DND: [What type of Muslim are you?]
TARIQ: I don't fit any of those groups. I'm just me. We're just Muslims, chilled out, go to college, saving up to buy a PS3.

Tariq just wanted to be recognized as an ordinary teenager. Like any other teen might be, he was enrolled in college and saving up to buy a Play Station 3. His words communicated the very ordinariness he experienced in being a Muslim in the East End. In a sense, I had been asking an improper question: why did I dwell on labels, when he was just being himself?

Tariq's comment demonstrates his embeddedness in the "ethics of authenticity" that pervade Western culture.[22] The value of individual authenticity was expressed by every young person I interviewed, Bangladeshi or Jamaican, in one way or another. I heard youth in my interviews convey in various ways the same general philosophy: it is important to be yourself and communicate that self sincerely to others. When I asked them which types of people they saw as very

[21] Jenkins (2008). [22] Taylor (1992).

different from themselves, many expressed a strong distaste for hypocrites, the opposite of authentic individuals.

Because individuality and authenticity are so prized, youth place a high value on identities that they have chosen for themselves. Many talked about coming to understand their Islamic or Christian faith for the first time as an adolescent or young adult, through a conversion or "born again" experience. Youth likewise devalued some of the identities that they had not chosen. For example, Jessica, an 18-year-old with a Jamaican father told me: "I'm not Jamaican. Jamaican is in me, but . . . " By this she meant that though she has Jamaican ancestry, it is not an identity she has chosen and invested with significance.

Another value that most London second-generation youth share, linked to authenticity, is the positive value of diversity and multiculturalism. Some expressed pride that they have a diverse circle of friends. Others told me about how they love the diversity and exciting multiculture of London as a city. Shahedul, a 23-year-old Bangladeshi youth, did not choose "English" as an identity when we went through the identity choice-and-ranking exercise together, yet he did choose "British" and "Londoner." I asked him, why not English? "When I hear English," he told me, "I think of White people. But when I hear London, I think multicultural."

In a similar vein, most youth expressed a high level of tolerance for people of other cultures. For example, many Muslim Bangladeshis were very careful to stress that, though they believe Islam is the Truth, the Qur'an instructs them that "there is no compulsion in religion."

Overall, the fact that virtually all Bangladeshi and Jamaican second-generation youth share values of individual authenticity, diversity, and tolerance simply bears witness to the fact that they have grown up in a modern liberal democracy (and, within that, in a vibrant cosmopolitan and multicultural city). It would be highly surprising, of course, if they did not positively affirm values such as authenticity and diversity. These values are the very basis for their own acceptance in plural British society.

CHOOSING MUSLIM FIRST

A total of thirty-five of my thirty-six British Bengali interviewees took part in the identity ranking exercise. I had developed the set of labels

Muslim First

Table 2.2. Labels used in the self-identification ranking exercise

Black	Asian	African	British	Muslim
Brown	Indian	West Indian	English	Christian
White	Bangladeshi	Caribbean	Londoner	Non-Religious
	Bengali	Jamaican		+ blank write-ins
	Sylheti			

(shown in Figure 2.1 and Table 2.2) through the extensive fieldwork in my first months of research, and they were intended to capture the most locally salient group identities.[23] In each interview, I would ask the interviewee to select all of the cards that he or she could "personally relate to." I also included some blank cards that young person could use to write in any identities important to her that I had missed. Once she had made all of her choices, she was asked to rank them in order of strongest identification down to weakest. I then asked her to explain why she had ordered them in this way. We entered a conversation about the meanings of specific chosen identifications and the relationships between them, also discussing the cards that had been excluded and any the interviewees considered especially different from themselves.

I had designed the exercise to generate a good conversation about self-definition and the interrelationships between identity options. I found it extremely useful for this purpose. The interview situation was, of course, a moment in which youth could tactically deploy self-identification in reference to how they perceived me, as a White American non-Muslim academic researcher. This does not make the exercise less valuable, but instead shows its value for studying particularly self-conscious presentations of identity.[24]

---

[23] These include labels from my comparative local fieldwork with young second-generation Jamaicans in Brixton (e.g. "West Indian," "Jamaican"), which is analyzed in the next chapter. I included the full set of identity labels together for the interviews with Bengalis and Jamaicans. Some labels had significant overlap across the two groups (e.g. "Brown," "British"), while others did not (e.g. "Sylheti," "Caribbean").

[24] While the choice and ranking method was well suited for observing certain aspects of self-identification, it inevitably occluded others. The identity label cards I produced were limited. I did not, for example, include role identities such as daughter, brother, wife, father, student, or activist, although some of these could have been important to the self-definition of my interviewees. I likewise excluded identities which are seldom spoken about among young East End Bengalis, such as class and sexuality, which could have prompted valuable discussions on what is

Easily the most resounding pattern from the ranking exercise was the strength of Muslim self-identification. A full thirty-one of the thirty-five young Bengalis ranked Muslim first.[25] Here is how Asma, an 18-year-old, explained the pre-eminence of her Muslim identity:

> For me, religion is really important. So I would say I'm a Muslim first. It doesn't matter what culture I'm from, what country I'm from. Because the person I am is I'm a Muslim person. And that's how I live my life.

Several of the points Asma makes in this brief quote are worth elaboration because they express attitudes common to Bangladeshis I interviewed. Asma found religion "really important." She shared this feeling with about half of her Muslim peers, who had high religiosity.[26] When Asma looked at the identity labels on the table and noticed "Muslim," it did not take her any time to think about putting it on top. In this quote she speaks of how Muslim identity relativizes all other identity commitments: "It does not matter what culture I'm from, what country I'm from." Other identities may fall second or third, but their actual distance to Muslim is great because Muslim is qualitatively different. Muslim defines a type of person, with a particular moral orientation: "the person I am is I'm a Muslim person." And this seeps into all areas of daily experience and action: "that's how I live my life."

Virtually all Bangladeshis, like Asma, chose Muslim immediately from the identity options and placed it first. A frequent theme in describing Muslim identity was its permanence. Shah told me "Muslim is first due to the fact that it's my religion and nothing can ever change that."

---

usually left unsaid. In my view, adding many more cards such as these would have made the prioritization process too cognitively challenging. However, I would later realize that I had made one critical omission—gender. Four of my female Bengali interviewees, and one of the males, chose write-in cards to identify with a gender (accounting for the largest total number of write-ins). The greater proportion of females than males who did this is intriguing in itself, as it seems to indicate the significance that gender has in structuring the life experiences of East End Bengali young women.

[25] This closely matches the results of other research that uses identity ranking: Thomas and Sanderson (2012).

[26] For the purposes of this study, I define high Muslim religiosity as praying five times a day and expressing a positive regard for this level of practice. While this definition is limiting in many ways, it was derived from the most frequent distinction young Bengalis themselves made of their peers: between being "practicing" and "non-practicing."

However, "Muslim first" meant somewhat different things to different people. Quoting Shah again, he thinks of Muslim identity primarily as an inheritance from his parents: "You know my family were Muslims, and followed the religion. So it's literally that's why it comes first." Another young Bangladeshi, Mahmoud, spoke of his Muslim identity in more spiritual terms: "I've put Muslim first because my main goal in life is my relationship with God." Mahmoud referred to his Muslim identity as having ultimate importance: "As a Muslim, I believe in the afterlife, so my plans go beyond just the future in this life. They go to the future in the hereafter as well." Youth most commonly identified with Islam for one of two reasons—its connection to parents and family, or its truth as a spiritual doctrine. For some youth, Muslim identity was more problematic. Shahedul is a thin young man who was wearing a tan English flat cap when we spoke. In our conversation he would often tap the table with his finger when he was making a point. Shahedul placed "Muslim" first in his identity ranking, almost as a default. Yet as we spoke more about religion a few minutes later, Shahedul asked if we could change his ranking. He said, "I'm not really practicing anymore or going to mosque" and asked if we could shift Muslim down to fourth place, putting it below British, Londoner, and Asian. He was one of only four youth who did not place Muslim first—although he only did so after reflecting on it more.

Another youth who did not place Muslim first is an 18-year-old named Karim. I met Karim in a park near Whitechapel Road where he was loitering with four of his friends. He is about 6 feet 3 inches tall and very skinny, with dark skin. He was wearing a white Nike hoodie and a light blue baseball cap covered with dozens of small New York Yankees logos. Karim's identity ranking was unusual: It began with Sylheti first, and then progressed to Non-Religious, Muslim, Asian, British, English, and finally Londoner. Karim's first identity, Sylheti, comes because his parents are from that region.[27] At his young age they largely define his sense of roots. He included Non-Religious because he is currently not practicing Islam by attending prayers. Karim placed Muslim third, and spoke to me about the identity with visible guilt. He said: "I can't put it first because I'm smoking weed all the time."

---

[27] Sylhet is a region in northeastern Bangladesh, where the Sylheti dialect is spoken. The vast majority of Bengalis in Tower Hamlets trace their roots to Sylhet.

Muslim identity was "first" for almost all second-generation Bangladeshi youth I interviewed. Even in the few cases where Muslim identity did not rank first, most youth acknowledged that they thought it should. Being Muslim, it seems, is the main orienting self-identification for Bangladeshi young people in the East End.

STRATEGIC INSTITUTIONS IN THE EAST END

Why are "Muslim first" identities so pervasive in the East End? Various institutional influences may contribute to this. It can be argued that Muslim identities have been reinforced by UK state initiatives and media coverage since 2001. Two of the most significant state-driven agendas have been community cohesion, which arose from the summer 2001 urban disturbances in Northern English towns, and Prevent, a soft counterterrorism response to the London bombings of 7 July 2005. Both agendas highlighted Muslim identities as a point of contact and provided the Tower Hamlets Council with funding that was partly distributed to Islamic institutions, among other partners. Cohesion and Prevent also had a negative result, because they conceptualized Muslim identities as potential sources of danger—as causes of monocultural, segregated communities and/or of violent extremism. They therefore unwittingly fed into media scaremongering about "no-go areas" and "homegrown terrorists."

I found that East End Bengali young people have been affected by these portrayals of Muslims from the state and from media, though usually in a distanced way. When I asked Salma which, if any, of her ranked identities came into conflict with each other, she answered without hesitation "sometimes British and Muslim." I asked what she meant. She said "After the 9/11, yeah. It does happen. I mean I have never experienced it, but I mean you've heard on the news that people were being harassed and whatnot." Salma is well aware of Muslims facing prejudice in Britain, though she does not expect to face it herself: "I mean I don't think you would ever, living here—there's so many Bengalis, so many Muslims. I don't think it would happen . . . I think that's a good thing about living in East London." Like Salma, most young people told me that they had not directly experienced anti-Muslim prejudice, though all were aware from news sources, text messages, or Facebook that it happens elsewhere. Even such secondhand Islamophobia can contribute to a sense of being an embattled community and strengthen "Muslim first" identification.

Muslim self-identification is also cultivated from within the local Bengali community. First-generation parents have brought Sufi-influenced Barelwi forms of Islam from rural Bangladesh, where Islam serves as a source of order, morality, tradition, and faithfulness. The Brick Lane Mosque, in a building originally built in the eighteenth century as a Huguenot church, is a now a major Bengali community hub and a space where men join together to pray. For many first-generation parents and elders, the Bengali cultural and Muslim religious functions of this mosque are closely intertwined in rituals and community gatherings, if they can be distinguished at all.

A few minutes' walk away on Whitechapel Road, the East London Mosque (ELM) has a distinctly different view of Islam and its role in society. The ELM is a prominent red brick structure, purpose-built in 1985 with a massive adjoining community centre, the London Muslim Centre (LMC), completed in 2004. The ELM/LMC promotes a deculturated Islam, influenced in part by Salafism. The mosque originates from the Jamaat-e-Islami movement of the Indian subcontinent and takes a programmatic yet pragmatic approach to political Islam.[28] The mosque premises are host to a variety of social services, youth programs, and community organizations. Importantly, the ELM provides prayer facilities for women, which greatly expanded with the opening of the adjoining Maryam Centre. The ELM leaders have developed increasing policy sophistication and broadened their contributions to society by partnering with the local council on initiatives such as community cohesion, raising school attendance, and tackling youth drug addiction.

Many of the young people I interviewed praised the ELM for the work it is doing. Salma, again, provides a good example. "If there's a charity event," she told me, "everyone goes there first... Because they've got space and they're good with this sort of thing." She said that the mosque is "doing quite good, especially with younger people who get lost in their identity." According to Salma:

> A lot of people get mixed up between am I British, am I Bengali, am I Muslim, you know, what am I? It can be quite difficult sometimes and confusing but I think with [the ELM] they help you to realize that, you

---

[28] Glynn (2002).

know, you are a Muslim but you are also British and whether you're Bengali or, I don't know, Moroccan or whatnot, I mean that's still part of your culture. Culture is still important. But I mean they just sort of show you the importance of religion I think.

The ELM, as Salma relates here, has actively promoted its particular view of what it is to be Muslim. There is a certain degree of pluralism in this view of identity: British, Bengali, Moroccan, etc., can all be accommodated. However these identities must be subsumed under a core, pre-eminent Muslim identity. This approach differs markedly from the more relaxed fusion of Bengali culture and Islamic practice taken by most first-generation parents, and epitomized by the Brick Lane Mosque. Indeed, the deculturating perspective of the ELM has led to frequent clashes with Brick Lane over symbolic events such as the Baishakhi Mela festival and practices like the veneration of *pirs*, or saints, which most ELM leaders consider idolatrous.[29] It is also worth mentioning the Darul Ummah Mosque, another significant institution in the East End known for its youth work. Darul Ummah shares a common Jamaat-e-Islami heritage with the ELM and, although sometimes seen as a local competitor, generally helps to reinforce the local consensus of political Islam.

In de Certeau's terms, the ELM is a strategic institution, acting from a position of power to promote a totalized vision of Islam. However, the ELM is far from the only strategic institution in the East End context. Rival mosques, first-generation parents, media, and the national and local state each vie for some measure of influence over second-generation youth. Through extensive investment in its youth work and facilities, the ELM has shrewdly positioned itself as a mediating institution between youth and most of these competing institutions. As youth reach adolescence, the ELM is able to supply an Islam that overcomes the seemingly simple-minded and syncretistic views of their parents. If youth are ever questioned about their Britishness, the ELM has an Islam in which they can be more fully British by becoming more Muslim. Thus the ELM is a strategically powerful institution among young people largely because it supplies them with flexible tactical resources to face other strategic institutions looming over their lives.

---

[29] Eade and Garbin (2006).

TACTICS OF MUSLIM IDENTIFICATION

The deculturated Islam propagated by the ELM and Darul Ummah has proven to be a versatile source for the tactics of identity. My estimate based on fieldwork including the interviews is that half of second-generation East End Bangladeshi youth are self-consciously deculturated. Most others evinced some degree of deculturation when they raised concerns about freedom from parents and the impurities of Bengali culture, while expressing their faith in a comprehensive, transcendent vision of Islam.

Young Bangladeshis tend to perceive deculturated Muslim identity as a source of empowerment. A Muslim young woman named Shany explained that her "Muslim first" identity is one that is free from any culture, thus breaking down barriers between people:

> [I chose] Muslim first because it is my most strong identity and I think it breaks down all barriers of every other identity. As a Muslim I don't have a color, I don't have a language, I don't have a nationality. It kind of bonds me to billions of other people without those barriers... It pretty much is quite an all-encompassing entity.

Islam provides an all-encompassing identity for Bangladeshi youth, connecting them to others around the globe. Bangladeshi identity can seem small and provincial in comparison.

The ways in which deculturated Islam is tactically used tend to differ among young women and men. Many young women find this Islam to be an empowering resource when they face their parents, especially in the issue of arranged marriage. Even Zahera, a young woman who does not habitually wear the headscarf or consider herself to be a practicing Muslim, sees Islam as providing freedom from oppressive cultural norms. Zahera says: "Within the Bengali community I'm told 'why are you not married?' and 'let me find you a husband.' Whereas from an Islamic perspective, I don't have to get married. I can actually choose to abstain from marriage."

One young woman named Rubina thought that her parents—though well meaning—had not been Islamic enough because they did not understand Islam as an abstract, transcendent system that can be applied anywhere. These differences are revealed most starkly in issues of gender and marriage:

> They don't understand the concept of [Islam] being a faith. Rather it's a, you know, a bunch of obligations that you must do... Like you have to

do this, you have to do that. Oh no, you can't marry someone lower class than you! But Islamically of course you can.

By purifying her Islam of Bengali culture, Rubina is able to do away with key cultural restrictions on her choices. When her parents attempt to control choices in marriage and family, Rubina can find in Islam empowering arguments. The issue of marriage is close to home for Rubina. She has already debated with her mother about Islamic and Bangladeshi conceptions of marriage, in relation to the marriage choice for her brother:

> My mum's looking for a bride for my oldest brother, because he doesn't have a girlfriend. So she wants to do an arranged marriage for him. And I think that there's plenty of [suitable] people, but they're not Bengali. I go "What's wrong with it then? Islam is saying that they need to be a good Muslim!" But [my mum is] like "Yes, but you know people are going to point fingers and say your son married out of the race." Like [I say] "Mum there's only one race which is the human race. You know that's what unites us all. You know there is no differentiation, you know we're meant to follow the Prophet Muhammad, you know he didn't differentiate between people. Why do we do it?" She goes "Oh you don't understand, you wouldn't understand. We lived here too long."

The mutual exasperation of Rubina and her mother show just how wide the gulf between generations can be, for young Bangladeshi women in particular. Rubina appeals to Islam as a source of transcendent values, hoping to resolve their dispute. Islam has become for her a source of tactical empowerment. It provides the most comprehensive, reasoned, and community-sanctioned solution for gaining control from her parents. Rubina's use of Islam as a faith system is a resource for living confidently within the modern sensibilities she has developed while growing up in London.

Bangladeshi young men tended to contrast religion with Bangladeshi culture not on issues of marriage and family, but instead in terms of Islam being more educated, more Western, or even more fun than a traditional Bangladeshi lifestyle. As Bangladeshi parents usually come from poor and rural backgrounds, many youth see them as not having the requisite knowledge to fully comprehend Islam.

When I met Farouq, he was standing in front of a chicken shop on Cannon Street Road, smoking a cigarette. He has spiked black hair and wore an oversized white puff jacket to look more intimidating. Farouq does not consider himself a devout Muslim, as he usually only attends mosque to pray on Fridays. He does rank Muslim first, however, and thinks of his Muslim identity in a deculturated way. Farouq told me that people in his parents' generation "are confused and mix tradition and religion together." In comparison, "the young kids nowadays are more focused on everything, more wise." Farouq said that Islam frees him from the constraints he would have felt to "make my parents happy, be a good boy, wear certain clothes, have certain haircuts. Like, don't have fun."

Another youth, Amin, does not think of himself as particularly religious either, though he does also identify as Muslim first. Amin expressed a similar view to Farouq's that the Islam of his parents is outmoded:

> Our generation's more Westernized. Whereas our parents' generation, they're more into the culture thing and everything. They're more into image and bad publicity and everything. They want to keep that under control... We want to have fun basically, we're Westernized.

Amin told me, further, that the Islam practiced by young people is a more knowledgeable one. "There's big scholars just studying religion and everything," he said. "We've learnt from them basically, and we know what's wrong and what's right." When I asked him who these "big scholars" are, he mentioned Sheikh Abdur Rahman Madani of the local Darul Ummah Mosque and Imam Abdul Qayyum of the ELM.

It is a tribute to the savvy youth programs and informal peer networks of the ELM and Darul Ummah that even "non-practicing" young men, like Farouq and Amin, take a deculturated view of Islam and associate it with knowledge and having a good time. Almost all Bangladeshi youth I interviewed had similarly superlative associations with Islam, regardless of how much they themselves fulfilled religious obligations.

For young second-generation Bengalis in the East End, then, deculturation has become a dominant framing of religion and culture. As Sadek Hamid has argued, this approach to Islam is attractive to British Muslim youth (and young men in particular) because it appears to be "intellectually rigorous, evidence-based and free of perceived corruptions of folkloric religion or the 'wishy washy' alternatives."[30] For British Muslim young women, this approach to Islam provides fresh

---

[30] Hamid (2009: 390).

arguments for expressing themselves in struggles over marriage and family.

AN EXCEPTIONAL CASE

While deculturation predominates among British Bengali youth, it is important to recognize that there are exceptions. One such exception is Yasmin, a young woman whose approach to self-identification is so different from most East End youth that it is worth describing in detail.[31]

I met Yasmin for an interview at a café on Whitechapel Road. She has deep olive skin, wore dangling gold hoop earrings, and had her hair up in a black headwrap, which at the time I thought of as an African style. Yasmin was 22 years old when we talked. In the first few minutes of our interview I learned that she is a professional dance performance artist. She was doing a solo performance that evening at an open mic night in the Whitechapel Art Gallery, just a few buildings along the road. She told me that dance allows her to connect with and explore her Bengali, British, and other cultural identities. In her own words: "It's about looking at myself as a young Bengali living in Britain and being in a city life... It's about how you express [that] in narrative. The narrative of living in London, the narrative of being a woman, being a Muslim. It's all these things." Yasmin attempts to articulate these various layers of cultural narrative through movement. For example, a dance performance might involve Western contemporary dance fused with South Asian styles, such as the North Indian storytelling dance form called *kathak*.

Very few second-generation youth make the exploration of cultural identity into a career vocation, as Yasmin has done. I tried to discern where she had developed her profound interest. A major influence has been her mother. Yasmin's father died when she was young, and she has had a very close relationship with her mother throughout her life. Her mother is a very artistic person who writes Sylheti poetry and sings traditional songs to maintain a living memory of Bangladesh. Because she does not speak English, she has relied on Yasmin and

---

[31] See Pearce (2002) on the value of anomalous cases, like Yasmin's, for understanding the bigger picture.

the other daughters in the family to be her points of connection into British life. In a reciprocal way, Yasmin links to her own Bangladeshi heritage through her mother. As she puts it: "Being a second generation, my connection to my ancestors has my parents between the two."

A turning point in Yasmin's life was her first and only visit to Bangladesh with her mother and sisters. It was through this visit that she fully realized her emotional connection with the country as "home":

> I was 11 when I went. We initially said we were going to stay there for six weeks, for the whole summer break, but it extended to six months. And that was purely because we didn't want to come back. Myself, my two sisters and my mum, we were in a house, and going there and seeing my father's grave, which is over there, and being in the village that my parents grew up in as husband and wife. That for me was a place that I needed to be at that particular time of my life. My sister felt exactly the same. I was 11, one of my sisters was 12 and my other sister was 18. The gap is quite large between myself, my other sister, and the 18-year-old. But we had a common ground, which was "We're home!" . . . It was really just seeing another life that was ours.

Although Yasmin was born and raised entirely in London, upon visiting Bangladesh she experienced "another life that was ours." Her close connection with her mother and her longing for her father may help to explain why Bangladesh resonated so deeply with her then. A sense of not fully fitting in among her peers in Tower Hamlets, as she would explain later in the interview, may also have played a part. As Yasmin spoke of the Bangladeshi countryside and the senses it evoked, her whole countenance brightened: "It was about walking the distance along the road," she told me. "It's where the wheat, it's where the mustard seeds are growing, it's where the cows are, the sheep, and the goats. For me that was the experience! It was so hot when we went. The smell is very particular."

Yasmin identifies herself as a Muslim as well, but speaks of this in an interesting way. She told me: "Muslim is a part of my identity that I can't deny." Her response of "can't deny" was much more passive than most of my Bangladeshi interviewees, who spoke with an active enthusiasm about being Muslim. As we spoke more, I learned that being Muslim is indeed significant to Yasmin, although not in the ways I was accustomed to hearing from other East End Bangladeshis.

Yasmin is a Sufi Muslim. She says that Sufi spirituality has deep roots on her father's side, and it is now quite actively maintained by her mother. She told me that in her view "the essence of Sufism is a spiritual sense, a perspective on how you see life ... And that for me is something I've got and will always carry." Her general life philosophy and her aesthetics as a performer are infused with this spiritual sense. Although Muslim religious practice is important to her too, she made clear to me that she does not follow this dogmatically. She prays three to five times each day "depending on how I'm feeling or depending on what I'm doing ... Prayer is like the center. [But] if I have to do something else, I don't create excuses."

Despite Yasmin's significant identification with Sufi Islam, she does not feel fully included among the Bangladeshi Muslims of the East End. I asked all interviewees to list their five closest friends. Yasmin's were two Jamaicans, a Nigerian, a Pakistani, and an Irish/Indian—making her stand out from other Bangladeshi interviewees, all of whom at least had a majority of friends who were Bangladeshi. She had met her diverse set of friends in university or through her performances.

Yasmin feels like something of an outsider among East End Bangladeshis. It is for this reason that she says she "can't deny" being Muslim. Her differences with her neighbors are rooted in differing views of religion and culture:

> Their perspective on the Bengali culture and their perspectives on religion are completely different [than mine] because there's a separation. There's a separation between what religion is and what culture is. In my mother's household we embrace the two, but in their household they divide the two. As I was growing up and connecting with other families they've always said that there's a contradiction in culture and religion. Coming from my own background I knew that there wasn't.

Yasmin believes that her family heritage and time spent in Bangladesh give her insight into the richness of Bengali cultural expressions of Islam. She contrasts this with the view of Islam that pervades the East End, which separates Bengali culture from Muslim religion and sets them against each other. She says of Islam in the local area: "In terms of culture, the food is there, the [Bengali] clothing is there underneath," she told me, "but things are getting diluted."

The fact that Yasmin's refusal to divide Bengali culture from Islam is at odds with other young people she knows demonstrates that she is an exception that proves the rule. The vast majority of British Bengali youth in the East End, as I have described in this chapter, perceive a clash between religion and culture, and Bengali culture does not emerge favorably. For Yasmin and a minority of local young people, these deculturated viewpoints feel like a betrayal of heritage.

DECULTURATION AND ITS LIMITS

While the religion and culture clash narrative is evidently widespread among young East End Bengalis, it is important not to overestimate its influence. Some of the young people I interviewed were in all likelihood repeating scripts about a religion/culture divide that they had frequently heard but not deeply internalized. Also, I am not claiming that Muslim self-identification in the East End is a wholly new phenomenon that has displaced earlier, Asian or Bengali, ways of defining oneself. Historian Jed Fazakarley has shown that Muslim political claims-making in Britain has a longer and richer history than is often assumed, much of this predating the Rushdie Affair.[32] British South Asians have at various times and places held different identifications simultaneously, tapping into those that can be tactically useful for political organizing. Indeed, it should be remembered that most young British Bengalis I interviewed chose "Muslim first" but not "Muslim only." While Muslimness usually rose to the top, for many youth it was complemented by diverse set of other ways they could choose to define themselves.

Deculturated Islam is not the only tactical tool British Bengalis have been using as a means of gaining freedom in young adulthood. Nabil, age 20, told me he has observed a trend of delayed marriage among his female peers. Some "girls... want to have fun messing about drinking or whatever," he said, "and they get married very young," unable to hold off family pressures. Nabil said education provides an alternative path. As he put it: "They use education as a means not to get married, 'cos no one would marry someone that's still in education, if you understand? They'd like, let her complete her education. So [she'll] use the degree as a shield." He said his cousin

---

[32] Fazakarley (2014).

had continued through Master's level to "shield" herself and maintain independence. In the Bengali East End context, educational attainment and Islam are often seen as closely intertwined, with young people speaking about Qur'anic injunctions to strive for *elm*, or knowledge.[33] Young women may attempt to maintain the virtues (or, in some cases, the façade) of being a good Muslim and good student at the same time. Schools in Tower Hamlets have dramatically improved since 1998, having "raised attainment well above national averages," a major achievement for an inner city borough in which many parents speak English as a second language.[34] At least part of this story has been the remarkable success of Bengali Muslim young women, who are the top performers among all subgroups and the most likely to attend university.[35] Young women in Tower Hamlets, it seems, are finding a degree of agency in educational and religious arenas that would not have been available to them in the domestic sphere.

Marta Bolognani and Jody Mellor have made the critical point that "when Islam is used as a tool to argue for greater rights for women, it does not always work."[36] In their study of "religion versus culture" narratives among British Pakistani women at a university in the North of England, they found that in some cases when young women used arguments about the importance of education in Islam to delay marriage, their parents simply overruled these and moved forward with the marriage plans regardless. In this respect, Bolognani and Mellor argue that is important to not simply ask "'who can speak?' but instead *who* is listened to and *how* particular voices are heard."[37]

Finally, there are other kinds of "limits" to the tactical use of deculturation. When taken to its logical extreme, it can challenge more than just Bangladeshi cultural identity. I met 19-year-old Khan on Brick Lane. We walked to the popular Sweet & Spicy Bangladeshi restaurant for some warm *nan* bread and an interview. Khan had

---

[33] The word for knowledge (*elm*, or derivatives from this root) is mentioned hundreds of times in the Qur'an. An often-quoted example is: "And say, Lord increase my knowledge" (20:114). The first words of the Qur'an revealed to the Prophet Muhammad concern reading, writing, and the transfer of knowledge (96:1–4): "Read! In the Name of your Lord, Who has created (all that exists), He has created man from a clot (a piece of thick coagulated blood). Read! And your Lord is the Most Generous, Who has taught (the writing) by the pen. He has taught man that which he knew not" (quotations from *The Qur'an* 2008, translated by M. A. S. Abdel Haleem).
[34] Woods et al. (2013: 2).   [35] Dench et al. (2006: 142).
[36] Bolognani and Mellor (2012: 217).
[37] Bolognani and Mellor (2012: 217).

shortly cropped hair and a modest beard, and was dressed professionally. His accent exuded an air of educated confidence. Early into our conversation, Khan took a more confrontational tone than I usually experienced in interviews. He spoke frequently and with disdain about "Orientalists," whom he defines as "people who are anti-Islam... who would like to distort the message of Islam."

In the identity ranking section, Khan asked "Can I choose just one?" He selected "Muslim" and placed that identity card alone on the table. To explain his choice, Khan contrasted it with combinations like "Bangladeshi Muslim" and "Black Muslim":

> You [could] have Black Muslim. So why do you need to put something ahead of Muslim? Before or after, there's nothing. You shouldn't put anything before or after Muslim. That's it. It's simple—you just worship your Lord, you do everything he has commanded you to do, stay away from everything that is forbidden for you to do, and that's it. That's why you're Muslim.

Khan supports the views of Anjem Choudary and the Islam4UK organization, which have advocated the enforcement of sharia law in Britain. He explained to me in the interview why he finds a future British Islamic state appealing, including the harsher punishments for criminals and the idea that women will be safer from men if they are required to wear *hijab*. Islam4UK, since the time of our interview, was proscribed in the UK as a radical organization and would re-emerge in the guise of Muslims Against Crusades, which was also proscribed.

Deculturation is a process that can take many forms. It can be held lightly in some cases, or act as a totalizing influence in others. Khan was one of three cases of Bangladeshi young men who expressed their support for radical organizations. One of these youth, Zain, had taken part in a Hizb ut-Tahrir protest march to advocate sharia in the UK. In cases such as these a deculturated Muslim identity has undermined all others, making a common purpose or basis of communication with non-Muslims a challenge.

ELASTIC ORTHODOXY

In this chapter, I have demonstrated that the tactics of religious identity are formed within a complex web of strategies and counter-strategies.

In the East End, Islamic institutions play an important part, providing many British Bengali young people with new tactical capacities to gain freedom from the demands of parents, the state, and media. At the same time, a small number of young people, like Yasmin, have drawn closer to family traditions and are questioning the styles of self-identification chosen by their peers.

Young British Bengalis in the East End have to a large extent adopted a style of self-identification that can be termed *elastic orthodoxy*. By this I mean that they accept the local social consensus on what it is to be a Muslim ("orthodoxy")[38] and then work tactically within this framework, stretching it to apply to new contexts and situations ("elastic"). The term elastic orthodoxy was coined by Michael Lindsay in his book on American evangelical Christian elites, to convey how these elites attempt to be doctrinally orthodox, and yet are flexible about whom they cooperate with on social and political projects.[39] I adopt Lindsay's term, but use it in a different sense here, because the elasticity I witnessed in the East End was not primarily relational but contextual. The elastic orthodoxy I have in mind is a skill young British Bengalis have developed for perpetually recontextualizing their revivalist Islam as new circumstances arise.

It is important to emphasize the recontextualization in this approach to Islam. Olivier Roy's theoretical account of deculturation may seem to leave people free-floating, untethered from culture, when in reality culture is inescapable. Deculturation from one set of symbols, norms, and practices will inevitably entail reculturation into another. In the East End, this reculturation into an elastically orthodox Islam is accomplished through many means including peer networks, religious ritual practice, and organizations that are geared towards youth, such as the Dawatul Islam Youth Group, the Young Muslim Organisation, and brothers' and sisters' circles for studying the Qur'an.

---

[38] Talal Asad (1993) defines orthodoxy as a "reordering of knowledge" in order to construct "a relation of discursive dominance." Rather than making judgments on what should be orthodox, I mean orthodoxy in this contestable and power-defined sense.

[39] Lindsay (2007: 216) defines elastic orthodoxy as "the ability to maintain a core set of convictions without being so rigid that [one] cannot cooperate with others who do not share them." On the pages that follow he makes clear that he restricts the term to this relational sense, differentiating Christian fundamentalists and evangelicals because the former primarily maintain relationships with similar others in separatist enclaves.

Elastic orthodoxy is subject to the same global forces that are influencing second-generation Muslims worldwide in a tendency towards pietization. Bryan Turner has described these processes well, and is worth quoting at length:

> The globalisation of the migrant labour market has been one cause of the globalisation of world religions, especially Islam, and the creation of new diasporic religious identities. Many diasporic Muslim youth, once outside their original homelands, have abandoned the traditional religion of their parents and have embraced various forms of renewal and revivalism. These religious changes often involve a greater emphasis on personal piety and stricter religious adherence to the reformed standards of modern Islam. Social and geographical mobility have produced a redefinition of Islam as a modern, transnational identity in a context where citizenship identity is often denied or delayed. These changes have been reinforced by the growth of literacy, the expansion of higher education, and the introduction of women into the formal labour market. In general, this amounts to a "pietisation" of religious practices, indeed to a new urban imaginary of anti-secular spirituality.[40]

For young Muslims in the East End, British citizenship identity can certainly appear to be "denied or delayed." Elastic orthodoxy provides a potent mix of some parts deculturation, some parts hybridity. It begins with strict deculturation to cut ties with tradition, then reculturates into an Islamic orthodoxy, before applying the results in myriad situational and hybrid ways. This particular combination of versatility and dogmatic certainty helps account for its lasting power. Elastic orthodoxy is a determinedly pragmatic—one might say very British—solution to the problems of integration, limited citizenship, and intergenerational relations.

In the next chapter I will investigate the degree to which young people identify as "British" or "English," setting this alongside the particular patterns of identity among young British Jamaicans. By now we have come to understand the appeal of "Muslim first." By the end of the next chapter, we will know why many youth choose "British second."

For the moment, however, it is worth pausing to recognize that elastic orthodoxy's success in the East End represents a significant development. It is a victory for the culture-stripped political Islam of

---

[40] Turner (2008: 139).

the ELM, Darul Ummah, and similar institutions in a long struggle with Bengali traditionalists and secularists. What remains to be seen is if this will prove a true victory for coming generations of British Bengalis, or a more Pyrrhic one achieved at the expense of rootedness in a rich Bengali heritage.

3

Looking for Black in the Union Jack

On August 4, 2011 police shot and killed Mark Duggan, a 29-year-old Black Caribbean man, in unclear circumstances in Tottenham, North London. Protests calling for justice quickly turned into violent confrontations with police. News of the Tottenham incident spread across Britain via text messages, social media, and conventional news media, triggering rioting and looting in Birmingham, Manchester, and parts of London including Chelsea, Bethnal Green, and Brixton. By August 11 the looting and burning of property and associated violence had resulted in millions of pounds of damage, four additional deaths, and thousands of arrests. According to Home Office figures, those charged with riot-related crimes were an ethnically diverse group skewed towards the young.[1] Around half of the rioters were under age 21, with a further half of this number aged 17 or younger.[2]

In the immediate aftermath of the riots, historian and public intellectual David Starkey gave his views on what had caused them. He told a live television BBC *Newsnight* panel that the riots had emerged from "a particular sort of violent, destructive, nihilistic gangster culture." He described this culture as a kind of "Jamaican patois that's been intruded in England." According to Starkey, this urban youth culture has pervaded all races so that, in his words, "the Whites have become Black."

Starkey's remarks show how British Blacks can suffer from pariah status, similar to British Muslims. In this chapter I continue the

---

[1] The ethnicities of those charged with riot-related crimes were recorded by the Home Office and Ministry of Justice as 46 percent Black, 42 percent White, 7 percent Asian (e.g. Pakistani, Bangladeshi, Indian), and 5 percent other. *BBC News* (2011).
[2] *BBC News* (2011).

discussion of second-generation youth culture and identity, shifting the focus to the British Jamaicans I interviewed. Before delving into these interviews, however, it will be useful to briefly set them in the context of race and immigration politics in recent British history.

RACE, IMMIGRATION, AND COMMUNITIES

David Starkey's language on "Jamaican patois," "gangster culture," and the alleged polluting influence of Blacks on Whites reveals pernicious racial undertones that are more often hidden in portrayals of Black British young people. Whites, Starkey implied, have a superior culture that is being tarnished by outsiders. Blacks have dangerous cultural traits of violence, destructiveness, and nihilism. They will ultimately be responsible for White misbehaviors. Such views, of course, are far from new. In Edwardian times, Prime Minister Arthur Balfour spoke bitterly of Jews as the "debilitated sickly and vicious products of Europe" that he feared would be "grafted onto the English stock." His government passed the 1905 Aliens Act for the first controls on UK immigration.[3] In 1968, Member of Parliament Enoch Powell gave his infamous "Rivers of Blood" speech in which he passionately declared British immigration to be a "rising peril." To Powell's mind, "[t]he West Indian or Asian does not, by being born in England, become an Englishman. In law he becomes a United Kingdom citizen by birth; in fact he is a West Indian or an Asian still."[4]

British immigration history testifies to the fact that, for many, it has not been easy being British. Paul Gilroy's classic treatise on race in Britain, *There Ain't No Black in the Union Jack*, takes its name from an old British racist slogan. Gilroy argues in the book that British identity from imperial times onward has been defined on White racial and Christian religious grounds, making it largely inaccessible for Blacks and other minorities.[5]

In contrast to British Muslims, British Blacks are seldom portrayed as a dramatic political threat. Instead they are more often cast, as in David Starkey's remarks, as a subtle cultural one. The ways in which this Muslim/Black distinction operates in Britain today have been

[3] Malik (2013).   [4] Quoted in Katwala (2008).
[5] Gilroy (1987).

profoundly shaped by political developments of the past two decades, particularly since Prime Minister Tony Blair's New Labour government took power in 1997.

Many researchers note that New Labour often approached Muslims, Blacks, and other groups as "communities." Such approaches, of course, have a much longer history than Blair's Labour government that has been informed by the demands of grassroots identity politics. Building upon (though departing from) the "political blackness" of the 1980s, and galvanized by the Rushdie Affair of 1989, Muslim political activists created nationally prominent organizations.[6] The most notable of these were the Muslim Parliament and the Muslim Council of Britain (MCB), the latter of which was launched in 1997. The MCB was a particularly effective lobbying group in the first term of the New Labour government (1997–2001), speaking on behalf of the Muslim "community" on issues such as making equal provisions for religious needs in schools, prisons, and hospitals and incorporating a religion question on the Census. Senior Labour politicians including Tony Blair and Jack Straw responded positively to Muslim approaches in this period, adopting a politics of balancing coalitions of cultural or faith communities.[7]

New Labour's early years in power also coincided with Sir William Macpherson's inquiry into the racially motivated murder of Black teenager Stephen Lawrence. The Macpherson Report, published in 1999, concluded that the Metropolitan Police Force had mishandled their original investigation into Lawrence's death and that the Force was "institutionally racist."[8] This heralded what has been called a "multicultural moment" with an unusual political and public openness to rectifying systemic racial and cultural disparities.[9] Lord Bhikhu Parekh's commission-led report on multi-ethnic Britain set a high-water mark in this period for its intellectual and political engagement with multiculturalism.[10] The Parekh Report spoke of Britain as a "community of communities" in which it was important to strive for a balance between equality, diversity, and cohesion. It

---

[6] McLoughlin (2005).

[7] For an account of the influence of Muslims and other faith groups on New Labour policy-making, see DeHanas et al. (2013).

[8] MacPherson (1999).

[9] Meer and Modood (2009a: 477).

[10] Parekh (2000). For a sophisticated yet accessible recent defense of British multiculturalism, see Modood (2013).

received resoundingly negative press coverage, particularly for its critical remarks on the cultural and racial content that is often implied in discussions of British identity.[11] Parliamentary sponsor Jack Straw distanced himself from the report on the day of its launch.[12]

The most politically influential understanding of "community" in the New Labour years would not be multiculturalism, but rather "community cohesion." In the wake of civil disturbances in Bradford, Burnley, and Oldham in summer 2001, Ted Cantle led a review team to investigate the events and how to respond to them.[13] The Cantle Report advocated a community cohesion perspective that foregrounded community differences, which were often rooted in culture. This focus on culture was a deliberate departure from existing ideas of social cohesion that had placed more emphasis on rectifying socioeconomic disparities.[14] The Cantle Report argued that some communities in the northern towns were so isolated by their cultural and religious characteristics that they seemed to be leading "parallel lives."

While some academic observers have been supportive of the community cohesion perspective,[15] many have been critical. Common criticisms are that the term "community" is highly ambiguous and the agenda allowed slippages away from addressing more meaningful race and class equality issues[16] or, similarly, that community cohesion (when paired with New Labour's active citizenship strategies) placed the onus for change on individuals and communities rather than on the state.[17] A frequent line of criticism is on the understanding of Muslim communities propagated by the agenda. According to Husband and Alam, the state has "actively promoted a programme of categorical stereotyping of Muslim communities through the ways it has formulated and implemented its policies on Community Cohesion. It is *their* perceived self-segregation and *their* wilful pursuit of parallel lives that has defined the purpose and method of Community Cohesion policies."[18] Any suspicions that Muslim communities are inherently separatist would only be exacerbated by the 7/7 2005 "homegrown" London bombings, and the counter-extremism Prevent policies that followed them.

[11] Pilkington (2008). [12] Uberoi and Modood (2013: 24).
[13] Cantle (2001). [14] Dobbernack (2014).
[15] For example, Thomas (2010). [16] Worley (2005).
[17] Burnett (2004). [18] Husband and Alam (2011: 58).

Returning our attention to the 2011 English riots, it is important to recognize that racial notions of "community" continue to play a role in how these events and their causes have been understood. Karim Murji and Sarah Neal persuasively argue that while these recent riots are consistently *described* as in line with the Brixton riots of 1981 and 1985, they are actually *understood* through the lens of community cohesion and the northern civil disorders of 2001. In other words, rather than focusing on race and policing (which would have been a true legacy of Brixton) political and media commentators have instead told the story of the 2011 riots as symptomatic of a British breakdown of "community."[19]

The past fifteen years of policy and media discourse have tended to portray Black British "problems" as issues of "not enough community" (e.g. the 2011 riots or violent crime). Muslim "problems" are instances of "too much community" (e.g. "parallel lives" or the alleged Trojan Horse plot in Birmingham schools).[20] In stating this, I do not deny that in some cases these concerns may have a grain of truth. However, whether done consciously or not, singling out groups for having "too little" or "too much" community will ultimately be unproductive because doing so merely shifts the blame (and the responsibility for action) to these groups while simultaneously disempowering them.

This brief overview of recent political history has shown that British Blacks and British Muslims are today—much more than in the year 2000—portrayed as belonging to pathological communities. Unfortunately such portrayals can influence how they think and speak about themselves, as we shall soon see.

JAMAICAN IDENTITY CHOICES

Race

Race matters to all the Jamaican second-generation youth I interviewed. When we completed the identity ranking exercise,

---

[19] This story, of course, does not only originate in domestic issues from the 2001 disturbances, but has also been influenced by the exploding interest in the "collapse and revival" of social capital since American academic Robert Putnam's (2000) writings on "bowling alone."

[20] Murji and Neal (2011).

introduced in the previous chapter, "Black" was the identity most commonly chosen by Jamaicans, chosen by all except one (who first considered it and then replaced it with "brown"). Those who chose "Black" routinely ranked it higher than either "British" or "English," again with only one exception. In two-thirds of cases (sixteen of twenty-four) "Black" was either ranked as the first or second component in identity. In most of these cases it ranked higher than "Jamaican."

The salience of Black identity, however, does not necessarily signal its strength. Thaddeus, age 21, ranked Black first. When I asked why he had placed it first, he said: "It's obvious, it's just me." He then explained to me what he meant: "Basically it's probably the first thing that you might notice from seeing me." Black identity for Thaddeus is something ascribed to him by the perceptions of others. This conception of being Black—that it is an identity given by others—was the most common way I heard Jamaicans speak about it.

Michelle spoke about being Black in more positive terms. "I'm very proud of being Black, for my culture, for what's happened in [our] past until now." For many Jamaican youth, a sense of Black history was important. Being Black connected them with past courageous generations, epitomized by endurance through the years of the transatlantic slave trade. Michelle mentioned other aspects of being Black as positive, such as the diversity captured within the term: "Some people may stereotype Black people for being all one way, but Black—the thing is that there's different shades of Black. We cover 500 shades from the very light to the darkest Black... Being Black, yeah, it's beautiful." Michelle also mentioned that Black people "can just do a lot of different things that I think a lot of the time society doesn't really celebrate for us. Like we can be academics, great in sports, great entertainers." Her affirmation of being Black, while positive, was nonetheless defined by a relationship with White members of society who may not recognize Blacks for their achievements.[21]

For some youth there was ambiguity as to what "Black" means. Naomi told me: "Sometimes I think Black is just a skin color. And sometimes I think it's a personality." There was a sense that one could "act Black," but that this was not predetermined. Mike, a mixed-race youth introduced in Chapter 1, had said: "I don't really 'act Black' like Black people do or 'act White' like White people do." Some youth

---

[21] Because I am a White American researcher my racial appearance may have sensitized youth to the ways they are viewed by others.

believe that race is declining in significance. Chanel told me: "I used to believe yeah, that being Black in England, you're underneath. Or you've got less chance. I used to think that would be a problem for me... I don't really think like that no more. I think we've got past that stage now." In her estimation, today "people are more interested in what qualifications you've got than what color your skin is."

The various ways in which Jamaican youth spoke about being "Black" captured a tension that has been present in the literature on the topic. In her book *Ethnic Options*, Mary Waters observes that Whites have freedom in choosing "symbolic ethnicities" based in their ethnic heritage.[22] Blacks, in contrast, encounter the additional issue of racial discrimination, which they are best able to face through "oppositional ethnicities."[23] Thus, Blacks are much more ethnically constrained than Whites. Claire Alexander questions this view in her book *The Art of Being Black*, writing that "black youths are concerned with the construction of new cultural alternatives, in which identity is created and re-created as part of an ongoing and dynamic process ... [providing] an alternative vision of black youth; not as a unified and homogenous, externally defined and structurally constrained entity, but a collection of individual lives, choices and experiences."[24] Mary Waters' position is broadly a "between cultures" view while Claire Alexander's fits within the hybridity research tradition.

Jamaican youth I interviewed seemed to sometimes confirm Alexander's perspective and at other times Waters'. Samuel, age 25, is a Jamaican youth who tried to articulate a post-racial perspective. He took a blank card and created the write-in identity of "human." Samuel ranked human first, then brown, Black, Jamaican, Londoner, and Christian. He told me why his identity as part of humanity came first: "Human because it's kind of like, I'm human. So it don't matter what race I am, what I do, what color. It all boils down to everybody bleeds the same." Samuel's positive affirmation as a person was a creative solution that appeared to transcend any concerns of race. Yet, when I asked Samuel if any of the identities he had chosen ever come into conflict, his answer revealed the continuing significance of Blackness:

DND: [Do any of these identities ever come into conflict?]
SAMUEL: I think the human and the Black. The human and the Black, you know. They come as a conflict.

[22] Waters (1990).   [23] Waters (2003).   [24] Alexander (1996: 18).

DND: Tell me why.

SAMUEL: Because I think regardless of "slavery's over" or "racism's finished," there's still an element of it about. I think it's subliminal. It's almost subliminal now... I'm saying, "I'm human." But they're saying, "No, you're Black."

As much as he wants to move beyond race, Samuel thinks that race remains important because racism persists. He speaks of racism as remaining in what he calls a "subliminal" form, perhaps what Eduardo Bonilla-Silva has called "implicit racism."[25] Samuel continued, speaking of how he thinks racism can be internalized by Blacks as self-image. This perpetuates the problem. "Our people do let us down," he said, "'Cuz it's like, it's weird—if you call someone something for long enough, they actually come to be that thing."

Other racial options were available as identities in the ranking exercise: "White" and "brown." Five Jamaicans out of twenty-four chose White as fitting somewhere into their identity. All did so because they have some White ancestry, including Mike whose mother is White. Clarise is also mixed-race, and chose White as important for this reason and also because she was raised by White parents in a foster home. The low number of youth who identify with White is surprising, especially in light of the dramatic growth of mixed-race relationships, including the fact that in Britain today there are more British children under age 15 with a White parent and a Black Caribbean parent than with two Black Caribbean parents.[26] Brown was a much more common choice among my interviewees than White, and was selected by two-thirds of Jamaican youth.

Most Jamaican youth showed significant creative freedom in their identity composition, as we have already seen in write-in identity of "human." Yet this generally hybrid and fluid approach to identity sometimes came in tension with a sense of the fixity of certain identities, especially "Black." I will illustrate this identity tension by first focusing on the apparently fixed cultural boundaries seen in the case of Mabel, before then giving a view into the creative and fluid identity composition of four young men.

---

[25] Bonilla-Silva (2001).
[26] Owen (2007: 4). For an overview of mixed race self-identifications in Britain and their potential implications, see Aspinall and Song (2013).

Mabel

Brixton was sometimes a challenging place to recruit new interviewees. Many of the young people I approached in hopes of interviewing were not actually Jamaican, but instead from Africa or elsewhere in the Caribbean. Yet Mabel broadcast her Jamaican identity to me all the way across Brixton Road. She was wearing a shoulder bag with a large and bright vinyl Jamaican flag as the opening flap. From a distance I knew immediately that she was Jamaican, and proud.

Mabel agreed to do an interview, and we sat down together at a nearby chicken shop. Mabel is short in stature, quick-witted, and very outspoken. She keeps her hair in lots of little braids that she calls twists: "When it comes to hair, me with my twists—no one does that, it's just me," she said. She was wearing a small "no guns" campaign badge pinned on the right side of her dark blue denim jacket. The badge resembled a round "no smoking" sign except with an image of a handgun crossed out in red. Mabel was on a gap year when we met. Having just finished secondary school, she was taking the year off to help at home before pursuing further work or education.

As we sat down, Mabel, unprompted, began talking about her love for Jamaica. I decided to probe further into the topic and to save some of my usual introductory questions for later. Mabel described Jamaica to me:

> Usually people think palm trees and beaches. There really is a lot of that. [But also] there's no pretenses or anything... That's why Britain and Jamaica are so different. Like, in Britain you can walk along the street and no one really acknowledges you. And fair enough, because they don't know you. But in Jamaica, like, they say "good morning" and "good afternoon," and they don't even know you. That's one of the things I love about it, it's just like the neighborly sort of community spirit.

Mabel contrasted the personal warmth and community spirit of Jamaica with Britain several times in the interview. She elaborated on her statement about Jamaicans having no pretenses: "I like people that are real, like don't pretend to be someone else... I really admire people who are true to themselves." In saying this, she was expressing the ethic of authenticity that was common to youth I interviewed. Jamaicans often use Patois, a variant of English, when they speak informally. Mabel likes Patois for the reason of its authenticity: "The way it's said—the expressions are so straightforward."

Mabel spoke of "family" and "discipline" as important Jamaican values. Much of Jamaican culture, she said, is captured in little sayings. One saying about discipline she mentioned is *"if you want all the bread go get it yourself, and if you want half a bread make somebody buy it"*—which means do for yourself anything that you want done properly. When Mabel's mother thinks that she has sage motherly advice that is falling on deaf ears, she will often say *"who don't hear, must feel."* The saying means that someone who does not hear wisdom will soon feel the consequences. Jamaican parents pass on culture and wisdom through sayings like these. They also use fables of Anansi the spider, which originate in West African oral traditions. Mabel told me: "He likes his money, that spider. He likes his money. But he always gets his comeuppance in the end."

If any of the Jamaicans I interviewed consider identities as fixed and discrete entities, Mabel is one. She views Jamaicans as having particular cultural traits such as straightforwardness that she highly values, especially being a Jamaican herself. She also has a clear sense of who she is not. Mabel told me "I have a problem with Africa." Although she identifies with the continent in terms of heritage, she told me that Africans rub her the wrong way in daily Brixton life: "African people—to put it bluntly, Nigerian people—get on my nerves, because I've had problems with them in the past, i.e. no one is going to tell me any different when I say Nigerian men tend to be perverts." She is often approached by Nigerian men on the street: "Even down to like when I was 15 years old, I'd say, 'I'm 15 years old!', and they'd still bother me... And African women like to watch you as well and give you these nasty looks. I'm not the only one that thinks that. A lot of Nigerians are not the most popular people, because of how they are. They're loud and just leery." It was true that Mabel was not the only Jamaican I interviewed who perceived strong differences with Africans—Thaddeus and Naomi also expressed negative sentiments. Naomi told me, regarding Nigerians in particular: "They are really, really loud and really, really over the top." These interviews and others indicate that there is some degree of inter-ethnic rivalry between Jamaicans and Nigerians in Brixton.[27]

---

[27] I interviewed a focus group of three youth from Ruach Ministries, who spoke about the rivalry they sometimes felt with Africans. This sense of rivalry is not perceived by all youth. Some interviewees have good friendships with Nigerians or other Africans, and indeed one was dating a Nigerian. However, the issue came up in

Mabel defines herself ethnically as Jamaican, in particular distinction from Nigerians and other Africans. Her maintenance of symbolic boundaries between ethnic groups helps keep her world in moral order.[28] She spoke about how sometimes Africans try to breach these symbolic boundaries: "A lot of Africans do try to pass off as Jamaican." She mentioned a recent issue with her Jamaican flag shoulder bag as an example:

> Even the other day a man said "Oh, I like your bag. I'd like to wear that." I'm just like, if you wear that then that's just going to cause people to misconstrue who you are. Because you are an African, be proud... I said "thank you" and everything, tried to be polite. But I'm thinking, there shouldn't be impostors. Be proud of who you are.

Mabel's perspective of "be proud of who you are" assumes a certain essence to identity. Each person *is* an African, a Jamaican, or someone of another ethnicity. It is important to know and accept one's identity, because to pretend otherwise means being an impostor.

Mabel thinks of the racial component of her identity in fairly essentialist terms. She spoke frequently during the interview from a "Black perspective." For example, when we talked about gang violence, she lamented: "Gang culture is just sad. And I speak from a Black perspective—it's all I can do because I'm that. Speaking from a Black perspective, it really does sadden me that I will see a group of Black boys congregate... We're killing each other, as Black people."

In line with Mary Waters' research, Mabel has developed her Black identity partly in reaction to not having a full sense of acceptance from White Britons. She spoke with some frustration about the experience of being Black in Britain: "They've got this thing 'There's no Black in the Union Jack.' And it's true, we don't come from here. It is true. But at the end of the day I am here. What are you going to do about it?"

In most of our interview, Mabel spoke of her identity in discrete terms. She finds acceptance in British society to be a problem because she perceives the society as defined in terms of Whiteness, from which she is excluded. She thus appears to be a youth who is caught

---

enough independent conversations to confirm that it is more than Mabel's isolated point of view.

[28] See Lamont (2000).

between cultures—or, more accurately, someone who is stranded on one side of a racial divide.

Yet, Mabel's identity is not as clear-cut as I expected from our initial questions. When she completed the identity ranking exercise, she did choose a racial identity as strongest. When she saw the cards with identity labels on the table, her first thought was to choose "Black." But she instead chose "brown," explaining this choice to me:

> I suppose the Black, I do use that term a lot. I think it's just a habit. I am brown [points to the skin on her arm]. That's Black [points to a black notebook]. So I do need to come out of the habit. I am brown.

Mabel was reconsidering her usual practice of self-referencing as Black. In a literal sense, her skin color is brown. Mabel had spoken adeptly about her Blackness throughout the interview, but at this point she questioned the very existence of "Black."[29]

Several young Jamaicans spoke about aspects of their self-identification, such as being "Black" or "Jamaican," as fixed containers of some cultural essence. Mabel did this perhaps more than anyone. Yet all Jamaican youth, even Mabel, at some point showed flexibility in their self-definition. Mabel recognizes "Black" as an identity that she has been branded with by White British people. However, when given "brown" as an identity option, she uses it tactically as a tool to critique "Black" and take on greater agency in how she defines herself. Even within the apparent fixities of Mabel's sense of identity there appears to be room for movement.

Moving with Music

If Mabel is on the fixed and essentialized end of the identity spectrum among Jamaican second-generation youth, then a set of four musically talented youth I interviewed are examples of greater fluidity. In this section I will describe these four young men and ways in which they use music to creatively articulate their self-definition.

---

[29] I capitalize "Black" and "White" throughout this book because these terms do not refer to a literal color, but instead connect people into social groups with shared histories. Capitalizing Black and White acknowledges that race can be just as "real" in lived experience as other self-identifications, such as Jamaican or Christian. I do not capitalize "brown" because young people tended to use this term to refer to a literal color in order to critique being "Black" (as Mabel does here).

Music is like life-blood to Damien. When we interviewed, he was age 20 and attending a London university to study Music Management. Damien is aiming for a career promoting gospel music artists. He has been actively networking on MySpace, Facebook, and industry-specific sites like GOSPELflava. Damien thinks he has reason to be optimistic—one of his brothers is a producer with his own small record label. Another brother lives in the United States and has promoted well-known artists like P. Diddy and India Arie. His large family, it seems, has always been musically talented.

Damien is of medium stature with a soft, gentle voice. He usually speaks slowly and clearly, but sometimes launches into flights of enthusiasm on the topics of music or his faith. When I laid the cards on the table for the identity ranking exercise, Damien labored at it for a long time. When he had made most of his selections, he asked to borrow my pen for a write-in identity. On a blank slip of paper he wrote "music." He placed this prominently—just below his faith and racial identity, and just above "Jamaican."

Damien had placed Christian first: "First of all I'm a Christian. My belief is very important to me. It keeps me going throughout the day. And my relationship with God, it's important, it's vital for me. It's what makes me who I am." He expressed this "Christian first" identity as the cornerstone in his life. It was not unlike how Asma and Rubina hold faith as the basis from which they live. Damien grounds this faith identity in his personal communion with God.

Racial identity for Damien did not seem to require much explanation. He placed "Black" and "brown" as a tie for second place in his identifications. For him, race was a label given by others: "Black, well, they say I'm Black." And as such, the label had questionable validity as an actual description of his skin color: "But really, I'm brown." Damien approaches race in very much the same fixed yet fluid terms that Mabel does.

And then there was "music": "Music is my heart, it's my passion, it's my love. From ever since I was a child, ever since I could remember I've just always been in love with music. Topics I've always loved and I talk about. My family is, especially my brothers are, associated with the music industry." For Damien, his write-in identity of "music" is something he holds as dear as his roots. His choice to add a personal interest and possible vocation amid a list of ethnic, racial, and religious identities shows just how strong individuality and authenticity have become as youth values.

Figure 3.1. A young man walking along Atlantic Road, Brixton

Damien's approach to identity is an unmistakably hybrid one. He combined a total of twelve identity components together, more than any of my other interviewees. He sees himself as an amalgamation of many different places and influences. These include British, African, Caribbean, Indian, and White, all of which he is able to trace in his heritage. Damien's stance on identity seems to be rather carefree and creative, with a sense that the more identity options there are, the better.

Damien was far from unique in his passion for music. Making and performing music (rather than just listening to it) was the most common personal interest mentioned by the young Jamaican males I interviewed (Figure 3.1). Several of them claimed to have real talent. Some go to recording studios, frequent open mic events, make CDs to pass around to friends, or set up MySpace pages to promote their own work. I often asked youth if they could perform a sample for me on our interview audio recording. Only later did I realize how much their performed music reveals about their approach to self-identification. Rap, as the lyrical component of hip hop music, is particularly revealing of processes of identification because rapping so often involves taking a stand and expressing an allegiance.

Adam is a tall, gaunt young man who wears diamond stud earrings. He was 19 when I first met him at a Jamaican restaurant across the street from Ruach Ministries, after we had both attended the youth service. Adam and I arranged to do an interview a week later, at a local café. In the first few minutes of our conversation at the café, Adam told me that he makes his own gospel rap recordings. He says he does this to help youth get "in a positive mindset... So they can see what I've gone through, and see where I got it wrong." While we sat there recording the interview, I asked him to demo his music for me. "What, rap now?" he replied. I said "Sure." Adam started a gospel rap from memory, at a brisk pace:

> Don't be wise in your own eyes
> The devil is a liar
> was my downfall
> That's the reason why we backslide
> so be careful
> Because he comes your way on a sly
> roaming through the world
> He'll try to hook you so stay wise
> Proverbs in the morning
> Psalms in the night
> It's warfare
> Making sure I'm putting on my war gear
> Don't go there, you know there's a hole there
> It's a trap
> The devil's trying to take you off track
> Life
> I need to try to get away from this hype
> The devil wants me
> I see it in my enemy's eyes
> Knows I've been fresh born since I got baptized
> But he can't touch me 'cos I'm covered by the blood of Christ...

Adam's full rap that I recorded continued on to about three times this length. It followed the daily trials of struggling with the devil and temptations. Adam explained to me his regimen of reading the biblical book of Proverbs in the morning and the Psalms at night. "Proverbs because it's a wisdom book," he said, "when you wake up in the morning it's good to read something that gives you wisdom for the day." In comparison, "Psalms is more like a warfare book. So what you do there, it's when you're sleeping that the devil tries to attack you."

With visible regret, Adam admitted: "To be honest to this tape, yeah, I have not been doing that recently [reading Psalms and Proverbs]... Recently I have backslided." The term "backsliding" means regressing from the ways of God. He told me that in the past year he's been smoking a lot of cannabis with his friends. "It's made me paranoid," he said. During the interview Adam's mood shifted like a man with multiple personalities, sometimes quoting scriptures fluently with confidence, and at other moments expressing guilt and anxiety. He asked me to stop the recorder at one point to get himself back together. Adam finds that he is living in a tension between the Christian morality preached by his church and the actions of his friends in "the world." Although Adam is now clearly troubled in his conscience, he told me "I believe that, by the grace of God, that God will pull me back up."

Johnny, age 18, is a Jamaican youth I met at a church who had a much more relaxed way about him. While Adam seemed to be in the fringe of his church community, Johnny is the son of a church leader. Every time I visited Johnny's church he was there. He seemed to know everyone. Johnny is musically talented and he invests much of his time and energy in writing and performing. When we conducted the interview, also at a café, I asked him to demo his music on my recorder too. Here is what I heard from Johnny, in a smooth and slow R&B sound that is more like the band Boyz II Men:

> I'll be everything you need
> And I'll be more
> If this love wasn't for you,
> Then what would I be doing this for?
> That I love you God,* that's what I want your heart to see
> Think of nothing else, but makes me think of you and me

Johnny has a melodious and powerful voice. I told him that I liked what I heard. Then I asked: "So that's a worship song of some kind, like a spiritual song?" He answered, "That's a song I made. Most of the songs are based around the people I know, so it's a lot of girls I know." I realized then that I had misheard the song: "Oh, that's a song about a *girl*!" Johnny had sung the words "I love you girl" but somehow I heard "I love you God" (marked in the song with an asterisk).[30]

Although my misinterpretation of Johnny's song was a small one, it revealed to me the kind of lens I had taken into our interview situation. Because Johnny was very involved in his church and is known there for his musical ability, I had assumed that he would demo a gospel song for me. Johnny told me that he does write a lot of religious songs too. But his choice to share a song about a girl with me showed the great ease he has in moving between the social worlds of church life and "secular" life. The fact that Johnny has written many songs—both sacred and secular—demonstrates his skill at what Elijah Anderson calls code-switching.[31]

Samuel, age 25, is a young Jamaican who also gave me a demo of his musical talent during an interview. He is the one who wrote in "human" as his foremost identity. I first met Samuel at the public library in Brixton. He comes from tougher circumstances than Damien, Johnny, or Adam. Samuel grew up an orphan, moving between boys' homes and shelters as a child. In his teenage years, he spent his days stealing mobile phones and wallets on the streets of Brixton to survive. He told me that he remembers what it was like to always be "looking for victims." But one day when he stole a man's phone and ran, the man chased after him. The man and a friend, both large and well built, caught Samuel when he was hiding behind a car. He was sure they were going to beat him up. Instead, the man talked with Samuel to understand his situation. He decided to let Samuel move in with him and his wife at their home, and he became Samuel's mentor. Samuel says he has been living as a Christian since around that time. He credits all of these events to the intervention of God. When I met Samuel at the library, he had been coming there regularly to search the Internet for employment opportunities. Although still dealing with issues of anger and impatience from his younger years, he thinks he can now hold down a steady job.

Samuel's transition from a street life to greater stability has not been easy, but music has played a part. For a while after his Christian conversion, Samuel volunteered at the Raw Materials Music Academy in Brixton. He was trained to mentor young people, helping them

---

[30] I misheard the word "girl" in the song as "God." I also misheard the last line of the song, which should say "Think of nothing else, but baby think of you and me."
[31] Anderson (1999).

develop talent while also counseling them into a positive lifestyle. Sadly, Raw Materials closed in 2007 after it was robbed several times of its equipment. Samuel wishes he could take up this kind of mentoring again, but does not know where he could do so.

When I asked Samuel to sing a sample of the music he writes, he sang two "rhymes" for me. One of the rhymes had an evident Christian content:

> Life's short,
> even shorter when you dis-tort
> reality, take it for jokes or for rash thoughts
> Instead of clowning around like you're a fool
> Just check yourself before you wreck yourself for good
> I know my date of birth but not by time of death
> That's why I'm in God's hands,
> I'm a part of God's plan
> Don't know the word "can't" cause I know that I can
> For I'm giving you extra like the Halifax man

In this rap, Samuel brings across the life and death reality of the streets. With crime and gang violence, you never know your "time of death"—it could be any moment. It was a message I often heard in Brixton churches, the need to turn to God in the face of death. As Samuel put it, "That's why I'm in God's hands." Yet his rap is not only about otherworldly concerns, but also the immanent and everyday. God enables success in worldly things: "Don't know the word 'can't' cause I know that I can." Samuel had told me that in his own life God is with him "like a friend." "He's taken me out of situations," he said. The rap ended with a humorous reference to Howard Brown, the Black spokesperson for Halifax Bank in Britain, who sings in television commercials about "giving you extra."

Samuel's take on Christian faith, as seen in this first rap, seems very close to Adam's. The Christian faith is a struggle, an adventure that requires the right moves to persevere. The adrenaline pumping style of his first rap came across also in the second one Samuel sang for me. The second rap had no religious overtones:

> Everyday I live this
> I move with this
> I have to take my chances, flow . . .
> Flows never boring
> To the skies soaring like a bird that flies

> Looking down at the earth my view's bird's eye
> And I ain't talking captain, about macky, just mackin'
> Engineering the sounds, we make crazy hits man
> Studio's so hot, turn on the rotating fan
> Play back our vocals, hear that baseline bangin'
> Even like my man said, get that freed up. Yeah, yeah.

This second rap is about "flow." It is about moving with the current and the rhythm. Samuel told me that it is a rap he created while free-styling at an open mic event. The very act of free-styling—creating fresh spontaneous lyrics in front of an audience—is about flow. Young Black men judge each other at open mic events on speed, style, and wordplay.

From listening to Adam, Johnny, and Samuel demo songs that they have written, I could discern two styles by which Jamaican youth bring cultural references together to compose rap and R&B music. The first is flow, the quick-witted, natural movement from one thought or situation to another; a fluid ability to adapt. The other style could be called steadfastness. It is the style of Adam's rap or Johnny's R&B, with the single-minded devotion to God or to a girl. Both styles are important to how second-generation Jamaican young men express themselves and earn respect from their peers (flow) or communicate their loyalty (steadfastness). While both styles can work together, the master style is flow. All of my Jamaican interviewees who sang their own original songs for me had written diverse repertoires of music, both Christian and secular, which gave them the adaptability to choose the right song for the right moment.

Natasha Warikoo writes about second-generation youth who demonstrate "multiple cultural competencies."[32] She argues that young people in urban New York and London schools who are simultaneously skilled in the cultural symbols of school and of hip hop are poised to succeed in both contexts. Youth who are not able to achieve the "balancing act" between these situational contexts tend to suffer either in the esteem of their teachers or the esteem of their peers.

Rapping is a verbal demonstration of a youth's multiple cultural competencies. Johnny and Samuel both show the ability to feel at home in the cultural worlds of church and of hip hop infused street life. Adam has honed these skills as well, but in his time spent with peers he has developed habits that make it harder to sincerely

---

[32] Warikoo (2011).

perform the cultural scripts of church. He feels guilt in contexts where he must demonstrate his faith, and for this reason does not attend church consistently.

These examples from young men and their hip hop music provide important clues about the nature of Jamaican second-generation youth self-identification. These are not young men caught between cultures, but instead they show dexterity in moving smoothly between cultural worlds. Yet hybridity may not be the ideal description of their identities either—at least if hybridity implies mixing, or syncretism. The youth tend to keep songs about Christian faith distinct and unpolluted by street life. There may be some overlap, as in Samuel's first song, but in general the street and Christian symbols are part of different genres of music. The skill lies in developing one's repertoire and choosing the right song for the right time. Perhaps a better term than hybridity for these youth is *situational identities*. Jamaican youth build repertoires of identity scripts that are each appropriate to particular situations or contexts.

Anne Swidler describes the process of moving between cultural scripts or frames, relating this to changing vessels on the sea:

> [A] person operating within one set of assumptions comes to a problem he cannot handle within his dominant scheme. Then, after floundering for a while trying to adapt his frame to unexpected difficulties, he may quite abruptly jump from one frame to another. This does not signal a loss of confidence in the first vessel, but simply a temporary abandonment of one craft while one navigates choppy waters in another.[33]

In Swidler's view, the ability to use different cultural frames to match situations is not a sign that one has lost confidence in a particular frame. In the same way, the fact that Jamaican youth can code-switch in different contexts is not necessarily an indication that they are insincere or not steadfast in any of their identities.

The situational nature of many young Jamaicans' identities—especially young men—became clear to me after I had completed the identity ranking exercise with all youth. I had recruited six Jamaican young men in church contexts, and seven in secular contexts. Five out of six that I first met in a church situation told me that they rank Christian first in their identity. All seven that I recruited in secular situations instead chose an identity *other than* Christian to

---

[33] Swidler (2003: 31).

rank first. Of course variability is to be expected—I was much more likely to select highly religious people in a church. Yet it also seems that the church context heightened in youth the awareness of the Christian part of their identity, leading them to foreground it in the interview situation. Adam would not have been as likely to place Christian first as an identity if we had met in a different situation, such as in a local gym. The church context of our first meeting gave him a sense of obligation to act and speak as a Christian.

Jamaicans overall showed a high level of flexibility in composing their identities. Even Mabel, who had quite "fixed" views about identity, was able to step outside the bounds of her Black identity and question it. In most cases self-identification appeared to be situational. In some cases, such as mixed-race youth, identity was also hybrid. Young Jamaicans also demonstrated a relative lightness and creativity to identity composition. Damien had chosen "music" as central in defining himself. Johnny, the young man who writes R&B, chose various ethnic and racial identities in the ranking exercise that included Asian. He told me that Asian fit into his identity because "I actually like a lot of Asian stuff... I'm a big fan of manga, from Japan, and like Chinese stuff." In Johnny's case, self-definition does not have an organic, assumed nature to it. It is very much the product of individual choice and composition, in which personal hobbies are legitimate options alongside race and ethnicity.

Claire Alexander found that the "art of being black" in Britain is an "ongoing and dynamic process."[34] My findings closely resonate with hers. The process is so dynamic, in fact, that when we reached the identity ranking exercise I found it almost impossible to predict which self-identifications a Jamaican young person would foreground.[35] Table 3.1 provides a summary of which identities were chosen "first" by second-generation youth.[36] Whereas Bangladeshis

---

[34] Alexander (1996: 18).

[35] I make this statement in particular about Jamaican youth I recruited in secular contexts, who chose a wide variety of identities as first in importance. The youth that I first met in churches (particularly males) more often chose Christian first.

[36] Table 3.1 shows responses from youth recruited from "secular" contexts such as streets and markets. It excludes the youth I recruited from religious institutions who could be expected to prioritize religious identification and therefore would skew the results. As I explain in the Introduction, my sample of interviewees was not random. Therefore, while these figures are useful indications they should be interpreted with care.

Table 3.1. Self-identifications chosen "first"[a]

Jamaicans	Bengalis
Black (4): 25%	Muslim (19): 82.6%
Christian (4): 25%	Asian (1): 4.2%
Brown (2): 12.5%	Bangladeshi (1): 4.2%
Jamaican (2): 12.5%	Bengali (1): 4.2%
African (1): 6.25%	Sylheti (1): 4.2%
British (1): 6.25%	$n = 23$
Human (1): 6.25%	
Londoner (1): 6.25%	
$n = 16$	

[a] From the youth recruited in "secular" contexts (not the full sample).

predominantly chose Muslim first, Jamaican youth made a range of different choices for their primary self-identification, such as Black, Jamaican, Christian, or brown.

Mary Waters found that White Americans have a broad freedom in defining themselves because they can choose ethnic identities that are symbolic of their own personal affinities.[37] Blacks, she argued, do not have the same freedom but are instead constrained by racialized society to respond with a race-based identity. In more recent work, Waters has found that second-generation West Indians in New York have greater freedom from American racialization because they are able to ground themselves firmly as West Indians, distinct from African Americans.[38] The Jamaicans I interviewed in Brixton also seem to be less constrained by racial definitions. Brixton's second-generation Jamaicans represent well what Stuart Hall has called "new ethnicities," with more situational and hybrid ways of defining themselves and more freedom of movement. It is perhaps less clear, however, who they have been freed to be.

NOT SO BRITISH?

Having grown up in London, the youth I interviewed typically spoke with the same London accents and mannerisms as their White British peers. Some were quintessentially British in their interests—playing

[37] Waters (1990). [38] Waters (1999).

cricket or watching television shows such as *East Enders*. None of this should be surprising. All of the youth I interviewed are full-fledged British citizens who were educated in London schools and exposed to British media and public culture.

I provided youth with "British" and "English" as options in the identity ranking exercise. Virtually all youth chose at least one or the other. Only two Jamaicans and two Bangladeshis could not relate to either English or British. This very high level of general identification with the nation of citizenship suggests that (besides a few exceptions like hyper-Islamic Khan) these are not youth who hold completely oppositional identities, or who live ghettoized lifestyles fully separate from the state.

Identification with "British" was especially widespread (twenty of twenty-four Jamaicans; thirty-three of thirty-five Bangladeshis). The actual rankings youth gave this identity varied considerably. Only one, a Jamaican 20-year-old named Martin, chose "British" first. On the other end of the spectrum was Damien, mentioned earlier, who placed "British" 11th and "English" 12th in his list of twelve identities. Identification with "English" tended to be less likely than "British." Fifteen of twenty-four Jamaicans chose "English," while only eleven of thirty-six Bangladeshis did so.

Although almost all youth chose "British," "English," or both, their actual levels of attachment to these identities could be quite low. Mike had told me "I'm not a very patriotic person... Coming from a mixed-race background, I like everywhere." Leonard likewise did not take much pride in his British identity, saying that: "Being patriotic don't seem to really hit home with me about British, or being British. It more seems to hit home with me about Jamaican." Almost all youth were like Mike or Leonard: they either identified a bit with "everywhere" or, more commonly, had other identities that meant more to them than being either English or British.

When I asked youth who chose "British" why they had done so, easily the most common response was "because I was born here." For many, "British" was primarily an indicator of geography—the context in which they were born and have grown up.

Near the end of the interviews, I also asked a related question about Britishness: "What does your British citizenship mean to you?" Youth tended to be surprised by this question. Most paused to consider their answer for a while. Chanel told me "It's just the color of my passport really. I got a British passport, that's what it means." Amin's view was very similar "I've got the red passport, that's it... And you get to go to European places without a visa." When asked about British citizenship, in most cases youth either had nothing to say or associated citizenship with their passport, their freedom to travel, or their protected status when visiting another country.

If Britishness tended to be greeted with indifference, Englishness was more often problematic. Some thought of "English" simply in terms of the language, and in these cases could identify with it strongly. Yet those who consider "English" to be cultural identity tended to feel excluded in some way. Shany, a young Bangladeshi woman, told me that she is "definitely not English." She said "I think it's just because I'm not White... It's more of an ethnic thing that I don't relate to, because I don't look the part."

Frequently youth spoke of how racism or labeling by others shapes their access to English and British identity. Shah told me that "I'm Asian rather than being British... I was born and brought up here, but people would label me as [Asian] before I'm British." Mabel expressed her frustration that in Britain "they've got this thing 'There's no Black in the Union Jack.'"

When youth tried to give cultural content to Britishness or Englishness, the most frequent image that came to mind was the English pub. Bangladeshi Muslim youth often singled out the pub as an English institution that would remain alien to them, due to Qur'anic prohibitions on the consumption of alcohol. Some Jamaican youth, particularly churchgoers, felt equally unable to relate to pub culture or binge drinking. Mabel said that she could appreciate British culture, but that British history tends to be one-sided: "I resent that they do not teach about people like Marcus Garvey and Immanuel VII in history classes, but they'd rather talk about Henry VIII."[39]

While most second-generation youth did not evince much interest in English culture or history, there were a few who were enamored with all things English. Shany was studying English literature at university. She told me that her favorite books tend to be from classic authors: "I think I'm a bit of an old fogy. I like reading traditional things. I like reading my Charles Dickens, and my Jane Austen, and my Mark Twain and stuff like that." Belal is a devout Muslim young man who grew up in the Bangladeshi community in

---

[39] Marcus Garvey and Immanuel VII are founding figures in the Pan-African movement.

Whitechapel. As a child he devoured English literature, his favorite book being Roald Dahl's *Danny, Champion of the World*. Belal had managed to develop a highly intellectual English accent from watching BBC television. Although he did not identify himself as English, he spoke with admiration of the English culture of a bygone era:

> I am not an Englishman. [But] it is a culture I really like... The way their culture used to be. I'm talking about a post-war Britain, where cricket used to be played in the long summer hazy days. Boarding schools—I'm a really big fan of that. Manners, family, strict discipline. I really love it. I've never done the hunting before, but all that tweed jacket thing with the hunting—I'm a big fan of that.

In a similar vein, Clarise told me she thinks Jamaican values *are* British values. Underneath Jamaican culture she said there is an "infrastructure" of British values that has carried over since the days of the slave trade. "Watch old movies and you'll actually see what old Britain was like. Very rigid, and very 'this is what's right' and 'this is what's wrong.' And if you look at Jamaicans now and their culture— like back home Jamaicans, not the ones here [in Britain]... They're very 'this is what's right' and 'this is what's wrong.'" It is notable that for these youth it was the Englishness of days past—whether portrayed in old movies, Victorian literature, or men in tweed hunting jackets—that resonated most. This nostalgic Englishness seemed to carry a greater weight of discipline and moral responsibility that they could readily identify as connected with their own.

The questions from the beginning of Chapter 2 are important to raise again. Second-generation youth tend to rank other identities above British and English—whether these are religious, racial, or ethnic. Are these youth "not so British"? Are issues of civic loyalty, like those raised by Timothy Garton Ash and the episode of *Panorama*, actually well founded?

It is important to recognize, first, that Caribbeans and South Asians actually have higher rates of identification with Britishness than the native White population. When given choices of only national (and not religious) identities in the General Household Survey, most White people selected English, Scottish, Welsh, or Irish identities instead of British. Most Caribbeans and South Asians identified most strongly with British.[40] Ian Bradley documents that a range of surveys reveal

---

[40] Bradley (2007: 176).

strong British identification among Britain's Black and Asian ethnic minorities.[41] It is when the choices are broadened beyond national identity, particularly to include religion, that identification becomes more complex.

The United Kingdom is, of course, a political union of four nations: England, Scotland, Wales, and Northern Ireland. It is difficult to conceive of a cultural content to British identity because Britain has historically been a political-legal entity more than a self-consciously cultural one. It is for this reason that recurring government efforts to define a cultural substance to British values inevitably fall flat.[42] As Lord Anthony Giddens argued in a House of Lords debate about Britishness and British values:

> I suggest that we drop the dead donkey; that is, drop the idea of Britishness. The very term "Britishness" is odd... [W]e should speak of Britain as a *citizenship nation*. That is what holds the nation together and gives us a coherent identity. If you speak of Britishness, you are looking for an elusive, essential identity which does not really exist.[43]

Giddens recognizes that Britain is a citizenship nation, where citizen status rather than particularistic Britishness is the "glue" that joins the diverse society together. Just as English and Scots bring their own cultural content to the table as British citizens, the same can be expected of other ethnic and religious groups in Britain. Britain as a citizenship nation is fundamentally a polity of dialogue between multiple perspectives.[44]

The fact that Britain is a citizenship nation helps to explain why my interviewees often had difficulty articulating the value of their "Britishness," beyond a set of rights and opportunities.[45] Britishness—if it is anything—is a set of citizen rights, opportunities, and responsibilities. Yasmin, the young Bangladeshi dance artist, told me that she thinks of being British as a "space to develop." It is within the norms

---

[41] Bradley (2007: 177). The finding of higher identification as British among ethnic minorities is also supported by more recent research from Nandi and Platt (2013).

[42] At some point during their tenures as Prime Ministers, Tony Blair, Gordon Brown, and David Cameron have all attempted to rearticulate "Britishness" or "British values."

[43] Giddens (2008), emphasis added.

[44] See Modood (2013: 117) on "dialogical" (and indeed "multilogical") citizenship.

[45] See also Hussain and Bagguley (2005).

and rules of the British state that one is free to develop an identity, and eventually to make a civic contribution.

If "British" is a civic definition that joins people with other identities they hold as core, then it is not problematic if British youth choose "Muslim first, and British second." In doing so, they are following the accepted norm by which most Scottish would choose "Scottish first, British second." Accepting that this is a valid way to prioritize identity, it becomes important to understand the various meanings youth articulate if they choose Muslim first, Christian first, or Black first (for example), as I have attempted to do here.

Second-generation youth approaches to identity range from Damien's all-inclusive list of twelve identities down to Khan's singular and all-encompassing Muslimness. Jamaicans tend to have more open, flexible, and situational identities, while Bangladeshis were somewhat more sparing in their choices, almost always placing Muslim first. These broad trends have implications for what youth will bring to the table as British citizens and for their potential levels of political participation.

Islam is an orienting identity for East End Bangladeshis. The process of deculturation, spearheaded by the East London Mosque, the Darrul Ummah Mosque, and other local organizations, is a reflection of broader currents of global revivalist Islam. Deculturation has spread to different degrees among different youth, but I was struck in my interviews by the fact that virtually every young Bangladeshi recognizes the argument that pure Islam should not be mixed with Bengali culture. Deculturation and other overlapping processes like *da'wa* (missionary activity) and political mobilization have largely eliminated the competition for primary allegiance in the East End. While Bangladeshi youth may interpret or practice Islam differently, very few would question its ultimate truth or its enjoining of particular actions. Muslim identity is therefore wide, and sometimes deep, as a foundation for collective political action in the East End.

The dynamics in Brixton are significantly different. Brixton Jamaican youth can choose from a wide array of possible identities. Jamaican youth identities take the form of "new ethnicities" which are more situational and hybrid than those of most Bangladeshis. Young men such as Johnny and Damien are skilled in multiple cultural contexts, and as such they may be well poised to succeed in different social worlds.

Yet the freedom and flexibility of "new ethnicities" makes for a shifting terrain of identities, in which common political agendas are elusive. Brixton is fragmented into various ethnic communities, some of which—such as Jamaicans and Nigerians—exist in rivalry or tension. The 1970s and 1980s were years of commonality in a Black political agenda. In more ethnically complex times, no common identity, whether political, religious, or otherwise, has been able to carry the same unifying power.

4

Rooted Religion

It was one of my first visits to Brixton. I had braved the chilly November afternoon, wandering the streets and markets to build up a picture of the diverse area. Now at the end of the workday I made the circuit back towards the main strip of Brixton. I crossed Windrush Square, the central green space that commemorates Black immigration to Britain. After walking by the popular Ritzy Cinema, I passed the KFC on the corner and headed towards Brixton tube station. Dozens of Caribbean, African, and other workers in coats and scarves were queuing for their buses home. Nearing the tube station, I noticed a narrow covered shopping passageway that cut directly through the building to my right. The sign above said "Reliance Arcade."

The Reliance Arcade is a long passage lined with independent booths on each side, selling items like greeting cards and flashy LED mobile phone accessories. As soon as I stepped into the arcade I was greeted by the familiar sound of African American gospel music blaring from speakers on the right and about ten yards down. The music came from a booth with the sign "The CD Bar." Literally set up like a "bar" for CDs, the booth had headphone stations for customers who could lean against the bar to sample hip hop, reggae, R&B, or Christian music before making their purchases.

There was a Black youth leaning on the bar. He seemed to be second or third generation, and at first I thought he was a music customer. But as I walked past I realized he was there for quite a different reason. He was receiving spiritual advice. Behind the bar stood the CD seller, named Reggie, whom I was soon to meet.[1] Reggie

---

[1] In this chapter and the next I use pseudonyms for the names of all people I met in research fieldwork, with the exception of religious leaders.

was mentoring the young man on a private matter and spoke with a knowing compassion. As I walked by I overheard Reggie give words of counsel about sexual temptation and the spiritual dangers of living in "the world."

I relate this experience to introduce Reggie, the CD seller, whom I came to know in the early weeks of my research fieldwork. Reggie is a tall man in his mid-30s of Nigerian origin, with a warm and easy air about him. He always wears a tan Kangol flat cap. I would come to see Reggie as an example of what Elijah Anderson calls an "old head," an adult role model that youth in Brixton can look to when facing the moral dilemmas of street life.[2] Reggie sees himself much in the same way. He would tell me later that he thinks of his job as a CD seller as a setting for Christian ministry. Reggie is known to have a knack for bringing almost any conversation around to ultimate questions of life, death, judgment, and Jesus.

The main streets of Brixton teem with a diversity of spiritualities. Older dreadlocked Rastafarian men roam the sidewalks, gathering in groups at the benches of St. Matthew's Park, sometimes speaking out words of worship to Haile Selassie. An African man stands near the tube station and silently distributes business cards for a local witch doctor psychic. Black Muslims stroll in family groups towards the Brixton Mosque and its religious primary school. Evangelists for many causes—Christianity, Falun Gong, or a recent conspiracy theory—can often be seen belting out messages in the main intersection by the KFC. Two middle-aged women on the street corner encourage each other that the Lord is faithful.

In his book *Streets of Glory*, Omar McRoberts writes about the Four Corners neighborhood in Boston, Massachusetts, as an example of a "religious district" because it contains such a larger cluster of storefront churches within a small radius.[3] Brixton would make the shortlist of places in London that could be considered its "religious districts" (Figure 4.1). The wards of Whitechapel, Spitalfields, and Shadwell in the East End of London, my other case study area, would also belong on such a list (Figure 4.2).[4] Both places are host

---

[2] Anderson (1999).   [3] McRoberts (2003).
[4] Other potential "religious districts" in London include Southall, Golders Green, Stamford Hill, parts of Newham, and sections of Southwark such as the Old Kent Road and Peckham Rye. Greg Smith (1996) has argued that Newham has the highest geographic concentration of places of worship of any London borough.

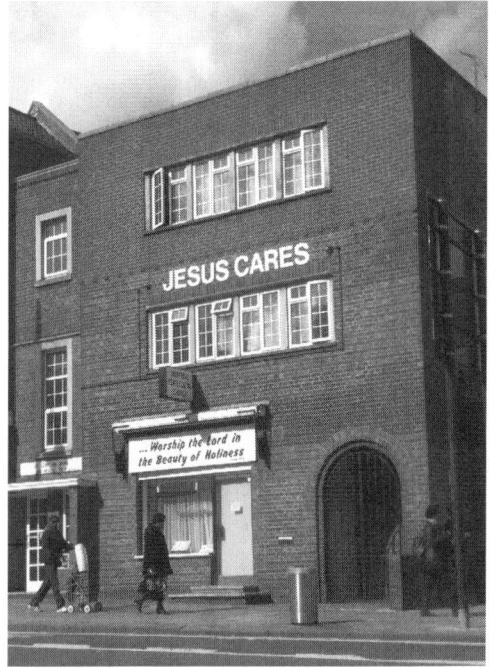

Figure 4.1. The Universal Pentecostal Church on Acre Lane, Brixton[5]

to various churches, mosques, or other religious institutions in historic buildings or converted premises, and to street cultures that are highly assertive of spirituality, especially considering Britain's privatized religious norms.

In this chapter and the next, I will investigate how religious institutions shape youth citizenship, focusing on two churches in Brixton and two mosques in the East End. This chapter focuses on two institutions that connect to the ethnic and cultural origins of the immigrant first generation, and their "rooted" religion. My emphasis will be on the particular visions of the citizen that are upheld by each place of worship.

Few studies in Britain have addressed how religion can shape believers into particular kinds of citizens. An important exception is

---

[5] The "Jesus Cares" message on Universal Pentecostal Church-Brixton (which is not one of my case study institutions) exemplifies the forthright street presence of some Brixton churches.

Figure 4.2. The Brick Lane Mosque (right, brick corner building) and Christ Church Spitalfields (left, with steeple)

Nicole Toulis' book *Believing Identity*, an ethnography of a Pentecostal New Testament Church of God (NTCG) congregation in Birmingham, England.[6] The Birmingham King Street NTCG congregation is predominantly first-generation Jamaican and largely female. Yet rather than viewing gender, ethnicity, or generation as their common ground, "their identity as Christians serves as the basis for their interaction with others in British society."[7] Members of the congregation view themselves and each other as "spiritual citizens." This identity allows the congregation to avoid "debates about how, and on what terms, African-Caribbeans may be included in the British nation, for [their] inclusive spiritual nation is not premised on racial differentiation."[8] The members of the NTCG congregation feel a satisfying sense of spiritual affirmation and civic belonging.

In a related manner, Peggy Levitt in *God Needs No Passport* investigates how spiritual perspectives shape the practice of citizenship,

---

[6] Toulis (1997).   [7] Toulis (1997: 210).   [8] Toulis (1997: 210).

creating citizens with different degrees of tolerance for religious pluralism.⁹ Therese O'Toole and Richard Gale observe that religion provides British youth (primarily young Muslims) who engage in politics with more globally oriented "grammars of action."¹⁰ Yasmin Hussain and Paul Bagguley investigate what they call "citizenship identity" noting that first-generation Pakistani Muslims in Britain tend to think of themselves more as temporary "denizens" whereas the second generation identifies with the rights and opportunities of being British citizens.¹¹

I will now further develop a concept I call "imagined citizenship" that has been germinating in the work of Toulis, Hussain and Bagguley, and others. Citizenship, in a legal sense, entails rights granted by the state, usually accompanied by concurrent civic responsibilities. I understand imagined citizenship to be: *constructed subjective membership in an imagined community of citizens, providing one's frame of reference for civic engagement.* This definition builds on Benedict Anderson's thesis that self-identifying with a nation or group means belonging to a community that is "imagined," and may not be directly experienced.¹² Imagined citizenship will not necessarily be spiritually or religiously based, but religions are important sites of its production because they so often confer transcendent narratives of membership.

The moral directives and congregational cultures of religious institutions can help us discern the kinds of imagined citizenries they will cultivate. Constance Flanagan and her colleagues build from the work of Michael Walzer to observe that schools are "mini-polities" in which the opportunities and resources of school-citizenship become templates for state-citizenship.¹³ The same may be true of religious organizations.¹⁴ For some young people, religious organizations will have a more long-standing influence as "mini-polities" than schools will, simply because religious involvement can extend beyond school age to continue reinforcing civic habits over time.

Before delving into the analysis of particular churches and mosques, we will return to The CD Bar in Brixton. It was there that a conversation early in my fieldwork gave me a first view of how to select religious institutions as case studies.

---

⁹ Levitt (2007).   ¹⁰ O'Toole and Gale (2010, 2013).
¹¹ Hussain and Bagguley (2005).   ¹² Anderson (1983).
¹³ Flanagan and Gallay (2014); Flanagan et al. (1998); Walzer (1989).
¹⁴ See Foley and Hoge (2007).

THE RELIGIOUS SCENE IN BRIXTON

On the cold November day that I first walked past The CD Bar, I had noticed that Reggie and the young man were engaged in a private spiritual conversation. I left the Reliance Arcade, returning ten minutes later to find Reggie alone.

I approached The CD Bar and introduced myself to Reggie. We struck up a conversation about music, culture, and Jamaican young people in Brixton. After a few minutes we were joined by Reggie's colleague and boss Vernon, age 30, who is a stockier man of Jamaican origin. Vernon is something of a foil to Reggie. He began to lose his Christian faith in early adulthood—around the same age that Reggie had a born-again faith experience. Vernon's winsome personality and ironic sense of humor make him a good match in conversation with Reggie's relaxed yet steadfast evangelical zeal. Vernon laughs often, with a hearty bellow of a laugh.

I piqued Reggie and Vernon's interest when I explained my research with second-generation youth. Ten minutes into our conversation I asked if I could record it with my digital recorder. They agreed. Then Reggie surprised me by pulling out his own larger, more advanced digital recorder:

> REGGIE: Yeah, I've got one here as well. [places his digital recorder on the bar]
> DND: Well, look at you!
> VERNON: Mine's bigger than yours! [All laugh]
> REGGIE: Yeah, but I won't record you all.
> DND: Your [recorder] is probably a little higher level than mine.
> REGGIE: Nah, nah.
> DND: But actually it's got good quality. So don't let that change what we're talking about or anything. And even if there's nothing useful, I'm just gonna keep [it] on.

I began by asking general questions to gain an orientation of the religious landscape in Brixton. Vernon—himself a Jamaican from the second generation—was only five years beyond my chosen demographic. The three of us had a very animated and wide-ranging conversation for more than an hour, speaking loudly to hear each other above the gospel and R&B tracks playing on The CD Bar's speakers. Reggie, who was tending the bar at the time, occasionally took a moment to sell a customer a CD.

Vernon told me about his own experiences growing up in a Jamaican-led church that was mostly influenced by first-generation immigrants. He spoke of these types of churches as "very Victorian." This was because "women were expected not to wear trousers or jewelry, expected not to relax their hair or manipulate it or change the texture." Vernon continued:

> I think it's an old fashioned approach to Christianity. Where you're supposed to be separated and, you know, "come out from among them." And you're supposed to look different from the world. This whole thing about "the world!" People in the world looking a particular way. You know they're very bejeweled, they're dressed up in the latest fashion. So the approach to Christianity was very conservative. That as a Christian you should dress "modestly." Which is a word that is very often mentioned in the Jamaican church.

Vernon spoke with considerable sarcasm about the protective environment of the church in which he grew up. It was a place that required its congregation to dress "modestly" in order to shelter youth from the "bejeweled" influences of the outside world.

In Vernon's view, churches of this more "conservative" variety have difficulty retaining the younger generation. He had himself felt his church was too strict and close-minded. He stopped attending as a teenager. I asked if there are churches today that more effectively tap into youth culture. "It's a big thing now," Vernon said, "influenced by Americans like Kirk Franklin," a gospel music artist. In fact, Kirk Franklin was about to perform a major show that weekend at London's largest music venue, the O2 Arena. Vernon and Reggie agreed: "He's a massive influence" on youth.

When I asked about which particular churches in Brixton successfully attract young people, Reggie and Vernon immediately thought of a local mega-church called Ruach Ministries. Vernon explained how this church had a much more relaxed and open atmosphere than conventional first-generation churches:

> When I was going to church you would wear a suit and tie every Sunday and go. It was showing reverence to God. And nowadays, churches like Ruach are very youth oriented. They allow youth to come as they are. You can come in jeans if you want. You don't have to dress up. They say "it doesn't matter how you come. Just come to church."

I noted to myself that Ruach Ministries would be a good place to meet Jamaican youth. It seemed that Vernon had identified an important distinction in the congregational cultures of British churches—the difference between the first-generation West Indian churches that emphasize reverence and modesty, as compared to the more youth-oriented churches that may better reach and retain the second generation.

As we continued to talk, a Trinidadian man with his hair up in a raised dreadlock style approached The CD Bar. He spent some time listening to music on the bar headphones, and then joined our conversation about Brixton youth. Speaking in a lilting island accent the man expressed pessimism about the state of Black youth in Britain. He did not believe there are viable role models for young people: "You know who youth look up to?" he asked rhetorically, without pausing for an answer: "50 Cent, [the American rapper] . . . As a Black youth in England, you have nobody who you can say you aspire to be."

Reggie agreed with this negative take on the circumstances of Black British youth. As an indefatigable evangelist, he explained the issue in the spiritual terms of the "doctrine" that young people hear preached by rap and hip hop artists like 50 Cent:

> REGGIE: To the very impressionable youngsters and the gullible ones, they are spewing out a doctrine that is a little dodgy. Because, you know, they're talking about—
> VERNON: It's just culture Reggie.
> REGGIE: [imitating a rapper]—"Yeah, we're popping the champagne! You know what guys, I'm driving my Ferrari!" And then they're moving from there and they're saying "You know what, I got money! You want money?"

Reggie objected to the "I got money" lifestyle of some Black music artists, and to its influence on youth. I noted the irony that posted behind him on the back wall was a list of the top ten grossing Black music artists worldwide (all of them American). In fact, Reggie is a bit like a teetotal bartender: he sells CDs from millionaire musicians, yet he remains wary of the "doctrine" of conspicuous consumption many of them preach.

The Trinidadian man standing with us began to talk about how the "I got money" lifestyle can transfer into Black churches in Britain. He mentioned the recent moral downfall of a Caribbean pastor elsewhere in London. The pastor had been diverting funds for his personal use: "A Ferrari pop up in the yard, a Porsche. His daughter was on the director's board, the wife, everybody." Reggie and Vernon immediately recognized this type of scandal. As Reggie put it, "You're living in a mansion, you have incredible power." It is easy for successful pastors with power and charisma to be lured into exploiting the trust of their congregations.

Our conversation at The CD Bar had identified a general pattern in Black British churches. If the more "traditional" and first-generation dominated churches overemphasize moral austerity, then churches at the other end of the spectrum—more "contemporary" churches with a large youth segment—face the opposite danger of excess and conspicuous consumption.

As we neared the end of our conversation, Vernon drew some of the threads together to provide his view of the main problem facing Black British youth:

VERNON: We must ask ourselves why is it that our children are so affected, so influenced by 50 Cent? There's nothing wrong with 50 Cent saying what he's saying—

REGGIE: There's something wrong with it, but it's not really the root of the problem is it?

VERNON: Yeah. Why is [a Black young person] so, so vacant that he's occupying his mind so much with 50 Cent to become so influenced by it? And that's a question for our community. He should be in sports, he should be doing his homework, he should be going on some kind of trip somewhere, or in the arts. You know what I mean? And be doing so many other things like so many other Black children are doing in the city.

There is a deeper problem among Black youth, according to Vernon. It cannot simply be blamed on indulgent Black musicians or flashy wayward pastors. Reggie offered his opinion: "The root of the problem starts with the family institution." Vernon was not so sure about this. But he believes that finding a solution is the collective responsibility of the Black community. "The Asians have their lobbying group, the Muslims do," he said. But for some reason the Black community had not been able to organize as effectively around these issues.

"What we need to do is *pray*!" Vernon joked, bursting into a raucous laugh. "Black mothers are always on their knees praying for their kids," he continued. "We need political and financial industry." For one reason or another, there has been limited advocacy on the issues that are shaping Black youth. Vernon thinks that more direct political action is the best way forward—which might mean taking a leaf from the lobbying successes of South Asian Muslims.

CASE STUDY CHURCHES AND MOSQUES

Our conversation at The CD Bar set me in a good stead for identifying case study churches in Brixton. In the months that followed, I visited several churches in Brixton as well as mosques in the East End where I undertook participant observation. I attended each religious institution during a service or prayer time, took detailed field notes, met youth and other people from the congregation, and informally met lay religious leaders or clergy. The full set of religious institutions that I visited for these initial observations is listed in Table 4.1.

From these first participant observation visits, I went through a gradual selection process to choose two churches and two mosques for in-depth case studies. My criteria for selection are broadly based on the selection logic that Nancy Ammerman has used in her multi-congregation studies.[15] I sought out congregations that (1) were large enough to be influential, exerting a substantial influence on second-generation young people and (2) captured something of the variation in the local area's religious institutions. The primary basis of variation, shown in Table 4.1, was between "traditional" churches that largely carry over the preferences of first-generation adults from their countries of origin, and more "contemporary" institutions that due to style or offerings have made substantial inroads among second-generation youth. This traditional–contemporary continuum was the main difference Reggie and Vernon had identified, and was a clear distinction I could discern in my initial months of participant observation. The distinction is of great importance to religious institutions' relationships with, and influence on, second-generation youth.

Table 4.1. Religious organizations visited for participant observation

	Church	Mosque
"Traditional": Predominantly first-generation adults	Brixton Seventh Day Adventist Church[a]	Brick Lane Mosque[a]
	New Testament Church of God (NTCG), Brixton	Christian Street Mosque
"Contemporary": large segment of second-generation youth	Ruach Ministries[a]	East London Mosque[a]
	Universal Church of the Kingdom of God (UCKG), Brixton	Darrul Ummah

[a] The four case study organizations.

[15] Ammerman (1996, 2005).

In practice, this selection process was at times quite simple and straightforward. It was clear from the beginning that two particular religious institutions are highly influential and youth oriented: Ruach Ministries and the East London Mosque (ELM). At the time of research, each of these institutions was estimated to draw about 4,000 worshipers during its main religious services day each week (Friday for ELM, Sunday for Ruach). Even if the 4,000 total was optimistic, Ruach and ELM undoubtedly drew weekly numbers in the thousands, making them exceptionally large congregations for London and Europe. The ELM is probably the largest mosque in Europe in terms of weekly attendance.[16] Ruach Ministries is one of a set of dynamic and growing African or Caribbean led churches in London, and the fourth largest church in Britain (see Table 4.2).[17]

Table 4.2. Mega-churches in Britain, with estimated weekly attendance (2005)[a]

Church	Attendance
1. Kingsway International Christian Centre (KICC)[bc]	10,000
2. Kensington Temple[c]	5,500
3. Hillsong Church[c]	5,000
4. Ruach Ministries[bc]	4,000
5. House of Praise, Woolwich[bc]	3,000
6. St. Thomas Crookes, Sheffield	2,500
7. Holy Trinity, Brompton[c]	2,490
8. Jesus House[bc]	2,200
9. All Souls, London[c]	2,000
10. Holy Trinity, Cheltenham	1,680

[a] From Peter Brierley (2006: 275-6)
[b] African- or Caribbean-led church
[c] Based in London

---

[16] With the completion of the Maryam Centre, adding additional prayer space for women, the capacity of the East London Mosque has risen to 6,000 with the congregation sometimes reaching over 7,000 and overflowing onto the surrounding streets (East London Mosque 2014: 8).

[17] These 2005 figures are estimates from Peter Brierley (2006: 275-6), an expert on British church statistics. Many of the churches in this table will have grown significantly while others have decreased in numbers in the decade since 2005, and may find themselves at a different point in the ranking today. For example, the Sunday attendance at Holy Trinity Brompton is now around 4,500 while at Ruach it is around 5,000 (Brierley 2015, personal communication, June 14). I have chosen to retain the 2005 figures in this table because they come from a single source, making them comparable, and because they provide background for my research in Brixton churches which took place primarily in 2007-9.

Sometimes the selection process proved more difficult. At one point, I considered selecting the Brixton branch of the Universal Church of the Kingdom of God (UCKG), a highly successful Pentecostal denomination that is known as the IURD in Brazil. The UCKG has a unique basis of operations compared to other British churches: it has established "Help Centres" that are open twenty-four hours each day, providing prayer, spiritual advice, or other assistance to anyone who wishes to visit. All of the UK church branches also hold four religious services every day of the week with particular themes (e.g. Monday is about financial problems, Tuesday spiritual healing, and Wednesday personal development). I attended the Brixton UCKG church for its largest Wednesday service, and learned that it has a substantial segment of youth as well as highly developed youth programs. Unfortunately, after a long process of persistent communication with the central church office of the UCKG, I was never allowed further access to the Brixton congregation for research. London branches of the church have been embroiled in various controversies over the past decade.[18] Although these issues were completely unrelated to my intended research with the youth ministry, they may be the reason for the cautious gatekeeping I experienced in my interaction with the church hierarchy. My experience was not dissimilar to Sophie Gilliat-Ray's failed attempts to access the "closed worlds" of four Deobandi Muslim seminaries in Britain.[19]

As my knowledge of Brixton deepened, I realized that the UCKG would not have been the ideal case study pairing with Ruach Ministries in the present study. Both churches can be classified as neo-Pentecostal, and it was important to broaden my research to include other potential forms of youth religious experience. I chose to attend the Brixton Seventh Day Adventist Church as a more "traditional" church pairing with Ruach. Seventh Day Adventism is the largest

---

[18] The most high-profile controversy for the UCKG church was its alleged lack of intervention to help Victoria Climbié, aged 8, who died from her guardians' abuse in 2000. The girl had brought problems to the attention of a UCKG pastor. In a much smaller controversy at the time I was doing research, the UCKG was intending to renovate a historic cinema in Walthamstow, but received significant opposition from local residents.

[19] Gilliat-Ray (2007). According to Sophie Gilliat-Ray (2014, personal communication, December 12), a generational "shift" has occurred in Deobandi leadership that has made them much more open to serious researchers, to the extent of actively approaching researchers for collaboration. I can only hope the same will happen for the UCKG.

Christian denomination in Jamaica, and the denomination is thriving among British Blacks. Because many second-generation Jamaicans will be brought to "traditional" churches by their parents, this particular church allowed me to tap into a common experience for Jamaican youth.

I likewise chose the Jamme Masjid (Great Mosque) on Brick Lane as a complementary case study to the ELM due to its "traditional" first-generation influence. The mosque is located at the center of the Bangladeshi "heartland" in London on Brick Lane, a street famed for its curry houses. This mosque is one in which many Bangladeshi youth first learn to pray and attend Qur'anic recitation and Arabic classes. Like the Brixton Adventist Church, it maintains transnational ties with the country of origin, serving as an ethnic community hub for its local area.

I will now profile each of the two churches and two mosques in turn. My goal will be to elucidate the kinds of imagined citizenship they communicate through their religious messages, and the practices and resources that might constrain or enable youth citizenship, in ways either overt or subtle.

BRIXTON SEVENTH DAY ADVENTIST CHURCH: THE DUTIFUL WEST INDIAN CITIZEN

Some residents of Brixton may be unaware of the large Brixton Seventh Day Adventist Church (Figure 4.3). It lies just north of the major Tesco grocery store on Acre Lane, but is nestled within quiet residential streets that have rows of identical Victorian terraced houses. The Adventist church is on Santley Street, in a building originally constructed by the Church of England in simple Decorated Gothic style in 1881.[20] The Anglican congregation in the twentieth century aged and declined, with the building declared redundant in 1980. The Adventists were able to acquire the Santley Street church through a property exchange for their smaller church on Ferndale Road (built in 1958). Today the main sanctuary does feel like a historic church. It is well kept and spacious, with seating for the choir behind the podium and many rows of dark wood pews for the

[20] Sheppard (1956).

Figure 4.3. The Brixton Seventh Day Adventist Church, Santley Street

congregation. The room is carpeted in a regal red color. New flower arrangements are regularly provided to match the seasons. It was in this sanctuary that the Brixton church hosted the then Prime Minister of Jamaica Bruce Golding, himself married to an Adventist, to speak from the pulpit in May 2008.

Adventists celebrate Saturday each week as their Sabbath, or day of rest and worship. At the Brixton church the main worship service takes place on Saturday morning, followed by a community lunch, and then an Adventist Youth Service (AYS) in the evening. From attending these services and events various times, I would estimate that the church reaches a maximum of about 300 attendees on an ordinary week.[21] Members of the Brixton Seventh Day Adventist Church know it simply as "Brixton." Their affectionate nickname conveys the church's intention to represent the best of what Brixton is (or should be) about.

---

[21] I also attended the church during a revival campaign when numbers swelled substantially, but new attendees at campaigns such as this are not necessarily representative of the regular congregation.

Jamie Gittens is the youth pastor at Brixton Seventh Day Adventist Church, a role that she holds in a voluntary capacity. Jamie's parents came to England from Barbados and St. Vincent, and she traveled with them when she was three years old. When I met Jamie to interview her about youth work at Brixton, she was in her late twenties. She wears glasses, keeps her hair back in a ponytail, and has a gentle manner. Jamie joked with me that the young people at the Brixton Seventh Day Adventist Church can never guess her age, usually guessing older, but sometimes a bit younger.

Jamie said she had first started volunteering as the youth leader because: "I've seen that my generation's left. They're all gone." For one reason or another, all of her childhood friends of the same age either left for another church or drifted away from faith altogether. "Now that I'm 28," she continued, "my passion is that as that next generation comes out they don't do the same thing."

The Brixton Adventist Church has a Sabbath school class for teenagers. There is also a more loosely organized set of events for youth in the church which include people in their twenties or early thirties, which is largely organized through Facebook. The AYS on Saturday evenings is, in reality, only for "youth" in name. I attended the AYS several times, and each week it functions largely as a smaller transplant of attendees from the morning service who are choosing to spend their whole day in church activities. The attendees at all services at the Brixton church are almost all Black. At least 60 percent are female. The largest specific demographic within the church is composed of older first-generation West Indian women. Women wear nice dresses and many wear church hats, while most men wear suits. As Jamie had mentioned, although there are children and adults in the church, there is a noticeable absence of young people in their upper teens and twenties.

I asked Jamie why, in her view, young people so often leave the church when they reach their late teens. She thinks that generational issues are a big part of this issue. "Sometimes young people can be very sensitive about comments on their dress," she said, implying that the modest and fairly formal dress code can be a barrier. I noticed myself from attending the church that I never saw anyone wearing earrings or other jewelry, including young women. Jamie believes that there is a generation gap within the church. She has tried to help heal the divide when possible. She once held an event where members of the different generations were gathered together to air their differences "but no one would talk. It didn't really work."

Most of Jamie's work is with the regular teen Sabbath school class, and she remains optimistic overall that youth ministry can make a difference. She was aware of my research on citizenship. When I asked her about the main goals of her ministry work with youth, she expressed these partly in civic terms: "First and foremost is on a spiritual level, that they become closer to God," she said. "And second of all, that they become *active citizens of the church*. And by that, they'll also be developing their talents that they've been given and use that in the community" (emphasis added).

The core of citizenship, according to Jamie, is located in the church as an institution. It is through involvement in this institution that youth develop skills that they can apply to national citizenship more broadly.

Jamie explained to me further what she means by "active citizenship of the church" and how this can carry over as the use of "talents... in the community" beyond the church walls. Being part of the youth ministry at Brixton Adventist Church "helps you become a good member of society." In her own experience: "I wouldn't be able to do presentations, or write songs, or write poems, or do public speaking if it wasn't for the skills that I developed when I was younger from the AY youth program."[22] Youth ministry is a place in which useful skills can be nurtured that one can apply to the benefit of society.

How well are Jamie's civic goals for youth actually accomplished by the youth work and general ministry of the church? To answer this and related questions I visited Brixton Seventh Day Adventist Church regularly for participant observation.

On the first Saturday Sabbath that I visited the church, I planned to attend the pre-service Sabbath school but I was slightly late. As I approached the building, a street evangelist paced back and forth outside the church. He was preaching a message of repentance and the End Times in order to convince passersby and draw them inside. I smiled politely as I walked in. Immediately upon entering the church sanctuary I was greeted by a charming middle-aged woman wearing a white dress and a black and white scarf. She discreetly funneled me to Sister Alma's class for newcomers, already in progress. The sanctuary space had been divided into perhaps half a dozen

---

[22] AY stands for Adventist Youth. The Adventist Youth Service that takes place in the evenings at Brixton is part of a well-resourced curriculum and strategy for youth work developed by the British Adventist Church.

Sabbath school classes. Groups sat on pews in different areas of the room to study the Bible together.

Sister Alma is an elderly West Indian lady, with a voice that is both kindly and stern. She was wearing a dress and a large church hat, perfectly matched in peacock blue. Sister Alma regularly teaches the newcomers' class. I sat down alongside about ten others who were new to the church. The Bible study was, in large part, Sister Alma's own spiritual instruction to us. She executed this with aplomb. When she checked for questions at the end, one woman sitting in our section raised her hand to speak. The woman said that she had attended Pentecostal churches in the past and asked if there was any difference. With a motherly tone of concern in her voice, Sister Alma explained that the Adventist Church takes very seriously the authority of the Word of God. She mentioned spiritual practices that might happen in a Pentecostal church, such as speaking in tongues, and chastened our class that we should recognize these as inappropriate in a church setting because (paraphrasing 1 Corinthians 14:33): "God is not a God of disorder. He is a God of order."

In the several weeks that I attended the Brixton Adventist Church for observation, the theme of orderliness came across consistently. The services were very carefully structured. Following the service plan, different members of the congregation stepped to the podium to lead singing, make announcements, or to give a musical performance. This structure also provided a sense that the service was a "family" enterprise, as many different members of the congregation of different ages were responsible for leading different sections from the podium. Before and after the service, when friends or acquaintances met they would shake hands and share the common greeting of "Happy Sabbath!"

Services at the Brixton Adventist Church regularly make mention of the West Indian origins of the congregation, usually using this term rather than "Caribbean" or the more specific "Jamaican" (although Jamaicans do compose the largest single ethnic group in the congregation). For example, early into the first service I attended, an Elder came to the front to initiate the service. He reminded the congregation of the importance of being punctual: "They say there's a 'West Indian Time.' Well, there is no West Indian time. There are no excuses for being late to church."

The model of a good young citizen that is expressed by the church has a particular ethnic character—it is a good, young *West Indian* citizen. This is because the descriptions, models, and injunctions expressed in church for what is good and right for a young person to do are often expressed as West Indian values. There is a cultural specificity to good citizenship within the Brixton Seventh Day Adventist Church, as I will explain further when I describe a skit I observed at one Sabbath AYS.

The church's West Indian values are combined with a strong emphasis on being Adventist. Seventh Day Adventists accept the foundational Christian belief in Jesus Christ as Lord and Savior, as outlined in the New Testament. In their scriptural hermeneutic they believe that it is likewise incumbent upon believers to follow Old Testament law. Adventists are distinctive from most other Christians in their attempt to carry on the Old Testament Jewish tradition of beginning Sabbath at sundown on Friday and celebrating it throughout Saturday. In an effort to uphold the Mosaic Law in scripture, Adventists do not drink alcohol and maintain a careful diet. Several members of the congregation told me that they try to avoid processed foods, while some were vegetarian. Based on the importance placed on detail in dates and laws by the Adventist founder, Ellen White, there is a frequent message of readiness for the End Times and Jesus' return to judge the world. The strong emphasis on following particular practices as a minority within the broader context of Christian tradition can have the effect of "ethnicizing" Adventism. By this I do not mean that Adventism becomes a distinct ethnic identity in its own right, but rather that the symbolic boundaries of Adventism further facilitate the ethnic distinctiveness of West Indian identity.

The emphasis on Adventist distinctions was frequently expressed in church services. At one communion Sabbath that I attended, Head Pastor Hamilton Williams preached about the meaning of the communion meal, as established by Christ himself. Pastor Williams is a tall and broad-shouldered Jamaican man of middle age, with glasses and a meticulously shaven head. He speaks with great force and verbal dexterity, intermixing frequent quotes from the King James Bible with his own words that have a potent biblical tenor (e.g. "the martyrs were torn asunder!"). In this particular sermon about communion, Pastor Williams took pains to communicate that at the Last Supper Jesus and his disciples "had just eaten bread and *unfermented* wine." He made it unequivocally clear that drinking wine and other alcohol is not a permissible indulgence in one's earthly life. Jesus himself said, in the theme verse of the sermon: "I will not drink henceforth of this fruit of the vine, until the day when I drink it new with you in my Father's kingdom" (Matthew 26:29). The sermon's resounding message was one of delaying gratification. It is necessary to maintain discipline and patience until it is time to be reunited with the Lord.

The requirements for self-control, patience, and modesty, as I have conveyed, were communicated often in the Brixton Church both as tenets of Seventh Day Adventist faith and as traditional West Indian values. One example of these values being taught in reference to youth was through a skit in one evening AYS. Entitled "Imitation of Life," the skit was performed by young people from the congregation, largely in their mid to late twenties. The skit stars a young man in the role of Johnny, who is growing up in a stereotypical Adventist West Indian family. It is based on the scripture verse Proverbs 22:6, which says "Train up a child in the way he should go: and when he is old he will not depart from it."

At the beginning of the skit, Johnny is a teenager and a good member of his family. He passes an important exam at school. He prays devotedly: "Dear Lord, the only real peace that I have is in You." His West Indian mother may be a bit overbearing in her faith—when Johnny faces a difficult situation, she advises him to "just praise the hurt away!" Johnny's father is perhaps too neglectful—he sits at the kitchen table in his bathrobe to read the newspaper, often forgetting his own children's names. These adult characters, portrayed by youth actors, received much of the laughter from the young people in the audience. But the overall message was serious: Johnny lived in a relatively happy and secure family.

Johnny goes away to university and falls in with the wrong crowd. He spends his time with three young men who are portrayed as delinquents: a Rastafarian, a youth in the Pan-African movement, and another friend who is into hip hop. "Just forget what your mummy tell ya," they say. Soon Johnny is smoking weed with these friends and skipping his classes. To uproarious laughter from the audience, he starts to take on Rastafarian mannerisms, yelling out expressions like "Jang Rastafari!" Johnny, while on a drug high, writes a letter to his mother that reveals the depths of his condition: "Dear Mum, I have decided to become a Rastafarian. Christianity is no longer a thing that I do. Re-spect! Stay blessed in Selassie." As the skit closes, Johnny remains estranged from his parents. A narrator quotes again the Proverb about training up a child. Perhaps Johnny's parents had not done enough for him.

After the evening AYS, a middle-aged West Indian woman asked if I had liked the skit. I told her yes, I thought it was funny and had a good message. "Oh, you understood it?" she replied. "You know, that really can happen!"

The "Imitation of Life" skit communicates well the Brixton Adventist Church's approach to socializing its youth into good believers and citizens. The Proverb of "Train up a child in the way he should go" that bookends the skit conveys the church's highly pedagogical and family-centric approach to young people. The skit also reveals the main peril that the church perceives to this socializing mission: a permissive youth culture that can steal away young people from Christian faith, life achievements, and parents. The use of Rastafarianism, Pan-Africanism, and hip hop as competitors to the Adventist faith show the particular symbolic boundaries by which the church defines itself in opposition to others.

The kind of citizenship modeled in the Brixton Seventh Day Adventist Church is a dutiful citizenship that honors the place of family and traditional values. It is a citizenship with a particular ethnic tinge to it, as it is hoped that youth will locate themselves in the heritage and values of the West Indies. Not always distinct from these cultural values are the doctrines of Seventh Day Adventist Christianity, which are considered the ultimate guidelines to an upright life as a citizen of the church and greater society. An ideal youth "graduate" of the Brixton Church, then, will be a dutiful Adventist West Indian citizen. There is much to hold together in this model of citizenship. It faces the challenge of being heavily reliant on intergenerational transmission. As Jamie had suggested—and as the relatively low level of youth involvement in the AYS makes clear—this transmission process has been a tenuous one.

BRICK LANE MOSQUE: THE DUTIFUL BANGLADESHI CITIZEN

The religious building that now houses the Brick Lane Jamme Masjid (Great Mosque) was originally constructed as a French Huguenot church in 1743. The building is frequently noted as an architectural symbol of Britain's multicultural and multi-religious immigrant history (Figure 4.4). The substantial rectangular brick structure stands on the corner of two streets—stately Fournier Street lined by tall Georgian

Figure 4.4. The Brick Lane Mosque

town houses, and energetic Brick Lane blazing with the neon signs of its curry restaurants. A sundial placed high on the external wall of the building bears the inscription *Umbra Summus*, or "we are shadows." Huguenots originally placed the sundial inscription as a reminder of the fleeting nature of earthly life. The phrase also captures well the historic transience of immigrant communities through these streets.

The Huguenots who built this place of worship in the eighteenth century were Calvinist Protestant refugees fleeing persecution from Catholic France.[23] Although initially facing exclusion from British society, the Huguenots eventually assimilated and intermarried. When building their church, they specified that the building should not "be used for any other purpose but for the worship of God."[24] Incredibly, this religious designation of the space has been honored through time. The building spent a decade in the early nineteenth century as the home

---

[23] Huguenots were persecuted in France after the 1685 revocation of the Edict of Nantes, which had extended tolerance for their beliefs. Many secretly fled, often at great risk to their lives, to settle in places including Britain, Holland, and the New World colonies.

[24] *The Economist* (2003).

of a Wesleyan missionary society to Jews, and then became a Methodist Chapel in 1819. By the end of the nineteenth century, the Jewish population of the East End had grown rapidly, in part due to the pogroms that followed the 1881 assassination of Russian Tsar Alexander II, and in part due to economic migration.[25] Jews purchased the Brick Lane building and it functioned as the Machzikei Hadas Great Synagogue from 1898 until the 1970s. At one time there were more than 100,000 Jews living in the East End of London. Yet as members of this community also incorporated into society or grew more affluent, they moved to other parts of London. Bangladeshis, who began settling in the East End in significant numbers in the 1960s, purchased the building to convert it into a mosque in 1976.

The same building on the corner of Brick Lane and Fournier Street, then, has been a Huguenot church, Christian missionary society, Methodist chapel, Jewish synagogue, and Bangladeshi mosque. Over the years it has been an important center of both religious and community life. The building has come to represent the part religion can play in rooting immigrant communities in their new home, providing them with spirituality and a secure community space that may facilitate their successful incorporation.

The religious building on Brick Lane has undergone physical changes over time that testify to its succession of occupants. Its Huguenot builders were Protestants who conscientiously demonstrated their difference from Catholics by *not* orienting worship towards the East. They instead built the pews and altar to a rational design facing north, aligning the building with its entrance from the south. The eventual Jewish heirs renovated the space to bring worship to face in an approximate eastward direction towards Jerusalem. A final reorientation was achieved by the present Muslim Bangladeshi owners, who have precise needs to pray towards the *qibla*, or direction of Mecca. This change was the most radical, and involved setting carpeted rows for prayer diagonally across the space with a *mihrab*[26] in the southeast corner of the building. To convert the space into a mosque, pews were removed, prayer carpeting was inserted, and rooms in the basement were repurposed as areas for *wudu*, or Islamic

---

[25] For a concise and lively overview of Jewish immigration to the East End, see Silver (2014).

[26] A *mihrab* is a prayer niche placed in a mosque to establish the *qibla*, or direction of prayer towards Mecca.

ceremonial washing. The most evident change to the exterior has been the erection of a tall silver minaret-like structure at the corner in 2009.[27] Today the large main prayer room on the ground floor of the mosque is covered in a sea of aquamarine prayer carpeting. The carpeting abuts beautiful massive dark oak doors from the eighteenth century. As Bangladeshi men bow down to pray, they worship beneath glorious golden candelabra-style chandeliers.

The leadership of the Brick Lane Mosque referred me to Sajjad Miah, a mosque Vice President, for my questions about second-generation youth. On the day I had arranged to meet Sajjad I entered the mosque to find him gathered with the leadership board in their main office. There had been an incident of pickpocketing at the mosque only minutes earlier and the board was arranging their response. Sajjad is a Bangladeshi man in his sixties, slight in frame, with glasses and closely shaven gray beard. He was visibly preoccupied by the pickpocketing situation. We realized it would be better to postpone the interview to the following week.

I found Sajjad the next week at the mosque office again. We ascended the dark oak central staircase in the center of the building. Carrying our two English teas, we entered a large and bare multipurpose room upstairs to sit down at a plastic foldable table for the interview.

I asked Sajjad to describe his experiences of coming to Britain and living here. He arrived as a teenager in 1967 with his father. As is true of most Bangladeshis in his generation, Sajjad's original intention was to stay in Britain temporarily and for economic reasons. Over time this "myth of return"[28] evaporated:

> My initial understanding was that after short while we'll go back to the Bangladesh. We'll go back to the Bangladesh after a few years or so. There was no intention of settling here in the beginning. But by the time passed, my other brother and sister and my mother came to this country. By then we realized that [laughing] we'll not be able to go back to the Bangladesh!

---

[27] Because it does not issue a call for prayer, the tall silver beacon is technically not a minaret. However Sajjad Miah of the mosque leadership told me that it is an important symbol that draws attention to the relatively plain brick building as a mosque, enabling the Muslim Bangladeshis of the area to stake their claim on public space.

[28] On the myth of return, see Anwar (1979). Interestingly, young second-generation Bangladeshis are so committed to their lives in Britain and to being distinct from their parents that when speaking about Bangladesh many repeat a "mantra of non-return" (see DeHanas 2013b).

His early years in Britain had been exciting times. There was a real pioneering spirit among the men who arrived to take jobs. At first they would join together for prayer in houses and various places. Sajjad was part of the process of purchasing the religious building on Brick Lane, which was at that time a synagogue with declining membership. He told me: "The Jewish people knew that this building would be used for a mosque, and because of that it would be used for a religious purpose. So they gave us a discount." Over the years, many of the wives of these Bangladeshi men arrived and the single men got married. Sajjad had himself started a family in Britain. When we spoke, his four children ranged in age from 33 to 9.

Yet the early years were also challenging times for Sajjad and his Bangladeshi compatriots. In the 1970s, skinheads from the National Front were harassing the growing number of Bangladeshi residents around Brick Lane. Sajjad had helped to form the Bangladeshi Youth Association (BYA) for young men to protect the community. The BYA also bought snooker tables and other recreational equipment to help men pass the time. It was one of several youth-oriented groups of the 1970s that would give Bangladeshis the infrastructure they needed to politically organize and mobilize.

Sajjad's memories of facing off racism in the Brick Lane area coincide well with those of his contemporaries, several of whom were interviewed in an oral history project by the Swadhinata Trust.[29] For these mostly male Bengali first-generation elders, the 1978 May election season proved a pivotal time. The National Front had slated about fifty candidates in wards across Tower Hamlets in their efforts to intimidate non-Whites in the area.[30] In the tense atmosphere of election night, a young Bengali garment worker named Altab Ali was walking home through a public park in the grounds of the former St Mary's Whitechapel. Ali was confronted by skinheads and stabbed to death on the spot. News of the murder spread rapidly through youth organizations, labor unions, and other channels. Bengalis joined with other anti-racists to organize a massive demonstration in solidarity against racism (Figure 4.5). More than 7,000 people flooded the streets of the East End in a "Black Solidarity Day" that echoed the 1936 Battle of Cable Street, which had seen off Oswald Mosley's fascist blackshirts in nearby streets.[31] Many

---

[29] Eade et al. (2006).   [30] Jones (2006).   [31] Rahman (2006).

Figure 4.5. The Altab Ali protest on Brick Lane, 1978 (photograph by Alan Denney)

participants in the 1978 Altab Ali demonstration marched from Whitechapel to Parliament to have their voices heard. The St Mary's Whitechapel gardens, where Ali had been killed, would be renamed Altab Ali Park in commemoration. As Abdus Shukur told the Swadhinata Trust interviewer: "The battle of '78 was very relevant, because it was a turning point for the community, it was a point, which said that, 'we are here to stay, we are no[t] going to be going back.'"[32]

Since 1978 Bengalis have entered Tower Hamlets politics with increasing confidence. Sajjad Miah himself would go on to successfully run for election in 1990 as a local councilor for the Liberal Democrat Party. In doing so, he was one of the forerunners of a broader trend: in 2002, Bangladeshi councilors became the majority of the Labour ruling group and in 2006 they became the majority on the Council, a status they continue to hold today.[33]

Yet although Sajjad Miah as a young man had taken an active part in major phases of East End Bangladeshi history, today he finds it difficult to relate to British Bengali young people. The main difference

---

[32] Shukur (2006).
[33] For much more detail on the increasing political consciousness of Bangladeshis in Tower Hamlets from the 1970s onwards, see Sarah Glynn's (2015) political history.

between youth in the 1970s and today, he noted, is that now they are involved in "drugs and anti-social behavior" to a much greater degree. He said that some young people are trying to bring their wayward friends "to the community." But in many cases, these youth are continuing to smoke or drink alcohol, sometimes in open defiance of their elders. The main problems Sajjad perceives—the substance use, the delinquency, and the generation gap—are almost identical to the issues raised in the Seventh Day Adventist skit "Imitation of Life."

At the root of these problems, according to Sajjad, is that "nowadays the youth don't care about Bangladesh. They are more London or English." His comment interested me, because at that time I had been asking second-generation youth how they prioritize their identities. I asked Sajjad himself about which components of identity are most important to him. He considers "Bangladeshi" to be his core identity. He follows this with Muslim second, and Sylheti (his region in Bangladesh) third. Sajjad spoke with great enthusiasm about the natural beauty of his country of origin. In his heart, Bangladesh remains his home.

The Brick Lane Mosque maintains continuity with the Bangladeshi way of life. Sajjad told me that the primary purpose of the mosque is to be a "place for the community." It is also, of course, a place of worship. For Sajjad the Bangladeshi cultural and Muslim religious functions of the mosque are closely fused together. The mosque inculcates an image of the good Bengali and the good Muslim through its *khutbas* (sermons). First-generation fathers may bring their children to teach them to pray at the mosque, and religious socialization of children occurs through years of prayer, *khutbas*, and close-knit community relationships. The mosque also reaches a youth segment directly through its separate classes for 10- to 15-year-old boys and girls to learn to read and recite the Qur'an. Sajjad estimates that about a hundred youth take part in these classes, where "the imams give speeches on what is right and wrong." The mosque endeavors to teach young people an integrated vision of the good Bangladeshi Muslim—a kind of model citizen of the local community and also of Bangladesh.

The Brick Lane Mosque is embedded in the Barelwi tradition of Islam. This means that it tends towards Sufi spirituality and cultural traditions of South Asia. The Barelwis of Bangladesh venerate the great Sufi saints, called *pirs*. These saints, such as Shah Jalal, first brought Islam into the Bengal frontier. The Brick Lane Mosque maintains spiritual practices and styles of worship suffused with Bengali traditions. For example, each year it celebrates *mawlid*, the birthday of Muhammad, through exuberant communal singing. Some Muslims of the East End consider such Barelwi traditions to be actions of *shirk* (idolatry). Indeed, it is utterly impossible to imagine a Bangladeshi *mawlid* being celebrated at the more theologically restrained ELM.

The cultural continuity of the Brick Lane Mosque has meant that it is deeply appealing for many men who have immigrated from Bangladesh, especially older men. The mosque has space for up to 4,000 worshipers in prayer. In my estimation attendance rarely exceeds 1,000 for the main Friday *jumwa* congregation. There is, nonetheless, a steady of stream of men entering and leaving the mosque on Fridays and some men around the prayer times every day. Most of the people I observed at these times were older bearded men in traditional flowing Bengali clothes and prayer caps. It was very rare to see a young person at the mosque of my research demographic of age 18 to 25. When recruiting young people to interview I would try to approach anyone who could be of the right age. In one early attempt I walked up to a man leaving the Jamme Masjid, who turned out to be in his thirties: "Oh no, mate," he said, in an attempt to be helpful. "There are no youths here. What you want is the East London Mosque."

One reason for the relative scarcity of young men at the Brick Lane Mosque is that the *khutbas* are given in Sylheti, the regional language of most East End Bangladeshis.[34] This language choice is a natural one for the community that the mosque has traditionally served. Yet because the sermons are not also spoken in English, they may be perceived as somewhat out of touch by second-generation youth, who while also being Sylheti speakers have grown up in the language and culture of Britain. In addition, youth older than 15 have no organized activities available to them at the mosque. The strong influence of first-generation parents on the mosque may conflict with the desires of youth for more freedom and independence from parents at this age.

---

[34] Although it shares words in common with Bangla (the most widely spoken language in Bangladesh) Sylheti is a fully grammatically distinct language rather than simply being a regional dialect.

Through continued effort to recruit young people leaving the Brick Lane Mosque, I managed to recruit and interview three who fit within my research requirements. Two of these young men expressed no real affection for the mosque. They told me that they were there simply because of its proximity to where they lived, and each was, in fact, more involved in the ELM. The third youth was a 20-year-old named Omar. He did express some appreciation for the Brick Lane Mosque, as he had experienced the Islamic education sessions there when he was younger.

Omar told me he gets along well with some of the older members in the Brick Lane Mosque. "One of them is my neighbor," he said. "He's good, he's funny. He's got his own jokes—classical jokes." Omar likes to talk with men in the older generation. Yet he believes that they have some limitations: "They haven't studied Islam," he said. Omar has gone through "Islamic studies, from the teachers in Whitechapel," by which he means teachers at the ELM. A youth named Amin told me that "older people go local for mosque," coming to worship on Brick Lane, but "young go more where there's a nice atmosphere." One reason he gave for the attraction of young men to the ELM is simply that "There are lots more PFCs [fried chicken shops] down on Whitechapel."[35] Another youth I met, who sometimes attends the Brick Lane Mosque, more often goes to the ELM because "there's more younger religious brothers around which can help you, which can guide you. And you feel more comfortable there, because there's a lot of people around the same age, who dress in the same way. With Brick Lane it's more like the older generations that came across here first."

The Brick Lane Mosque shares many similarities with the Brixton Seventh Day Adventist Church because both are first-generation dominated. In both congregations the cultural traditions, practices, and values of the first generation are faithfully maintained. Both institutions are transnationally connected with their countries of origin, bringing dignitaries and guests regularly to join in worship. Perhaps the clearest difference between the two is the gendered maintenance of religious tradition. At Brixton, the congregation is majority female. Women take on much of the leadership in teaching

---

[35] PFC stands for Perfect Fried Chicken, and is the name of several (unrelated) independent chicken shops in the East End. It has come to represent chicken shops in general.

Adventist and West Indian values to the next generation. The Brick Lane Mosque is, in contrast, an entirely male institution. Although it provides religious instruction to girls, it is unable to directly influence young women as they mature in adolescence.

The Brick Lane Mosque is similar to the Brixton Seventh Day Adventist Church in its espousal of an ethnic style of citizenship. The leadership of the mosque attempts to shape young people into dutiful citizens of the local Bangladeshi community, believing that this will make them better members of society. Yet, even from my interviews with youth I met at the Brick Lane Mosque, I found clear signals that the mosque has limited influence on young people in the middle teenage years or beyond, especially compared to the ELM. Likewise, the Brick Lane Mosque no longer retains the political vitality it once had as a hub for anti-racist activists and youth groups in the 1970s. It is to the East London Mosque and Ruach Ministries—two institutions that represent newer trends with far wider appeal among today's young people—that we must now turn.

5

New Religion

In April 2006, Prime Minister Tony Blair invited a select group of Black church and community leaders to a meeting at 10 Downing Street. The meeting was followed by a conference at Ruach Ministries, Brixton, where Blair was the keynote speaker. From the podium of Ruach, the Prime Minister praised Black churches and encouraged them to action:

> Churches such as yours have long been the bedrock of our local communities... Your organizations have a crucial campaigning role. They are not political in the sense that the parties are. But they do engage in the important issues of their day—they cannot but do so. They are political but with a small p.[1]

Tony Blair's recognition of Black churches was a milestone in British politics. It symbolically validated Black church political involvement, giving some of the leaders of these churches a seat at the highest government table. The following year the political significance of Black churches was further confirmed when Prince Charles chose to spend his 59th birthday with his wife Camilla the Duchess of Cornwall at Jesus House, a large Nigerian-led church in South London.[2]

This chapter concerns two large inner London congregations that have gained prominence on a national or even global stage: Ruach Ministries and the East London Mosque. These congregations exemplify a "new religion" in which believers are less preoccupied with transmitting culture or roots through the generations, and instead

---

[1] Blair (2006).
[2] Jesus House is the largest British church in the Redeemed Christian Church of God (RCCG) denomination. The RCCG, founded in Nigeria, is well known for its global extent and its commitment to the "reverse mission" of returning Christianity to post-Christian societies.

take religious texts and practices to have immediate, pragmatic relevance to everyday lives. Both institutions are at the top end in congregation sizes and have, at least at certain moments, been highly effective in leveraging their mega-scale to gain influence. Importantly for this book, both have extensive programs for young people that are seen to be savvy and highly successful. At the outset, at least, it seems these congregations hold out greater promise for shaping young people into active, participating British citizens than the more traditional first-generation congregations profiled in the previous chapter.

RUACH CITY CHURCH: CHAMPIONS AND AMBASSADORS

London has long been a fulcrum in the global development of Black Majority Churches (BMCs) outside Africa and the Caribbean. The first BMC in Europe was Sumner Road Chapel, founded in 1906 by Reverend Thomas Kwame Brem-Wilson in Peckham, South London.[3] London remained a node in multiracial Pentecostal networks in the early twentieth century through the encouragement of Brem-Wilson and his friend Cecil Polhill, the philanthropic missionary mobilizer. In Britain's 1950s and 1960s post-Windrush years of immigration, new arrivals from the Caribbean began to establish their own separate churches. Black Christian leaders have differed on whether this was because White churches were unwelcoming or simply could not adequately fulfill Black immigrants' needs for emotional support and more exuberant styles of worship.[4] Joel Edwards has characterized the early post-Windrush years into three phases: a fleeting "suitcase" phase (1950–65), a "letterhead" phase in which church identities were consolidated (1960–75), and a "business card" phase when churches expanded their networks of professional and political allies (1975–88).[5] Since the 1980s, developments in British Caribbean Christianity have become increasingly complex, for at least three reasons: more Caribbean churches have joined multiracial associations like the Evangelical Alliance; truly multi-ethnic

---

[3] Olofinjana (2010).
[4] For the former position, see Mohabir (1988); for the latter see Edwards (1993).
[5] Edwards (1993).

charismatic mega-churches have emerged, including London's Hillsong Church and Kensington Temple; and African-led churches have overtaken the Caribbean-led as the main engines of Christian growth.[6]

Peter Brierley's research has drawn attention to the remarkable contemporary growth of BMCs in London.[7] Despite a slight decline in Anglican attendance,[8] the overall number of church attendees in London increased at the highest rate in Britain (16 percent) from 2005 to 2012.[9] This growth has been largely fueled by BMCs and immigrant churches. Today nearly half of all weekly Christian worshipers in London are Black.[10] While the number of BMCs in the London borough of Lambeth (where Brixton is located) is not known, a detailed survey of the comparable neighboring borough of Southwark found more than 240 BMCs there.[11] Black church leaders have been drawn by London's status as a global city at the center of flows of power, talent, information, and financial capital and by its cross-cutting links with various diaspora networks. Church leaders such as Bishop John Francis of Ruach and Matthew Ashimolowo of the Kingsway International Christian Centre (KICC), the largest church in Britain, have found London to be fertile ground for building congregations at a mega scale and for establishing international broadcast ministries and conference circuits.

Ruach Ministries rose to its contemporary prominence from humble beginnings. John Francis, a second-generation British Jamaican, founded the church in 1992. For the first worship service, eighteen people met in rented space in the Carlton Halls building, behind the Morleys department store in central Brixton.[12] Bishop John Francis, as he is now styled, today leads the large multi-sited organization with his wife, Co-Pastor Penny Francis. Unlike most UK Caribbean-led churches, Ruach is independent of conventional Caribbean denominational structures. This makes it similar to many African independent

---

[6] For a nuanced analysis that picks apart trends in UK Caribbean and African churches see Osgood. (2006).

[7] Brierley (2013).

[8] Jackson and Piggot (2011: 1) find that in Anglican churches in the diocese of London "membership [is] continuing to grow strongly while attendance has begun to fall slightly, [indicating that] committed people may be coming to church less often." Their research is an important complement to Peter Brierley's work.

[9] Brierley (2013: 3).   [10] Brierley (2013: 11).
[11] Rogers (2013).   [12] Ruach City Church (n.d.).

neo-Pentecostal churches, and indicates their common influences from Black American neo-Pentecostal leaders, such as Bishop T. D. Jakes.[13]

Ruach Ministries changed its name in 2014 to "Ruach City Church" to accord with a new vision to "build a city." The church has been expanding and, in addition to the Brixton campus (since 1996), Ruach has active congregations in Kilburn (Northwest London, since 2007) and Walthamstow (East London, since 2010). It most recently bought a large site in Norbury (South London, 2011). Pastor Mark Liburd, who was serving as the main youth pastor in Brixton when I interviewed him in 2008, has since become the Pastor in Residence at Ruach's Walthamstow campus.

In his mid-thirties when we spoke, Pastor Mark Liburd somehow manages to balance warmth and youthful energy with an authoritative air. Mark is a second-generation Jamaican himself. He began his career in car electronics before taking on the Youth Pastor role at Ruach. At the time, the Ruach Brixton campus had an estimated 4,000 total attendees over its five Sunday services each week. One of these services is the youth service each Sunday afternoon at 2 p.m., which would draw 150 to 200 young people. It was an impressive achievement in the "rough" streets of Brixton, where it was the largest youth service. When we spoke Mark was actually one of two staff leaders of the youth ministry, but acted as its sole representative on the church's senior leadership team.

I met Pastor Mark at his office in Ruach for a 45-minute interview. We spoke at length about the problems faced by young people in Brixton, including gun violence and drugs, and the role that the youth ministry has in confronting these. Mark and some of the youth from his ministry do mission work and evangelism each summer in the poor council housing estates of the local area. Some of his young people regularly help staff a nearby youth club.

Early into the interview, Mark mentioned that his youth ministry helps young people become better citizens. I followed up with a question to gauge what he meant by this:

DND: What does involvement in the youth ministry, or their Christian faith, do for someone in their British citizenship?

---

[13] Osgood (2006). "Neo-Pentecostal" churches emerged more recently than the long-established Pentecostal denominations (such as Assemblies of God) and are part of the broader charismatic renewal movement (see Pew 2006: 2).

MARK: I think that [question] in itself is problematic... I don't think anyone knows what being British is! [laughs]... There is a lot of confusion for people, what is Britishness, what does that mean? Is it sitting in the Royal Albert Hall singing "Rule, Britannia," waving your British flags? Or is it just the fact that I'm just here, I'm just a part of contributing to the country?

For Mark, the concept of "British citizenship" is itself worth questioning. He expressed an ironic (very British) skepticism about the expressions of patriotism in the summer Proms concerts at the Royal Albert Hall and about the cultural content of "Britishness" in general. He thinks that a sense of national identity is not as important as one's contribution to society. Mark continued, expressing what he believes to be a superior alternative to citizenship based on British national culture (emphasis added):

> The citizen side of things [for the youth in my congregation] is really making them a better citizen for society, if you sign up to being British or not. It's more of a God culture. Where your *citizenship is really to heaven*. And your citizenship is signed up to that. Whichever country you are in you should be the best citizen of that country because you're an ambassador of Christ.

Mark's comments here reveal much about his approach to youth citizenship. He says that he wants the Ruach youth service to have a "God culture." The phrase "God culture" provides a sense of the kind of polity Mark hopes his youth congregation will be, one in which a consciousness of God is foregrounded. Within this general congregational culture, Mark specifies that his youth should develop a citizenship that "is really to heaven." In saying this, he is paraphrasing St. Paul the Apostle, who wrote to fellow Christians in the early years of the Church that "our citizenship is in Heaven" (Philippians 3:20). St. Paul was himself a Roman citizen, entitling him to legal protections and privileges that were highly valuable at that time. Yet he considered his spiritual citizenship as a Christian to be more important. Citizenship in heaven, as Pastor Mark uses the term, relativizes both one's loyalties to the nation state and one's valuation of the benefits of worldly citizenship. Pastor Mark conveys this approach to identity in a complementary metaphor from the New Testament—that Christians are "ambassadors of Christ" (2 Corinthians 5:20).

Mark thinks that spiritual citizenship is the ultimate locus of social membership, safety, and responsibility. Yet, being a citizen of heaven should not lead to otherworldliness. It has clear and tangible implications for the here and now. Mark continued (emphasis added):

> There's no way your country should look down and say "Oh my gosh, why are you tax evading, why are you?" You should be the best citizen of whichever country you are in cuz that's the law of the land. And you don't want to go against that. So for me, the citizenship side of things is to get young people to sign up to being a good citizen regardless of if you believe you're British, if you're not, or if you were born in Ghana. You're here. You may be here for the next five years. Are you British or not, or are you just Ghanaian? *It doesn't really matter.* You come here be the best citizen until you leave... It's really just making people a better person regardless of denomination, or if they sign up to being British, or Londoners, or Welsh or whatever. Be who you need to be in alignment to heaven.

Citizenship in heaven, as Mark expresses it here, is a radical relativizing of other forms of self-identification and membership. Mark speaks of "British," "Ghanaian," "Londoner," and "Welsh" as identity options, but more important is that underneath these one is becoming "a better person." In fact, Mark states that cultural or national identity "doesn't really matter"—much more important are one's actions while residing in one country or another. His view of the best approach for youth seems to emphasize being good denizens of Britain rather than citizens, at least when it comes to national identity.

In order to witness the civic environment and "God culture" of Ruach Ministries, I attended the youth service several times beginning in May 2008. The church is located on Brixton Hill, about ten minutes walk up from central Brixton. It is tucked away from the street in an unassuming warehouse-conversion next to a carwash (see Figure 5.1). On my first visit, I entered the foyer a few minutes early for the youth service that was scheduled to begin at 2 p.m. The foyer was crowded with young men and women socializing in little groups. The noon church service was running over time. Television screens throughout the foyer displayed that service on live video as Bishop John Francis, Ruach's lead Pastor, spoke and ministered powerfully to a very responsive crowd. As I waited in the foyer that afternoon, I met several young people including Mike (introduced in Chapter 1).

As the doors of the main sanctuary opened, hundreds of women and men with triumphant smiles streamed out into the foyer. Some exited the building; others lingered in the foyer or the adjoining Christian bookshop. Those who could not wait joined long queues

Figure 5.1. Ruach Ministries

for the lavatories. Although I cannot confirm whether 4,000 people were attending across the multiple services that Sunday, the building was certainly stretched to capacity.

I had met Mike in the foyer before the youth service. When we were allowed to enter the sanctuary, we went through the main doors and found seats together. The sanctuary is the main room of the warehouse-conversion, substantially deeper than it is wide. The room is fairly large and nondescript, with blue carpeting, white walls, a main stage with projection screens to each side, and no noticeable Christian symbolism. Around 500 seats have been carefully fit into the space. The Sunday youth service fills 100–200 of the seats near the front.

At Ruach youth services, ages range from 15 to the early thirties. On the average week the youth congregation is entirely Black or mixed-race. Within this seeming homogeneity there is significant diversity. Youth hail from many different Caribbean and African ethnic backgrounds. In my several visits to Ruach I met young people with ancestry from Jamaica, Barbados, Ghana, and Nigeria, among other nations. Sometimes this diversity is celebrated during the youth service itself. On one Sunday a Trinidadian music artist was visiting to perform a few Christian hip hop songs. As the MC introduced him, the two large projection screens displayed Trinidadian flags. The MC started his introduction by riling up the audience: "Are there any Trinis in the house today?! [some audience response]... Are there any Trinis IN DA HOUSE?!! [yells and applause]."

If a religious institution can be a place for cultivating "global citizenship" and expanding one's vision of the world, then the multiculturality of Ruach is important to how it socializes young citizens. Ruach's internationally-oriented character was immediately evident as I entered the sanctuary: the walls are adorned with dozens of hanging flags of countries from around the globe. It was an intriguing selection—flags from Ireland, Brazil, Ghana, Belgium, France, Greece, Denmark, Italy, China, Japan, India, Barbados, and Australia—but no Britain, no Jamaica, and no further Caribbean or African countries. The flags display the global mindset that the church hopes to cultivate, which is simultaneously wide in its extent while unconcerned with specific national borders. The flags are representative symbols of "every nation, tribe, people, and language" (Revelation 7:9) whose histories will all culminate in God's Kingdom that transcends all boundaries. As Pastor Mark Liburd had told me in our interview, heavenly citizenship is more important than the specificity of earthly national identity on earth: "Are you British or not, or are you Ghanaian? It doesn't really matter."

In that first youth service I attended at Ruach, Pastor Mark served as the preacher. He preached with the title "A Champion on the Road." The sermon provided a clear message about the kinds of young citizens Pastor Mark hopes to raise in his congregation.

Pastor Mark's sermon was undeniably funny and given in an inspirational style pitched to his Black British youth audience. The sermon was based on 1 Samuel 16, a section of the Old Testament in which the elderly prophet Samuel visits David to anoint him as the King of Israel. The biblical episode breaks with conventional expectations. The Israelites had in fact chosen a king for themselves: Saul, a tall and handsome warrior whom they could picture in that place of leadership. Yet Saul had grown increasingly corrupt and distant from the God of Israel. In choosing his replacement, Samuel visited a very unlikely candidate. David was a mere shepherd boy. He was the youngest and smallest of his brothers. Pastor Mark illustrated for his congregation just how unlikely and unexpected Samuel's anointing was, couching this in a contemporary illustration: "Imagine you were being groomed to be king. It would be like if Gordon Brown and the Queen came to you in McDonald's, to groom you to be king."

"But David was *a champion on the road!*" Pastor Mark bellowed. Humble he would not remain. Mark used examples that appealed to the young men and women in his audience. In a saccharine tone, he spoke of the heartbreak David may have felt as he left the lambs he was raising as a shepherd—including, apparently, the especially cute "Larry the Lamb." Part of the congregation oohed. But, Mark went on, David needed to grow up and face the challenges of life. The big challenger was Goliath, the Philistine giant who was facing down the army of Israel.

"Goliath was not just a big geezer," Pastor Mark continued, smiling. He paused for a moment, and then continued in his booming voice, "he was *a big geezer with demonic powers!*" The congregation responded well, laughing and giving each other knowing glances. Mark clearly knew his audience. He knew how to place a good rhetorical punch.

Pastor Mark quoted significantly from Biblical scripture in the sermon, tying these references to life as a young person in London. Mark spoke of how David, the champion, had been the representative of his entire nation when he faced Goliath. He paraphrased the words of David to Goliath in their showdown: "I'm not an ordinary youth, because the Spirit of the Lord is upon me!" Pastor Mark explained that David was victorious because he was favored by the Lord. If you are a champion on the road, Mark told his young people, then likewise "no weapon formed against you can prosper."

Mark also drew from pop culture and contemporary examples. He played a short film clip from *Rocky*, in which Sylvester Stallone, training for the big fight, runs through the streets of Philadelphia and up the stairs, ending in his iconic pose with hands raised in the air. In the same way, Mark told the congregation, youth need a training regimen in reading and learning the Bible if they are to develop into champions. Mark spoke of debates he has had with atheists and people of other faiths when he has represented Christianity. His training has prepared him for these. There is no need to be fearful about facing such challenges in faith if youth remember that "Goliath won his battles through intimidation."

The message of triumphal living as a "champion" was a consistent theme in all preaching I heard at Ruach. The church places an emphasis on the "faith gospel": that one's faith in God should to be tangibly manifested through personal victories.[14] The theological core of the faith gospel is that suffering, poverty, and ill health are all evils, and that Christ has defeated these evils through his death on the cross and his victorious resurrection. As believers grow in faith, they can expect to gain more freedom from evil and a greater capacity to achieve God's personal plan for their lives.

One week after the sermon on being champions, Pastor Mark preached about how faith grants freedom from evil in a sermon called "Desperate for Deliverance." In this sermon he asked youth to consider if the struggles in their own lives could be attributed to spiritual forces—particularly demons. Mark identified demons as causes of sinful emotions such as anger and jealousy. He said that these supernatural entities can root into a person's life in "strongholds" that make them difficult to remove. Mark encouraged youth to be desperate for deliverance from the demons in their lives, praying fervently and fasting for a period of time if necessary. At the end of the service there was a long session of ministry. The whole youth congregation cried out loud in desperation about their struggles, some gesticulating or playing out personal supernatural battles. People were encouraged to come forward at this time for prayers of deliverance. Mark spoke over their voices: "Be confident that this is something you can overcome!"

Ruach's motto, displayed on its printed Sunday programs, is "Where Everybody Is A Somebody." There is a focus on applying faith to the achievement of personal goals (like a champion) and to the overcoming of personal struggles (such as demons). Does the church, then, promote a brand of the "prosperity gospel"? At the time I was attending, the Ruach bookstore prominently displayed Joel Osteen's prosperity bestseller *Your Best Life Now* and a book called *Prosperity Gospel: A Defense of the Theology*. Yet, in my experience of attending the youth service several times, the themes of health and wealth were seldom mentioned. Much more common were themes of self-actualization through school success, the use of talents, and career achievements.

The congregational culture in the Ruach youth service is decidedly middle class. As I met dozens of young people in the foyer before youth services, I learned that virtually all in the appropriate age

---

[14] Gifford (1998, 2004).

bracket are attending university. Although Ruach does not enforce a dress code, youth typically do dress well. Suits and ties are not uncommon. In the first week I attended, a young woman came to the front of the church to give a testimony. She spoke about God's goodness in helping her achieve beyond her expectations on A-Levels, the British subject exams taken by secondary school students with university ambitions. It is usually ambitions of this kind—modest, bounded, and professional—that are the most celebrated in the Ruach youth service.

There is some mismatch between the middle-class culture of Ruach and the socio-economic deprivation in surrounding areas of Brixton, such as the infamous Angell Town public housing estate. The mismatch exists because the young people who attend the Ruach youth service are predominantly not local residents. Most of the youth I spoke with travel by tube or bus to the church each Sunday, some having come from a significant distance. Youth were most often attracted to Ruach by the quality of the youth services or to the spiritual character of the church, including the "anointing" of Bishop John Francis, a figure who has great confidence and power. Yet the fact that youth are not locals themselves has implications for the church's outreach work in the locality. Similar to the geographically dispersed congregants that Omar McRoberts met in the churches of Four Corners in Boston, Massachusetts, regardless of how effectively Ruach ministers to its youth attendees, its influence on the local Brixton area is questionable after they have all taken their buses home.[15]

The youth that Ruach attracts are pleased, grateful, and often astonished at their encounters with God on a regular basis. Damien told me that he was drawn to Ruach because: "I could just see how God is just moving, and just having this way, and just off the rails, and just having liberty in the church...I just love Ruach. It's an outstanding ministry." The spiritual effects of Ruach on young people were something they spoke about with glowing passion. These effects did not seem to reduce down to goals fulfilled or social connections gained.

Pastor Mark Liburd spoke of his youth ministry as inducting young people into their "citizenship in heaven." The meaning of this phrase

---

[15] McRoberts (2003).

at Ruach can be better understood through two of Mark's specific goals for his youth—that they become "champions" and "ambassadors." Ruach youth services encourage youth to strive for a victorious life in which faith helps them meet and overcome challenges as champions. The services also teach them to share the message of faith with others, acting as ambassadors for heaven. It seems that Ruach's youth are mastering the "champion" side of this role, as many are fulfilling aspirations for personal success and emotional adjustment. More questionable is their success in the ambassadorial side of the role—at least if being an "ambassador" means bringing a faith perspective into politics and local community engagement.

EAST LONDON MOSQUE: ISLAMIZED CITIZENS

The East London Mosque (ELM) can lay claim to being Britain's busiest mosque. In the average week tens of thousands pass through its doors, with numbers increasing to an estimated 300,000 people over the full month of Ramadan.[16] The main building is a purpose-built red brick structure with tall minarets, constructed in the 1980s on noisy Whitechapel Road (Figure 5.2). The lineage of the mosque can be traced significantly earlier. A London Mosque Fund had been established in 1910 to rent and then buy sites in the East End.[17] The directors of the Mosque Fund successfully raised the finances for the current building in part from the much-expanded community of local London Muslims. They were also aided, somewhat controversially, by a generous gift from King Fahd of Saudi Arabia. The ELM is one of the few mosques in Britain to broadcast its *adhan*, or call to prayer, over external loud speakers. With its regular *adhan* and unmistakably Islamic architecture, the mosque asserts a powerful claim to visual and audible space in the East End of London.[18]

A major expansion of the ELM took place in an adjoining site to create the London Muslim Centre (LMC), opening in 2004. The LMC is a six-storey building that has an impressive gate-like main entrance with a curved blue and white Islamic tile motif above. The completion of the LMC significantly expanded the prayer space of the mosque.

---

[16] East London Mosque (2014: 8).
[17] See Ansari (2011).   [18] Eade (1996).

Figure 5.2. The East London Mosque (left, with minarets) and London Muslim Centre (center, white entrance, and right, large building) after Friday prayers

The LMC building also made new community facilities available, adding a boys' school, a day care unit, office headquarters for organizations including Muslim Aid and Islamic Forum Europe, large event spaces and classrooms, a restaurant and café, housing, and a sex-segregated gym. The LMC is the base for broadcasting Muslim Community Radio every Ramadan, as well as a radio show called *Easy Talk* throughout the year. The LMC's many facilities and activities also include various programs for young people, work placement assistance, pro-bono legal advice commended by Britain's former Chief Justice Lord Phillips, and beekeeping and honey production on the mosque roof. The joint work of the ELM and LMC led to victory in the Islam Channel's UK-wide "Super Model Mosque" competition in 2009, in which various British mosques were pitted against each other in competitive brackets for public votes. Another expansion project for the mosque, called East London Mosque Phase II, broke the record for single-day fundraising on an "ethnic" television channel, when it brought in more than £1 million in one day on the Islam Channel. Phase II has now been completed. It includes the large Maryam Centre for women's activities, improved facilities for funerals, and a multi-storey parking garage.

I first visited the main ELM prayer room with a friend in summer 2007. We entered through the automatic glass doors of the LMC under the blue and white Islamic tiles. Inside the grand LMC lobby, my friend and I removed our shoes and set them aside. We walked through the corridor on the left towards the main prayer room. The prayer room is a large space about three storeys in height with white walls. Its floor is covered in blue carpeting with red decorative motifs at regular intervals. Looking up at the ceiling, one can see the interior of the mosque cupola around which there is a circle of Arabic calligraphy attributes of Allah. The main prayer room is reserved for men alone. A women's prayer room, located on a higher floor, overlooks the much larger main prayer space through a one-way glass. When we arrived, the previous congregational prayers had recently been completed. There were perhaps two-dozen men scattered across the room, most of them older and of the first generation. Some men were prostrating in additional prayers. Others lingered on the sides of the room to read or recite the Qur'an. One elderly man sat with rosary-like beads that he used to guide his devotions. A group of seven young men were seated in a circle at a back corner, quietly engaged in discussion. The atmosphere was still and serene. Men took their own time and space to engage in personal acts of devotion or study.

I began to understand the ideological vision of the ELM by regularly attending public events at the LMC. The LMC has a very active calendar, including hosting open days and dinner events for the public. These open events are always executed to an impeccably high standard in the LMC's well-equipped seminar suites and public spaces. The events are often designed to educate about Islam, build a reputation for transparency, and aid the mission of *da'wah*, or spreading the Islamic message. By frequenting such events I was able to meet men with varying degrees of involvement in the mosque. I was particularly fortunate at one LMC dinner to sit next to Ehsan Abdullah Hannan, who at that time was an ELM imam.

Ehsan does not match stereotypical portrayals of imams in British media. In his thirties, he keeps his hair at a fashionable medium length and his beard carefully cropped and styled. He was wearing a fine suit and tie when we met. Ehsan had recently started studying for a PhD at the University of London's prestigious School of Oriental and African Studies (SOAS), where he specialized in the writings of Islamic scholar Ibn Qayyim Al-Jawziyah. He was a presenter at the LMC dinner event on the evening that I met him. An urbane public speaker, Ehsan quotes with equal ease from Islamic scholars and Western cultural icons like the Beatles.

Some weeks after our first introduction, Ehsan and I met for a recorded interview about the mosque's work with second-generation youth. We climbed the main stairs of the LMC to sit on couches in a modern upper foyer. Ehsan held the position of community relations imam, acting as the main mosque representative for various local outreach efforts and partnerships. His work often involved young people. For example, he was meeting later that day with the Brick Lane Youth Development Association (BLYDA), to discuss their efforts to break Bengali young men out of gang and drug dealing lifestyles. Ehsan's own understanding of young Bangladeshis comes from being a member of the "1.5 generation" himself: he arrived in England with his parents at age 9, spending his formative years in British schooling.

Ehsan and I spoke about many of the problems faced by young Bangladeshis in the local area, including drugs, violence, and limits to academic achievement. To his mind, "the challenges are generally identity challenges." Problems most often arise when Bangladeshi youth develop "the sense that they have a very distinct culture" from the greater British community around them. Ehsan explained his own theory on how such isolationist identities can develop:

> Many Bangladeshis when they were growing up would have been told "Don't forget you're Bangladeshi. Don't ever forget that you're Bengali." Not necessarily "Don't forget you're a Muslim." I think it's parents using a safety harness, so they don't lose their children. But because it didn't define what being Bangladeshi is or isn't, all it defined was ascribing yourself to a particular group of people... If a person is told they are Bangladeshi and it's drummed into them, on an unconscious level they've divorced themselves from greater society.

The problem is largely Bangladeshi self-segregation. According to Ehsan, Bangladeshi identity is not filled with a particular moral content, so youth are left both isolated from the mainstream and unmoored from any value orientation.

The issue centers on negative self-image because "the large majority of the Bangladeshi community come from the rural backgrounds of Bangladesh and are not very well educated." Ehsan said that youth who do not have adult role models beyond their parents' immigrant generation can be mired in thinking: "This is our lot. We're an inferior class. A race that's treated in an inferior way. They are not us, we are not they. They are White. We are Bangladeshis." As such, there is little motivation to do well in education or to contribute to broader society.

Ehsan believes that the solution comes from youth developing a strong core Muslim identity. The ELM promotes Islam as this core, which he thinks will help youth navigate the challenges of growing up in their generation:

> If they were to be told "You're a Muslim, keep your faith, be sincere, etc., etc. Remember your mother tongue. It's up to you what you want to call yourself [ethnically]. That's not an issue, as long as you're good to everyone and you respect everyone." Then they might start seeing people coming off the train, and that they've been working all day, working very hard. That these are also my role models. And life's about working hard. They will start taking experiences of life from a greater pool of people.

Ehsan's message here closely resembles the words from Mark Liburd at Ruach about being a "citizen of heaven." Ehsan, like Mark, thinks of all specific ethnic identities as equally valid choices. What matters deep down is that "you're good to everyone and you respect everyone." Ehsan believes that Muslim identity provides the best way to achieve this virtuous internal character.

It is worthwhile to also compare Ehsan's perspective, as a representative of the ELM, with the words of Sajjad Miah of the Brick Lane Mosque. Sajjad sees Bangladeshi identity as the source of good values in which children should be raised. In fact, he believes that the erosion of this cultural identity is the cause of youth drifting into delinquency. Ehsan, in contrast, locates the problem *in* Bangladeshi cultural identity, which he argues has led to segregation and low aspirations. Later into our interview, Ehsan posed the rhetorical question: "After how many generations are you going to say you're Bangladeshi?" It is an unsustainable identity. It is much better to realize that "you're one people now, you're British, you're part of society." Islam can provide a singular and unifying way to do this, eliminating ethnic differences to allow youth to take on role models from "a greater pool of people." Sajjad and Ehsan—and by extension, the mosques they represent—are on the opposite ends of an East End debate about religion and culture.[19]

The model of a good citizen that is upheld at the ELM is the "Islamized citizen." Ehsan's comments provide a view into this style of citizenship, which I would see reflected across the many sermons, events, and personal conversations through which I encountered the mosque.

A mosque can make its most consistent impact on believers via the *khutbas* (sermons) delivered at the main Friday afternoon congregational prayers. At the ELM, these are most often given by senior Imam Abdul Qayyum, although the mosque also hosts visiting preachers. Because Friday prayers are so large at this mosque, I spent significant time getting to know the mosque at other times during the week before attending Friday prayers for the first time in May 2008. I arrived quite early for the prayers, entered one of the large secondary prayer rooms, and sat down on the carpet at the back of the room. Men of all ages began to enter, some in Arab or South Asian style dress, others in Western casual or professional clothes. They followed the practice of filling in the next available space at the front in rows, shoulder to shoulder. Some Bengali boys in their early teens stayed in the back area where I was sitting. I was not quite prepared for the sheer numbers as the large room filled to capacity. Imam Abdul Qayyum, a gray-bearded first-generation Bangladeshi man, delivered the *khutba* that preceded the physical act of prayer. He was broadcast to us via live video projection.

Abdul Qayyum's talk was the first *khutba*[20] I heard at the ELM, and I was immediately struck by how different it was in style from

---

[19] It is interesting to trace how this debate about religion and culture has developed over the years. Two decades ago, a research team led by John Eade (1994a) for the Centre for Bangladeshi Studies published a report based on twenty interviews with young educationally successful British Bengalis. Reading the quotes from these interviews, I am struck by how purported negative qualities of Bengali culture today such as low aspirations, insularity, or backwardness do not seem to feature in this glimpse back to the 1990s. As I have argued in published research based on the interviews for this book, some Tower Hamlets Islamic institutions—particularly the ELM, Darul Ummah, and smaller mosques and organizations—have been highly effective in planting seeds of doubt in many young people's minds about the merits of Bengali culture. This issue is examined in Chapter 2 and in DeHanas (2013b).

[20] *Khutba*, as explained earlier, is the Arabic word for a sermon given in a mosque. Because this section of the chapter includes many Arabic Islamic words, I will footnote definitions of each at their first occurrence.

sermons at Ruach, a similar institution in terms of its appeal to youth. The imam delivered a message of about seven minutes in length in three languages: in Arabic, then Bangla, then English. He thus did not attempt to "warm up" his hearers with an introduction, as Mark Liburd often does in his approximately 40-minute Ruach sermons. Instead, Abdul Qayyum took us straight to the heart of the *khutba*: "Brothers and Sisters, [this message is about] the *adab*[21] of the house of Allah," he began. Then, raising his voice with added sternness: "The *masjid*[22] is the house of Allah!"

Abdul Qayyum's sermon concerned the *adab*, or manners, of the mosque. As it was an Islamic message, the version he delivered in English made frequent use of Arabic Islamic terms and interspersed quotes from the Qur'an and *ahadith*[23] (also in Arabic). Abdul Qayyum spoke of how small actions to keep the mosque clean are honorable deeds that will be rewarded in the hereafter. He mentioned several matters of Islamic etiquette. He gave a dour injunction to arrive punctually for prayers, making the comment about "West Indian time" I had heard at the Brixton Adventist Church seem light and airy. As he put it, quoting from a translated *hadith*: "The Prophet said: 'There are some people always late, and Allah will make them late everywhere in righteous deeds. Allah will make them so late that they end up in *Jahannam*!'"[24]

The imam's *khutba* was serious in tone, though not humorless. Later into the talk Abdul Qayyum explained with some exasperation that "The sock is a very big problem. Every summer I talk about the sock! The sock carries a very bad smell. Sometimes one person's sock can trouble this whole house." Nor was his *khutba* behind the times: he spoke about how there is usually at least one worshiper who has left a mobile phone on during prayer time, and that if the phone rings it will "nullify their *jumwa*."[25]

This first *khutba* I heard from Imam Abdul Qayyum had the same tenor as the others he would give in the weeks I attended. They were

---

[21] *Adab*: manners, comportment.   [22] *Masjid*: mosque.

[23] *Ahadith*: The plural form of *hadith*, which is a compilation of the Prophet Muhammad's words and deeds. Various *ahadith* are available and Islamic scholars have differing valuations of the weight of particular collections.

[24] *Jahannam*: hell. The opposite eternal condition of *jannah*, or paradise.

[25] *Jumwa*: the main congregational prayers that take place on Friday afternoon each week. It is considered obligatory for Muslim men to perform these prayers together with others at the mosque if they are able.

messages about the *deen* of Islam: the set of religious micro-practices that fit into all areas of life. The concept of *deen* includes the full scope of Islamic practices such as prayer, modesty of dress, manners in the mosque, saying *bismillah* (in the name of Allah) before embarking on any action, and eating and drinking with the right hand. *Deen*, as the comprehensive blueprint of pious behavior, is an extremely important concept at the ELM. The idea of *deen* was often conveyed to me by youth who would say that "Islam is not just a religion. It's a way of life." Most of the sermons I heard at the mosque were primarily aimed to provide guidance on correct behaviors in the Islamic *deen*, carefully proof-texting this with Qur'an or *hadith* references.

The imagined citizenship that the ELM attempts to cultivate is that of the "Islamized citizen." It is by a daily regimen of following the *deen* that one's behaviors and outlook will progressively approach their Islamic ideal.

Imam Abdul Qayyum delivered a *khutba* several months later, in January 2009, that sheds light on another aspect of the ELM's vision of the citizen. The *khutba* was given in the immediate aftermath of the three-week Gaza War of December 2008 and January 2009. Abdul Qayyum spoke about the resilience of Muslims in Gaza throughout the Israeli incursion as evidence of divine intervention: "Allah *subhanahu wa ta'ala*[26] helped them. That's why they survived," he said. "That's why they defended their land and their people." He urged his congregation to be steadfast in prayer, in the hope that Allah would intervene further:

> We must pray to Allah. May Allah complete the victory of our brothers and sisters. May Allah make [it so that] the house of Allah—Bayt Al-Maqdis, Al Masjid Al-Aqsa[27]—is freed from this illegal occupation. May Allah free [this mosque] so Muslim *ummah* can pray there and glorify Allah *subhanahu wa ta'ala*.

Imam Abdul Qayyum spoke to his congregation as members of the *ummah*, the global community of all Muslim believers.[28] He was urging prayer for the Al-Aqsa Mosque, an Islamic holy site of great

---

[26] *Subhanahu wa ta'ala*: "glorious and exalted is He," a phrase often used after the name of Allah that can be abbreviated as *swt*.

[27] Masjid Al-Aqsa (Bayt Al-Maqdis): the mosque on the Temple Mount in Jerusalem.

[28] The *ummah*, when used in this sense, is the objectified global community of all Muslim believers. The term *ummah* has different potential connotations. Charles

importance in Jerusalem. The mosque is currently regulated by Israeli authorities, who allow prayers there but reserve the right to restrict entry and times. Abdul Qayyum was making a political statement that fellow believers should petition Allah in prayer, requesting that Muslims regain control of the mosque.

Yet prayer was not the only form of action the imam encouraged in relation to Gaza and Jerusalem. He said that "Allah *subhanahu wa ta'ala* [has] given sincerity to the Muslim population." Muslims were already acting in various ways to come to the assistance of Palestinian brothers and sisters in the *ummah*. He commended his fellow Muslims for "how they were doing *dua*,[29] how they were generous to donate for their suffering brothers and sisters," his voice cracking with emotion. He spoke of "how they were participating in all these demonstrations and they'll continue. This the Muslim *ummah* have shown."

Ummah-membership enjoins political action, especially when others in the global Muslim community are suffering or threatened. Political activism on behalf of Islamic causes is assumed to be the natural outworking of *ummah* solidarity. Abdul Qayyum had spoken of praying, giving charitably, and participating in demonstrations as actions that Muslims take for the *ummah*. Yet these actions must be underwritten by a pious heart. Citing an example of the Prophet's piety when faced by the territorial struggles of his day, Abdul Qayyum reminded his listeners that "our relationship with Allah is number one. That makes [sure] our financial contribution is accepted. That will make [sure] our participation in all this picketing is accepted."

The ELM attempts to develop worshipers into Islamized citizens. A first aspect of this process for second-generation youth is the adoption of an all-encompassing Muslim identity. Imam Ehsan had told me that such an identity displaces narrowly defined ethnic identities (Bangladeshi in this case) connecting youth to "a larger pool of people" and to a sustainable moral orientation. A second aspect of the process of Islamization is the continual practice and development of *deen*, the Islamic micro-practices of everyday life.

Tripp (2006) argues that the use of *ummah* as a global brotherhood in this sense developed in the late nineteenth century.

[29] *Dua*: petitionary prayers. Within the highly uniform framework of Islamic prayer, there is a period of *dua* in which personal petitions and devotions are appropriate.

One's entire life should be Islamized, from large life decisions down to the smallest details of cleanliness or eating. Third, an Islamized imagination of citizenship is embedded in a global community, the *ummah*. Membership in the *ummah* is demonstrated by solidarity, including the willingness to take action or make sacrifices for the sake of fellow brothers and sisters. An Islamized citizenship is a comprehensive one—it reaches deeply into one's self-identification, daily practices, and community of belonging as it becomes the main frame of reference for civic engagement.

CONCLUDING DISCUSSION

Classic studies such as Oscar Handlin's *The Uprooted* and more recent work by Kershen, Casanova, and others highlight the role of religion in the historic social incorporation of first-generation immigrants.[30] Nicole Toulis' study of immigrants in a Jamaican first-generation church finds, in line with other recent research, that religion is a rich source of meaning, belonging, and social resources for many contemporary migrants undertaking the journey and adapting to a new society.[31]

Yet the same religious institutions that serve as secure ethnic hubs for immigrants may be viewed with indifference or even scorn by their second-generation children. Will Herberg observed the phenomenon that while ethnic identification tends to decline in the first three generations, religious identification usually rises.[32] Second-generation adolescents and young adults who attempt to "break away" from their parents and adopt their own independent identities, are likely to favor institutions that emphasize religious identities over and above ethnic ones.

Indeed, the "ethnic hub" institutions of the Brick Lane Mosque and Brixton Seventh Day Adventist Church struggle to retain youth beyond the early teenage years. In part, this is due to the high expectations they place on the young. The civic imaginations upheld

---

[30] Handlin (1951); Kershen (2005); Casanova (2007).
[31] Toulis (1997). There is a very significant literature on this topic, with key debates summarized well in Foner and Alba (2008).
[32] Herberg (1955).

in these institutions tend to be too circumscribed and ethnically bounded to appeal to youth raised in cosmopolitan urban London. They are based heavily on responsibilities of good behavior rather than on the rights and privileges that could come from being a member. Farouq summarized his view of the mosque "citizenship" promoted by the first generation: "I make my parents happy, be a good boy, wear certain clothes, have certain haircuts—like, don't have fun." Similarly, Mabel, the young woman with the Jamaican flag shoulder bag I met on Brixton Road, gave her perspective on the Brixton Adventist Church she used to attend:

> There's a church called Brixton Seventh Day Adventist Church just around Santley Street, and most people have left there, because of stuff like, they will concentrate more on what a person's wearing than what's in their heart or what's on their mind, or the content of their character. And things like, in Pentecostal church, you can shout "Hallelujah!" as loud as you want to, you can praise God. Whereas in the Adventist church, they'd tell you to be quiet.

The religious institutions that have won the affections of second-generation youth are those which have conscientiously sought them. Ruach Ministries has developed a youth service closely attuned to the style and needs of young people. The ELM offers extensive youth activities as well, some of these run by the Young Muslim Organisation or the Islamic Forum of Europe. The mosque has further developed its reputation among Bangladeshi youth because of its partnership work to combat drug addiction, its respected scholars and facilities, and its position as dialogue partner for British politicians and as host to Muslim dignitaries. It would be difficult for first-generation "ethnic hub" institutions to compete with the enticing power of such large and well-financed organizations.

Yet Ruach Ministries and the ELM differ in ways that have implications for the kinds of young British citizens they produce. First, there is a difference in how moral authority is communicated. The youth service at Ruach promotes what I would call a "subjectified" Christianity. When the pastor of Ruach's youth service posits authoritative truth claims, these claims are made relevant to the individual subject in order to show that they are true. The means of this subjectification include idiomatic preaching, contemporary music, and the fact that at Ruach, as Vernon had told me, youth are allowed "to come as they are." The subjectification of Christianity is most radical in the ministry sessions at the end of Ruach youth services, when young people are encouraged to verbally and physically express their struggles by yelling, praying, speaking in tongues, and moving about the sanctuary. It is in these sessions that youth communicate personally, and at times physically, with the Holy Spirit.

The subjectification of Christianity at Ruach Ministries is not surprising, given broader developments towards subjectivity that have been noted in Western religion and spirituality[33] and in Pentecostalism specifically.[34] Christian Smith, in a study of religion among American emerging adults, observes that young people "simply cannot, for whatever reason, believe in—or sometimes even conceive of—a given, objective truth, fact, reality, or nature of the world that is independent of their subjective self-experience."[35] Ruach youth services do encourage youth to believe in objective realities by faith. But it can be a faith that is tenuously held, and reliant on fresh spiritual experiences for its renewal.

The contrast is great with the ELM. The mosque promotes what scholars have called an "objectified" Islam.[36] Objectification is the process of transfiguring the various historic and context-dependent streams of Muslim belief into a timeless, changeless, and singular entity of "Islam." Whereas experience often dictates the truthfulness of the Pentecostal Christian message, for practicing Muslim youth Islam dictates much of their experience. The Islamization process is a systematic restructuring of everyday life—one's daily schedule to meet prayer times, the gender composition of friendships, one's outward appearance and personal habits—so that these conform to the Islamic *deen*. Imam Abdul Qayyum makes little, if any, attempt in his *khutbas* to speak in terms that are "relevant" to young people. He regards the behavioral obligations of Islam as transcendent and immutable.

There is, in fact, a finer line between subjectification and objectification than this discussion indicates thus far. Ruach Ministries does preach a message of objective truth, and certain aspects of this message (e.g. the resurrection of Christ) must be accepted without first-hand experiential knowledge. Likewise, Muslim youth who

---

[33] For example, Wuthnow (2000); Heelas and Woodhead (2004).
[34] For example, Coleman (2000).
[35] Smith with Snell (2009: 46).
[36] Eickelman and Piscatori (1996); Starrett (1998).

New Religion 161

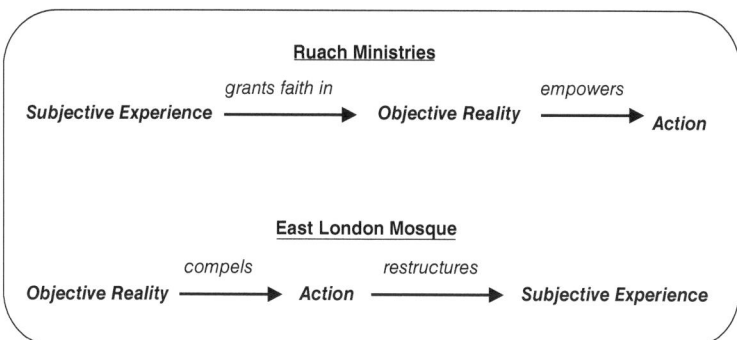

Figure 5.3. Relationships between subjective experience, objective reality, and action

regularly pray at the ELM may find that prayer is itself a subjective experience which feels so "right" that it confirms the objective truth of Islam. For these youth, the regular body practice of prayer feels "right" in part because it is a familiar path that has been well worn by repeated travel. Each act of prayer, in the context of thousands of acts before, adds to the internally referential veracity of Islamic experience.

Overall, however, the worship experiences at Ruach Ministries and the ELM rely on different underlying logics of the connection between subjective experience, objective reality, and behavioral action. I have diagrammed these differences in Figure 5.3. At Ruach, subjective experience grants youth faith in an objective reality (Christianity), which will in turn motivate them to action. At the ELM the process begins with an objective reality (Islam) that compels youth to perform particular actions that will, over time, restructure their subjective experience.

The objectification of Islam at the ELM gives the perspective on Muslim identity propagated there a comprehensiveness and power. At Ruach, because young people's own experiences are accepted as functional arbiters of truth, there is a greater freedom for youth to take on faith in a self-focused or piecemeal manner. This can mean that young Jamaicans include Christianity as one of many self-identifications, while Muslim self-identification tends to be more singular and all defining. It is also true that the implicit logics of belief in Figure 5.3 differ in the grounding they provide for action (and ultimately, for activism). Islamic social activism is grounded in actions that are understood to be instantiations of ultimate reality (prayer, *zakat*, and so on), while Christian social activism is most frequently based in the faith experiences of individual participants. This is a difference in the social mechanisms of activism that I will explore in greater depth in the next chapter.

Moving beyond the discussion of moral authority, a second major difference between Ruach Ministries and the ELM is in their notions of community. Muslims at the ELM conceive of themselves as members of the imagined community of the *ummah*, which is global in scope. Pnina Werbner has written of Muslims in Britain as having membership in an imagined diaspora, because their relationships with other Muslims are imbued with a sense of common ancestry or kinship.[37] Indeed, the "Islamic" styles of clothing worn by many second-generation Bangladeshi Muslims connect them globally with Arabian Peninsula clothing styles much more than with the traditional Islamic dress of Bangladesh. Through these clothing styles Bangladeshi Muslims develop an outward "family resemblance" to Muslim communities elsewhere in the world. Communal acts, such as regular prayer and fasting during Ramadan, are central mechanisms by which a sense of global, diasporic kinship is built and reinforced.

The ELM is quite deliberate in its cultivation of the imagined community of the *ummah*. A good example of the mosque's work to develop a unified sense of Muslim community in the East End is its Muslim Community Radio station (MCR, 87.8 FM). MCR is broadcast each Ramadan, with programs in both English and Bengali, including topical call-in shows, youth programs, limited forms of Islamic music, *fatwa* shows, and spiritual counsel for the challenges of fasting during Ramadan. The radio station is exceedingly popular in the local area. Bangladeshis of all generations listen in their homes or cars, and shopkeepers play it during the day. The broad reach of MCR during Ramadan helps to set the agenda for local activism, to instill a particular stream of Islamic interpretation, and to create a common sense of community, as Muslims across the borough listen to the same topics discussed each day.[38] The ELM also establishes a sense of community simply through sheer numbers. Every Friday,

---

[37] Werbner (2002).
[38] For an analysis of MCR and its role in political campaigning see DeHanas (2010a).

Whitechapel Road is transformed by the large crowds who attend congregational prayers. This visible presence is accentuated during Ramadan, when many local residents dress more "Islamically" and attend various events at the mosque.

Because so much of the ELM's cultivation of community happens through the common actions of believers, the result is probably best termed an *enacted community* (rather than simply an "imagined" one). With its strong community presence, the ELM can be thought of as the equivalent of an Islamic "cathedral" rather than a megachurch.[39] It has taken on the local area as its "parish" or "diocese" and now has significant sway religiously, socially, politically, and in public displays of piety.

In Chapter 1 we found that Bangladeshi Muslim youth are highly engaged in civic actions that are communally oriented, such as boycotting Danish and Israeli products, or signing petitions against the war in Iraq. Actions of these kinds are sometimes promoted by the mosque directly, or more often informally through the various social networks and organizations that are based there. As the ELM's community presence is so strong, its political mobilization efforts are important to explaining the robust levels of Bangladeshi youth civic engagement.

In comparison, Ruach Ministries' vision of "citizens in heaven" tends towards the otherworldly. It has not taken on a parish-like vision of the Brixton area, in which it would prioritize the care of souls and social problems within a limited local domain. Instead Ruach has operated on the "gathered" model that is common among (neo-)Pentecostal churches, in which "the world is [its] parish."[40] London churches have been threatened by three types of urban change in recent decades—global migration, suburbanization, and gentrification—which destabilize local demographics and make

---

[39] There is, of course, a long tradition of mosques serving as centers of the community, education, and society. The use of "cathedral" here is simply as an analogy familiar in Western tradition. For grand mosques in the same period as Europe's major medieval cathedrals—with the same vast social and cultural scope—see Daniella Talmon-Heller's study of mosques in Damascus, Aleppo, and Jerusalem (2007).

[40] Martin (2002). This phrase that David Martin uses to describe Pentecostals is, of course, not a Pentecostal one. It comes from the words of John Wesley (2013 [1739]: 55) in his journal: "I look on all the world as my parish; thus far I mean, that, in whatever part of it I am, I judge it meet, right, and my bounden duty, to declare unto all that are willing to hear, the glad tidings of salvation."

the "gathered" model of church an effective strategy.[41] In the case of Ruach, the congregation is gathered from across London and its suburbs, with individuals willing to travel large distances for the worship experience and the powerful anointing of its pastors. Whereas the ELM's vision of the *ummah* as the site of imagined citizenship is grounded in particular territories (e.g. Mecca, Palestine, Kashmir), Ruach's global vision is radically de-territorialized.[42] The Ruach sanctuary is lined with flags of the nations of the world, but the actual choice of nations seems to be arbitrary. Ruach's main aim has not been to establish a local presence or "imagined community"—rather, it cultivates within each believer a sense of individual *imagined communion* between her/himself and God. Pastor Mark Liburd refers to this aim as creating a "God culture."

The difference between "enacted community" (at the ELM) and "imagined communion" (at Ruach) is a significant one. A personal faith developed at Ruach can be a powerful motivator for individual change and achievement. However, as much as attendees at Ruach are sensitized to their individual needs for communion with God, they may at the same time be unaware of possibilities for community change and renewal. Ruach's approach to spirituality may inspire financial sacrifice as an act of commitment between oneself and God, but it will only rarely lead to a radical subordination of the self for a collective good.

When Tony Blair commended Ruach and other churches for practicing politics "with a small 'p'" he was speaking of a politics that was generally positive, and certainly in no way confrontational or threatening. He would not have wanted Black church politics to pose any real challenge to Third Way accommodations between the state and the market.[43] In this respect, Blair was using the small "p" as synonymous with "personal."

---

[41] Eade (2012).

[42] On these points I differ from Olivier Roy (2004) who writes of globalized Islam as the pre-eminent example of de-territorialization. This is true of the virtual Islamic communities on the Internet, for example, which he has studied. My experience in the East End is that issues of territory are highly salient, both in terms of local mosque competition for "areas" in the East End and especially in terms of a global vision of Muslim territories, including Palestine. The most interesting dynamic is the shift in territorial importance: Bangladesh is the place most often spoken about by first-generation "traditional" Bangladeshis, while Muslim "diaspora" territories are much more frequently mentioned in the context of the ELM.

[43] For Tony Blair's vision of the Third Way see Blair (1998). For a critical take see Rose (2000).

6

The Building Blocks of Social Change

On a Saturday afternoon in August 2009, about 300 people gathered at Westminster in London to march against gun and knife crime. The event was planned by the South London regional Seventh Day Adventist administration to take place on the Sabbath Day.[1] It also included some participants from other denominations and religiously unaffiliated supporters who felt passionate about the issue. The protesters marched silently past Parliament carrying signs emblazoned with the acronym LIVE: "Living Intentionally Versus Existing" (Figure 6.1). Some larger banners had pictures of knives and guns. Hundreds of camera-toting tourists, finding their route to Big Ben and Westminster Abbey temporarily obstructed, waited by the road with quizzical stares.

The march continued from Westminster across the River Thames, on a three-hour course into South London that followed blocked roads and police escorts. Although they remained silent through the Westminster portion, the marchers sang Christian worship songs together for the rest of their journey. The destination was Kennington Park in South London. There they were greeted upon arrival by free vegetarian food, a variety of booths and outdoor activities, and a program on the main stage of worship music, speeches against gun and knife violence, and the memorializing of victims.

In this chapter I continue the discussion of how religious beliefs and practices contribute to the development of young citizens in London. In particular, I consider the ways in which religion influences youth to take different approaches to bringing *change* to their

---

[1] Seventh Day Adventists practice a Sabbath of rest and worship from sunset each Friday evening until sunset on Saturday. This includes holding their regular worship services on Saturdays, unlike most churches in the Christian tradition.

Figure 6.1. The Seventh Day Adventist LIVE march

personal lives, to their communities, and (in some cases) to politics. In Chapter 1, I found that most Bangladeshi youth in the East End engage in politics significantly more than Jamaican youth in Brixton. By profiling the LIVE event and a comparable grassroots event in the East End, I will argue that religious understandings of change are an underlying cause of this political participation gap.

THE LIVE EVENT: OPPOSING GUN AND KNIFE CRIME, ONE PERSON AT A TIME

The Seventh Day Adventist LIVE march on Parliament, and the community event that followed in Kennington Park, were geared primarily towards teenage youth. These events provided an ideal setting in which to observe young people engaging in faith-based

The Building Blocks of Social Change 167

civic activism. I had originally heard about the event from some of my Jamaican interviewees at the Brixton Seventh Day Adventist Church. Johnny, an 18-year-old I interviewed months before, told me that the previous year he had marched: "It was amazing! We had so many people ask us what we were doing it for. We were making them think about how they live their lives."

The event in Kennington Park included various performances and activity booths that were run by the youth ministries of South London Adventist churches. The vast majority of congregants in these churches are African or Caribbean in origin, and this composition was mirrored that afternoon. In good Adventist fashion, the youth emphasis of the event was paired with an emphasis on family. Family members of crime victims were asked on the main stage to speak about how they keep going in light of tragic loss. An Adventist youth group performed a mime to dramatize the toll that gun crime takes on friendships and on families. A memorial service was held for the last half-hour of the afternoon, giving families time to remember together.

The main aim of the LIVE event, captured in the acronym "Living Intentionally Versus Existing," was to encourage youth to think through how they live their lives, rather than blindly sliding into peer pressure and violence. A plywood wall at the back of the park had been painted sky blue. Youth were invited to put their handprints on the wall in white paint, pledging that these hands would never touch a knife or gun.

Alan James, a Caribbean man affected by gun crime, gave a spoken word performance. His assertive, powerful lyrics were wrought with emotion. They captured some of the tenor of the event:

> Put down the gun. Don't want another brother die.
> Put down the gun. Don't want another mother cry.
> Put down the gun. Don't want to kill another wife.
> Put down the gun. Don't want to spill another life.
> Put down the gun. Don't want another sister dead.
> Put down the gun. Don't want another Mr. Lead.
> Put down the gun and stop acting like a clown.
> Put down the gun ... before the gun puts you down.

The crowd roared with applause.

I wandered through Kennington Park, visiting the LIVE event booths and talking with young people. I spoke with a group of three young

Black men, all aged 19, who told me that they attend Adventist churches in Peckham and Kennington. I asked if they could relate to the message of the event. How much of a problem was gun and knife crime in these areas of South London? The flurry of responses from the young men came so quickly that their replies interrupted each other:

A: It's *ser-i-ous*—
B: It's got worse—
A: You wouldn't believe it.
B: It's like, it's normal. Before when we hear of it we were shocked, but now it's normal… You just get used to it—
A: It's nothing new—
C: I'm not surprised at all—
A: It's everybody. Very dangerous.
B: That's why I'm glad this sort of activity is happening.

The three young men went on to tell me that they each have friends or acquaintances who had stabbed or shot someone else. They see youth violence as an urgent problem that is only getting worse. Even so, they expressed optimism about the LIVE event. I asked: what kind of lasting effect is it likely to have?

A: I hope this event really changes people's minds.
B: *Pray*, not hope, *pray*.

For these young people and others I met, the significance of the LIVE event was both the stand it took against youth violence and the power it had to change the lives of those gathered there. It is worth noting that they did not see it as part of an ongoing program of lobbying or activism, but rather as a day in which minds would be changed.

A talk delivered by Sam Davis was the centerpiece of the day's events, and essential to understanding their intended purpose. Davis, a second-generation Jamaican man in his fifties, leads the South England Conference of Seventh Day Adventists (SEC). He was dressed in suit and tie and was introduced on the main stage as an honored guest. When approaching the microphone, he held out his silver mobile phone. He would look down at the phone as his speech prompter.

Davis' speech was, in fact, a sermon. It was delivered in a confident preacher's cadence. He began by reading Matthew 13:24–8, from the New King James Version:

> Another parable he put forth to them, saying: the Kingdom of Heaven is like a man who sowed good seeds in his fields. But while the man slept,

his enemy came and sowed tares among the wheat and went his way. But when the grain had sprouted and produced a crop, then the tares also appeared. So the servants of the owner came and said to him: "Sir, did you not sow good seed in your field? How then, does it have tares?" And he said to them "an enemy has done this."

In these New Testament verses, Jesus Christ tells a parable of a man who sowed good seeds. Only later does the man discover that tares—or weeds—have sprouted up alongside his intended good wheat. Sam Davis began explaining the parable to his Kennington Park audience by describing the good world God created in the Garden of Eden. He said that God's intention was only for good to be sown in human lives:

> Everything that God had provided was just right. It was never God's plan that sin and death would enter that environment. It was never God's plan that mothers and fathers should weep for their children. Never in the script that young men should mow down each other over turf warfare. Never in the script that drugs and violence should mar this planet. God sowed only good seed in the earthly garden.

By preaching in this way, Davis was connecting with street life experiences and stories that would have been familiar to his audience. He was retelling these stories into a spiritual grand-narrative of epic struggle between God and a deceptive enemy. Just who was the interloper who had sown weeds in the field? Davis explained that this was the devil: "We need to de-mythologize the devil," he said. "We need to say he is real. We need to say the devil is not someone with horns and a tail, but he is real, and he wants our kids."

Davis recognized the devil as an agent actively at work in society, an agent with a cunning personality and evil motives. The devil had sown bitter weeds of sin and death on God's territory. These weeds were the underlying cause of youth violence and the other social problems in South London. To solve the social problems, therefore, one had to get personal. One had to take on an alternative life free from the devil's influence. Davis explained the solution in this way:

> Until we begin to teach our children that they have been made in the image of God, that God loves them and that they need to love their fellow brothers and sisters, society will have lost it.

Standing there in the crowd, it was at this moment that I realized what the anti-crime rally was deep down. It was a *revival meeting*. The central purpose was to change hearts and minds, one by one, so that they would come into a right relationship with God. If this sort of conversion was achieved, then social change could be expected as a natural outflow. I will return to how Davis expressed this view on change a bit later. For the moment, however, it is worth considering more generally if religious revival movements can be harbingers of real social change.

Some of the most powerful social movements in history have had a religious revivalist character. David Chappell argues that the American Civil Rights movement was *primarily* a religious revival in the eyes of many of its participants and central figures.[2] God was freeing His people from yokes of segregation and oppression. He was setting them in right relationships with their fellow men. It is well known that many of the other leaders of the Civil Rights movement were preachers, including the Reverend Martin Luther King Jr., and that the movement gained momentum through networks of churches, such as those in the Southern Christian Leadership Conference.[3] In the words of one of its towering figures, the Reverend Fred Shuttlesworth, the Civil Rights movement was "a religious crusade, a fight between light and darkness, right and wrong, good and evil, fair play and tyranny. We are assured of victory because we are using weapons of spiritual warfare."[4]

Just *how* does religion contribute to social action, both in Black Majority Church settings and elsewhere? Over the past few decades, sociologists have been particularly engaged in this question. Some of the earlier studies from Aldon Morris and Doug McAdam demonstrated the importance of church networks and resources for providing the structure that channels social movement growth.[5] Mary Pattillo extended the research scope beyond structure to include church culture.[6] She found that cultural practices in Black churches—including prayer, call-and-response, and the Christian imagery of songs and sermons—provides the motivation and meaning for community actions. She perceived that behind these cultural practices was a belief in an all-powerful, immanently active God who could galvanize change to surpass human limitations.

---

[2] Chappell (2003: 88).   [3] Morris (1986).
[4] Shuttleworth's address to the Alabama Christian Movement for Human Rights in Birmingham, Alabama, June 1958, as quoted in Chappell (2003: 88).
[5] Morris (1986); McAdam (1982).   [6] Pattillo-McCoy (1998).

Richard Wood builds upon these previous research studies of structure and culture in his comparative book *Faith in Action*.[7] Wood compares faith-based activist organization PICO with race-based activist organization CTWO, both in Oakland, California, and both advocating for the disadvantaged. CTWO attempts to unify the interests of members of various races, as expressed in its organization leaflet: "We are Black, Latino, Native American, Asian, and White people of all ages and economic backgrounds who demand... power over issues that affect our lives." The language here demonstrates CTWO's recurrent challenge to create common purpose and to forge unity from diversity. For faith-based PICO, in contrast, the cultural work of purpose and unity has already been achieved within its partner network of religious congregations. Wood concludes from the comparison that religious congregations provide advantages to social movement organizing. Congregations are advantageous both because they are pre-existing reservoirs of social capital and because they gather around beliefs and symbols that are rich sources of human motivation. Confirmation of Wood's research can be seen in the significant history of social movements that were at least partly congregation-powered. Twentieth-century examples in addition to the American Civil Rights movement include the Solidarity movement in Poland, the 1979 Revolution in Iran, and anti-apartheid in South Africa.[8] Michael Walzer has argued for an even greater influence of religion, tracing the origins of modern political activism to the Calvinist revolutions and reforms of early modern Europe.[9]

There may therefore be reason for optimism as we project the potential impact of the LIVE event. Sam Davis' speech certainly seemed to capture the imaginations of the audience that day. Returning to the speech, we have already seen that it took the form of a sermon in a revival church service. Casting everyday problems into a spiritual cosmology, it gave the audience evocative cultural resources and motivation that they might potentially use to resist gun and knife violence.

---

[7] Wood (2002).
[8] For essays on the role of religion in these and other twentieth-century social moments, see Smith (1996).
[9] Walzer (1982).

Yet the speech and event were, at the same time, inherently self-limiting. The limits were most evident as Sam Davis brought his sermon to its rhetorical crescendo (emphasis original):

> The politicians are looking for a solution, and they are saying that what we need is better social housing, we need more mentors, we need better education, we need more youth schemes and so on. But I want to say that *we have tried it all and it has failed repeatedly*. We have tried these things and found that none of them have been successful. And so my friends, I want to say to you today, having tried everything—having tried more social work, having tried to put more policemen on the streets, having tried better education, having tried better youth schemes—why don't you try *Jesus Christ!* [crowd cheers]

Davis was presenting Jesus Christ as the ultimate way out of youth violence. Within the terms of the spiritual narrative he had presented thus far, this solution fit perfectly. But Davis' words also set boundaries on the process of social change, suggesting that Jesus Christ *cannot* work for the good of society in mentoring relationships, improved education, and youth schemes.

Underlying Davis' words is a particular perspective on how change can be produced. He was arguing for *personal faith* as the causal mechanism that generates real and lasting change. I have already observed the importance of personal faith when discussing Ruach Ministries in Chapter 5. In the Brixton Seventh Day Adventist Church as well, faith was preached alongside discipline as an approach to change. I have diagrammed the logic of the personal faith approach in Figure 6.2.

Figure 6.2 follows what has been called the DBO model of human action—desires (D), beliefs (B), opportunities (O), and action (A).[10] The figure shows the internal states and external actions of two people, who are labeled with subscripts i and j. Personal faith begins with a desire (D) for some outcome or some state of relationship. This desire then shapes what the individual believes (B) is attainable in the outcome or relationship. The beliefs and desires are then able to work in concert and, if all goes well, they enable the action that the person desires. The mechanism is structurally equivalent (though not necessarily ultimately equivalent) to what sociologists have called "wishful thinking."[11] A person with the lived experience of "personal faith"

---

[10] Hedström (2008). [11] Hedström (2008).

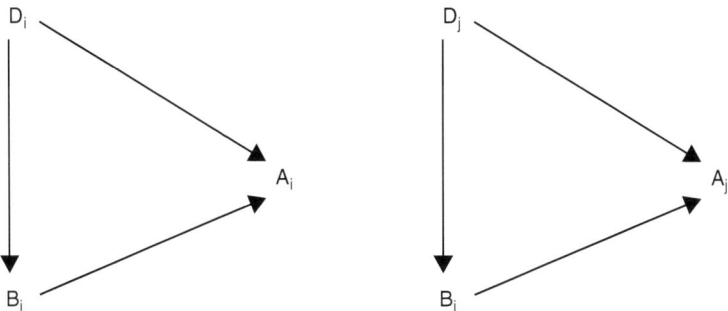

Figure 6.2. Personal faith as a causal mechanism of individual and social change

will perceive that there is a transcendent element—that God is at work in social change.

In the example of gun and knife crime, youth at the individual level are expected to take their desires (D) for a safe and non-violent society and to combine these with a faith that this is attainable (B). In doing so, they become capable of achieving social change through their actions (A). Religious conversion is a related variant of the personal faith mechanism and may influence violent crime more indirectly: an individual's desire (D) for God becomes a faith-held belief (B) that may influence later actions to be less violent (A). In both of these cases, the individual must place significant faith (B) in something not yet entirely substantiated to move the process forward. I have diagrammed the personal faith mechanism of two individuals separately in Figure 6.2, to emphasize that it tends to be an atomistic process.

With personal faith as the individual-level building block, social change occurs as more and more individuals act in faith.[12] The many small actions of individuals aggregate at the social level into what can be called *revival activism*. The narrative of revival activism—that as more people take hold of faith they will make society better—is one that I often heard among Jamaican youth and in their churches. I also heard a Muslim variant of the narrative in some of my interviews with Bangladeshi youth.[13]

---

[12] Christian Smith and colleagues (1998: 191–2) refer to this ideal scenario as the "miracle motif."

[13] For example, the revival-based model of change is a recurrent message of Hizb ut-Tahrir (HT), a radical political activism organization which seeks the re-establishment

The revival activism strategy for social change is certainly well intentioned. Personal faith and social revival were important in the powerful social movements for freedom and civil rights mentioned earlier in this chapter. Yet, those who believe *exclusively* in social change through revival activism are blind to structural factors. They are less likely to seek partnerships with other organizations, to initiate a long-term strategy of influence and activism, or to advocate for the structural changes (e.g. in education, the police force, or employment opportunities) that are almost always necessary to produce lasting change.[14] Even if personal discipline is added to personal faith (as it will often be in an Adventist approach to activism) the neglect of structural factors in the revival activism strategy will still be a weakness.

As the LIVE event neared its end, I spoke with an official representative at the information booth. I learned from her that the Seventh Day Adventist Church was partnering with a charitable organization called FAME (Families Against Murders Escalating) and sending donations from the event to further their work. This partnership has potential to make a positive impact. When I asked the representative about how the gun and knife crime initiative would be continued, however, the limits of the revival activism strategy again became evident:

DND: What are you guys going to be doing to carry this forward from here?

REPRESENTATIVE: As you see, all of these booths [at the sides of the park] are from different churches.

DND: Oh—these are all from different churches?

REPRESENTATIVE: Yeah... Depending on the area, we could connect you with the church in your area. And you could see whatever extra-curricular activities they have. For example, tomorrow in the Hatfield area, at Hatfield University, we are organizing a basketball tournament. We've done one earlier this year, and a lot of people who are not necessarily Christian have come and

---

of a Muslim caliphate. HT's propaganda and events frequently invoke a utopian vision of life under a caliphate, as a much more Muslim populace governed by sharia law finds itself free from crime, hunger, poverty, and other evils caused by not living under God's given system. A few of my Bangladeshi youth interviewees held similar views on the caliphate. Many others expressed a general faith that personal conversion or Islamic renewal made one into a better member of society.

[14] Tilly (1999).

played. So at least we are making connections with them. And, you know, they can see that "I don't have to be drinking, or carrying guns to make friends, or doing drugs to have a group of friends." You can have fun without being into one of those. You can be sober and still enjoy life. So we're at least connecting through events like that.

A strategy of personal faith and revival as the basis for change can build personal connections with youth susceptible to criminal involvement. Yet, with its exclusive reliance on this "one person at a time" approach to change, the Adventist Church dramatically under-realizes its potential influence on the violent crime issue. Reflecting on the LIVE march and event overall, one can see a strange ambivalence. The march resembled a typical protest march on Parliament to demand political change. Yet any message of change was somewhat neutralized by the event at Kennington Park, where the main speaker and the organizers expressed little faith in political action.

THE BIG IFTAR: BREAKING A RAMADAN FAST FOR THE HUNGRY AND HOMELESS

The Saturday of the LIVE march against gun and knife crime also happened to be the first full day of Ramadan 2009. As Seventh Day Adventists protested at Parliament, Muslims throughout London were fasting from food and drink. The East End areas surrounding Whitechapel Road and Brick Lane, where I was doing research fieldwork with Bangladeshis dramatically changed during the month of Ramadan. Friday prayers overflowed onto the streets. Some of the normally non-practicing Muslim young men I knew begin to wear prayer caps and to dutifully attend evening Qur'an recitations and prayers. After sunset, there was a tangible sense of relief as crowds of grateful believers descended on local curry houses and chicken shops for *iftar* meals.

During Ramadan 2009 I attended the Big IFtar, a Muslim civic activism event concerning the issue of homelessness. The community *iftar* meal was held outdoors on a cool Friday evening in early September. The IF Charity (also known simply as IF) organized the event to raise donations for meals for "homeless people in London as well as displaced communities around the world."¹⁵ The event took place in Altab Ali Park, a modest park near the Western edge of Whitechapel Road that has monuments commemorating Bangladeshi history.¹⁶ A crowd of about 200 people of all ages, largely Bangladeshi and Muslim, stood in the park for the introductory program. Most remained afterwards to share in the *iftar* curry.

IF had invited celebrities to serve as honorary chefs at the large white cooking tents. Baroness Pola Uddin, reality television star Syed Ahmed, and other notable Bengalis momentarily stirred pots of *iftar* dinner and posed for photographs. Across from the cooking tents stood the main stage, the focal point for the introductory program of speeches and performances (Figure 6.3). These included a stand-up comedian, a personal testimony from a Black Muslim convert, musical acts, and various speeches from politicians and charity workers.

The White English Muslim music artist Naseeha performed on stage in baggy hip hop style clothes and a gray beanie hat. He sang two *nasheed* songs with a vocals-only R&B sound.¹⁷ One of these, "Peace, Justice, and Harmony," had recently featured on the Islam Channel. It provides an account of the Prophet Muhammad's life and comprehensive social vision. The other song Naseeha performed was "Allah, Help Us Change": a prayerful request for repentance and change in the hearts of believers, one person at a time. This song

---

[15] IF is a charitable organization whose first sponsored event was the Gaza 100 of summer 2009, a 100-meter relay run that raised money to assist children in Gaza. The IF website provides little information about the organization's aims or ethos, but it is a Muslim organization at least partly intended for joining together the work of other Muslim charities in London. See <http://ifcharity.org.uk/> (last accessed June 26, 2015).

[16] Altab Ali Park has an emotional resonance for many Bangladeshis. It is named after the 25-year-old Bangladeshi man who in 1978 was murdered in a racist attack on his way home from textile work on Hanbury Street. Altab Ali is commemorated by a sculpted iron gateway at one entrance to the park. In a corner of the park is the Shaheed Minar, a replica of the monument in Dhaka to martyrs of the Bengali Language Movement. These martyrs set in motion the violent struggle in East Pakistan that culminated in independence for Bangladesh.

[17] *Nasheeds* are a contemporary form of Muslim music. In many cases these are sung without instrumental accompaniment (or with percussion, but no other instruments). The music takes this form to match particular Muslim views on which forms of music are permissible. *Nasheeds* have grown in popularity among Muslim youth in the West, especially those from popular artists such as Zain Bhikha and Yusuf Islam (formerly Cat Stevens).

The Building Blocks of Social Change

Figure 6.3. The Big IFtar charity event

closely resounded with the message of person-based spiritual change I had heard at the LIVE march.

Performances at the Big IFtar were largely, though not exclusively, aimed at young people. Along each side of the park there were additional information booths and activities. Most of these booths also had a youth theme. One booth advertised an Islamic comic series called *The Adventures of Hakim: Streetwise Champion* with the tagline "The hero for the Ummah is back!" Another provided print resources from the Young Muslim Organisation (YMO), such as manuals for students seeking to improve their school's or university's Islamic society.

I spoke with the Bangladeshi young man running the YMO booth. As with the LIVE event, I was hoping to discern the lasting effects this community event might have. He told me about his organization's partnership with IF:

> The main thing is that all of this [event today] is for IF. They're a Muslim organization that's trying to feed the homeless people. We set up a meeting with this organization, to come and join with them and work together. So that's what we're doing.

Organizational partnerships were an important contrast between the Big IFtar and the LIVE event. At the LIVE event, the only partnership outside the Seventh Day Adventist denomination itself was with FAME. In comparison, the Big IFtar was facilitated by an impressive list of organizational partnerships. IF had brought together various organizations for an overall initiative called IFtar 10,000 that would distribute 10,000 meals for displaced or homeless people around the world. Flyers explained that a gift of £10 would provide ten meals over the next ten days in ten world "countries": the United Kingdom, Somalia, Bosnia, Sudan, Iraq, Pakistan, Afghanistan, Bangladesh, Palestine, and Kashmir. In order to accomplish this sensitive global task, seven partner Muslim NGOs had been enlisted as *iftar* meal distributors.[18] For example, Muslim Aid provided meals in Somalia and Bangladesh, while Human Appeal did so in Afghanistan. The beginning of the UK meal distribution took place at the Big IFtar itself for homeless people from the local area. Additional UK meals were supported at four Christian and secular London charities for the homeless: the Salvation Army, the Whitechapel Mission, Providence Row, and Thames Reach.

How was social change on the issue of homelessness understood, and practiced, in the context of the Big IFtar event? In part, social change was seen as an outcome of a personal faith put into action, as expressed in Naseeha's song "Allah, Help Us Change." In this way, change could be achieved through a kind of revival activism. A second component of social change was through partnership with existing NGOs, demonstrated by IF's distribution of meals through a globally linked network of NGO affiliates. The third component, mostly left implicit during the event, was social change through what I call "pillared activism."

By *pillared activism*, I am referring to actions for social change built on the rituals of Islamic practice, particularly the Five Pillars of Islam. The Five Pillars are *shahada* (confession of faith), *salah* (prayer), *sawm* (fasting during Ramadan), *zakat* (alms giving), and *hajj* (pilgrimage to Mecca). Most of these pillars are repeated each day (prayer and confession during prayer) or each year (fasting and alms giving). Therefore if the Pillars are a basis for activism, the activism

---

[18] The seven Muslim NGOs that distributed *iftar* meals were Muslim Hands, Muslim Aid, Islamic Help, Muslim Charity, Islamic Relief, Human Appeal International, and InterPalestine.

The Building Blocks of Social Change

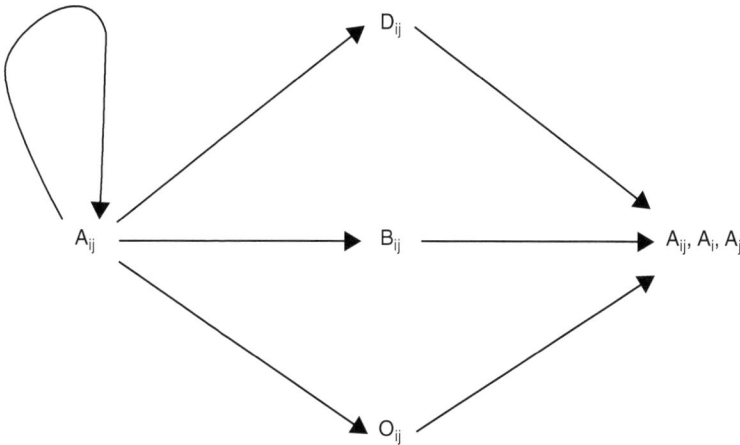

Figure 6.4. Solidarity through ritual as a causal mechanism of individual and social change

will have the consistency of regular communal practice. I will highlight two mechanisms of pillared activism: (1) solidarity through ritual and (2) social change through ritual.

The causal mechanism of solidarity through ritual was difficult to perceive at the Big IFtar simply because it remained in the background. I have diagrammed the mechanism in Figure 6.4. It begins with a collective ritual action (A) that is repeated regularly, as shown by the repetition arrow. The action (A) in the diagram has two subscripts together, for person i and person j, to demonstrate that it is collective. Muslim prayer is the archetypal example of a repeated collective ritual action. Many East End Bangladeshi Muslims perform prayer five times each day, with men being more likely than women to have the opportunity to do so collectively. A collective ritual action produces common desires (D), beliefs (B), and opportunities (O)[19] in the persons who engage in it, and the similarity of these DBOs is reinforced by the repetition of the action. In other words, participants

---

[19] The capacity of collective ritual action to form common desires and beliefs is easy to understand, but perhaps the formation of common "opportunities" is not. Some common opportunities can come out of collective action simply because participants are in the same place at the same time. For example, men who attend the same mosque for prayer may have a common opportunity to sign a petition as they leave the mosque, or their conversations after mosque may lead to other joint opportunities.

in the collective ritual develop solidarity with each other. The developed desires, beliefs, and opportunities are likely to cause further actions (Aij) that are taken in solidarity, as well as to produce some independent actions for each person (Ai, Aj).

Although prayer is the most obvious example of the development of Muslim solidarity through ritual, other Pillars of Islam can contribute to this as well. The common experience of fasting during Ramadan can draw Muslims together and provide an added social significance to breaking the fast in a communal *iftar*. Although many Muslims will only experience it once in a lifetime, if at all, *hajj* has a high potential to contribute to solidarity through the ritual actions performed in Mecca. Interestingly, the feeling of internal solidarity does not necessarily lead to intolerance of outsiders. A study of Pakistanis returning from *hajj* determined that they had developed both a greater solidarity with fellow Muslims *and* a greater tolerance for diverse others, because in their practice of common rituals they had been exposed to a great diversity of people.[20]

A sense of "kinship" develops as Muslims participate in collective rituals together over the course of years. Each additional collective action may further reinforce the feeling of brotherhood or sisterhood, and this may be felt even more strongly than kinship within the consanguineous family.[21] Due to this feeling of common kinship, many actions taken in solidarity do not need a rational motivation beyond the sense of common connection with others.

Solidarity through ritual, experienced by many Muslims as kinship, was an underlying mechanism of the civic action at the Big IFtar. Immediately prior to the event, many of the Muslims attending had engaged in Friday congregational prayers together at the nearby East London Mosque. As the *iftar* feast ended, it would be time to join in prayer again. The presence of prayer before and after the Big IFtar event seemed to draw individuals into a similar frame of mind. Solidarity could also be seen in the practice of the common *iftar* meal at the event, down to the small detail that everyone broke the fast together with the customary eating of a date.

---

[20] Clingingsmith et al. (2008).
[21] See DeHanas (2013b) for a more detailed analysis of how journeys to Mecca can strengthen young British Bengali Muslims' bonds with other Muslims. On the social construction of kinship, see Ebaugh (2000).

The second mechanism of pillared activism is social change through ritual. While solidarity through ritual can motivate actions for social change, in some cases Islamic rituals are themselves vehicles of social change. *Zakat* is a good example of social change through ritual. Finances given through *zakat* contribute to social change because they are part of an Islamic system of redistributive justice. *Zakat* can thus be thought of as a form of obligatory activism (if this is not too paradoxical).

Because Bangladeshis in the East End are so far from their country of origin, many give their *zakat* to British-based Islamic NGOs who redistribute it to the poor around the world.[22] This contrasts with Bangladeshis who live in Bangladesh, or even Maghrebi immigrants in France, who can more easily send funds to the poor at home through traditional means. Partly for this reason, the UK has the most well-developed Islamic NGO sector of any Western country.

The main collective civic outcome of the Big IFtar was voluntary charitable giving, a practice known in Islamic terms as *sadaqa*. Young IF Charity volunteers with donation boxes roved around the event soliciting £10 charitable gifts. Event speakers including the MC, performers, and the then Leader of the Council Lutfur Rahman[23] invoked kinship solidarity frequently to encourage charitable giving. Local councilor Abjol Miah's speech at Big IFtar showed his particular skill at mobilizing action through kinship solidarity.

Miah is a medium-build second-generation Bangladeshi man in his late thirties. He rose to prominence in Tower Hamlets politics when as a Respect Party candidate he defeated talented Labour politician and professor Michael Keith in 2006. Miah was a regular personality

---

[22] De Cordier (2009).

[23] Bengali Muslim politician Lutfur Rahman would rise to become the first directly elected mayor of Tower Hamlets in 2010. The controversies of Rahman's tenure as mayor dominated political discussions in Tower Hamlets from 2010 to 2015. Shortly before being elected mayor, Rahman had been expelled from the Labour Party following journalist Andrew Gilligan's *Dispatches* TV documentary "Britain's Islamic Republic" which insinuated that Rahman was abetting an Islamist takeover of Tower Hamlets. Rahman went on to win the election in 2010 as an independent candidate. He was then apparently re-elected in May 2014, although an election petition from local residents initiated an electoral fraud trial in which Rahman was found guilty and the election retroactively voided. To read the 200-page electoral fraud judgment, see *Erlam and others v. Rahman and another* (2015). For supportive takes on the judgment see Jeory (2015) and Ware (2015). For critical takes see Archbishop Cranmer (2015) and Izaakson (2015). For a helpful primer on the entire Lutfur Rahman political saga see Hill (2015).

on the local Muslim radio program *Easy Talk*. He identifies himself and his political stances primarily with Muslim issues. As Miah took the Big IFtar stage, he began his remarks by acknowledging the diversity of the crowd and stating that the occasion was significant:

> [Today's *iftar* is] a great opportunity for us to break our fast in an open way, remembering and sharing our meal with the homeless people in London... Today this *iftar* is a unique *iftar*, where we will be able to share with each other, people of all backgrounds, people of all faiths and no faith, where the concept of Ramadan will be shared.

With these opening words, Miah described *iftar* as a community meal that had brought together local ethnic, religious, and socio-economic diversity. Miah's words cited unity in a common humanity, using the term "people" to represent everyone in the crowd at Altab Ali Park. In his next section of the speech, the word "people" would undergo a subtle but significant shift in meaning, as Miah's frame of reference moved from local to global:

> But most importantly, let us not forget the thousands of lives who don't have shelter in the UK and around the world. And many who suffer under tyranny, under oppression, many who will have to break their fast in open cold, where there's no home for them to shelter. When we break our fast we know that there is room for many of us. But there are many around the world with no guarantee they will get their meal. So in solidarity with people around the world, for the people who suffer, for those who are homeless, this is a unique opportunity to break the fast.

Miah was now speaking the language of kinship solidarity. Although he said broadly that he sought "solidarity with people around the world," it was safe for him to assume that most of the audience understood these people to be fellow Muslims. At an *iftar* event that sponsored meals in Iraq, Afghanistan, Palestine, and Kashmir, the images Miah evoked were of the effects of tyranny and oppression on the Muslim poor. These words may have ignited in his listeners deep emotions of family connection and collective urgency. Kinship solidarity, which had been built through the communal practices of prayer, fasting, and fast-breaking, could now be channeled into charitable giving.

Miah's rhetoric of kinship solidarity mirrored what I had frequently heard in other Muslim fundraising and political events. The event provides an example of pillared activism (Islamic ritual practice merged with political practice), which has influenced the high rate of

The Building Blocks of Social Change 183

Bangladeshi youth political participation in the East End. As Abjol Miah concluded his speech about global poverty, he brought forward its implications for local area politics:

> I have with me Councilor Mamun Rashid from Shadwell Ward. We are Respect councilors working hard, to bring respect back into politics, to bring respect back into the community, to make our charities successful. And IF Charity is our number one charity at the moment. It has had the opportunity to unite all the other charities together.

Sam Davis at the LIVE event had eschewed calls to political action. Abjol Miah, in contrast, directly connects Muslim activism and charity with the agenda of the Respect Party. Unlike the revival activism of LIVE, Miah and other Muslim councilors with similar political commitments have had a sustained presence in local Tower Hamlets politics, ensuring that representation of their activist agenda remains ongoing.[24]

The collective action of the Big IFtar had been built on the solid support of pillared activism through fasting, prayer, and charitable giving. The giving that resulted was channeled through effective organizational networks. As such, the results of the Big IFtar event were tangible: it contributed to the delivery of 10,000 meals worldwide. Islamic practice and the solidarity that can result from it were central to enabling this effectiveness.

The Queen Mary University of London (QMUL) prayer room controversy, described in Chapter 1, has also developed into an example of pillared activism. When I interviewed Hamid in December 2008 he was helping to spearhead the Islamic Society's (ISoc) efforts for prayer room policy change. The QMUL administration had designated the former Muslim prayer room as a multi-faith room, an action that Hamid said has "really affected the work of the Islam Society." The ISoc had tried many methods of advocacy,

---

[24] In 2010 Abjol Miah stood as the Respect Party candidate for Parliament for the Bethnal Green and Bow constituency and George Galloway stood as the party's candidate in the neighboring Poplar and Limehouse constituency. Both lost their elections to Labour Party candidates (Rushanara Ali and Jim Fitzpatrick, respectively). Since that time the Respect Party's fortunes in Tower Hamlets have dimmed, and the party is no longer considered a major political influence in the local area. Many of the individuals formerly associated with Respect continued to be highly involved in local politics as independents, some having served in former borough Mayor Lutfur Rahman's cabinet.

including writing letters and signing petitions, but at that time did not believe it was ready for more confrontational measures such as protests.

Hamid has since finished his studies at QMUL. In autumn 2009, under new leadership, the Queen Mary ISoc took the prayer room controversy to a new level. The ISoc began to protest the administration's decision in a uniquely Islamic style. They organized outdoor prayers to take place in front of the main university administrative building. Dozens of young Muslim men stood together to prostrate in rows, praying in the public space to communicate their need for consistent prayer space. The prayer room campaign adopted the slogan: "The right to pray, throughout the day." Their argument was that space for Islamic prayer is intrinsic to the human right of freedom of worship.

The prayer protests were part of a coordinated campaign, organized through Facebook, YouTube, a campaign blog, and grassroots personal contact. By the end of the academic term a compromise was reached with the university. The administration granted more Muslim-specific prayer time in rooms around campus, but it retained the multi-faith room. The Queen Mary ISoc published an open letter on January 4, 2010, to explain the compromise. I include part of the letter here:

> After a semester of activities directed towards increasing access to prayer rooms for brothers and sisters, we would like everyone to be aware of what progress has been made...
> [list of specific agreements with the university about prayer times]
> We are working with the College, Student Union and other faith societies to ensure there is as little conflict as possible. This is not the final step; our goal [is] to expand opening hours, have a Qur'an rack and display posters. These are all goals which we will continue to work towards, via the multifaith centre user forum et cetera.
> Most importantly we would like to express our gratitude to Allah ('azza wa jal)—without Whom no good is possible. And after that, every single brother and sister who spent their time, money and effort—be it with their du'a, selling cakes, making banners, organising jumu'ah, printing flyers, publicising the campaign blog or even just by being there and voting with your feet. May Allah reward you all...

The Queen Mary ISoc prayer room campaign exemplifies creative and multi-faceted campaigning from young people that is, at its core, pillared activism. Cakes were sold and blogs were publicized. Yet all of these activities connected to the rock solid backbone of public communal prayers.[25]

CONCLUSION: THE HEART OF ACTIVISM

In this chapter we have considered how different understandings of social change rest at the heart of activism campaigns in South London and the East End. The LIVE event in Kennington was intended to revive the personal Christian faith of its participants and, in so doing, to enliven their dedication to opposing gun and knife violence. This "one person at a time" strategy may have left a lasting impression on some in attendance that August afternoon. Yet campaigns built on personal faith are unlikely to result in wide-scale or structural changes. They will seldom capture the imaginations of many outside church circles.

Indeed, the LIVE march and rally revealed a conflicted attitude— deep convictions about political issues juxtaposed with a lack of faith in political action. I had observed much the same ambivalence in the young British Jamaicans I met in Brixton churches. British sociologist David Martin perceptively explains why this can be the case:

> The paradox of evangelicalism (of which Pentecostalism is included for present purposes) turns on the way it embodies secularity and seeks a more thorough sanctification. Evangelicalism is the most expansive element in contemporary Protestantism and yet as it seeks [a] deeper appropriation of faith at the individual level it erodes the idea of a Christian society by dismissing the uncommitted majority as not Christian. Given that the democratic state increasingly reflects the comparative indifference of the majority, evangelicalism in principle abandons [the state] ... The "ideal type" of evangelicalism has to be constructed in terms of the restriction of religion to a voluntary sector unable and unwilling to propose [political] norms.[26]

---

[25] In the ISoc open letter, prayers are referred to with the Arabic terms *du'a* and *jumu'ah*. *Du'a* is the term for words of prayerful petition to God while *jumu'ah* is the term for Friday congregational prayers.

[26] Martin (2005: 134). David Martin is comparing the evangelical mentality of born-again conversion and personal faith to what Max Weber called the "church" mentality, where one is automatically born into a national church that extends across

In other words, evangelicalism is an extremely change-minded religious movement. It has hopes for deep individual-level heart change that culminate in the transformation of society. Yet, when confronted with societies where the vast majority is indifferent to their faith message, evangelicals can become deeply cynical about the actual potential for political and social change. Therefore most evangelicals in the West compartmentalize their influence to the voluntary sector (especially to their local church), or in some cases may campaign on a small set of moral touch-point issues. The evangelical faith—which overflows with ambitions for societal transformation—ironically tends to accept a highly circumscribed, and therefore secularized, role in society.[27]

The pillared activism I observed among East End Bangladeshi Muslims does not suffer from this lack of political confidence. At the Big IFtar event, public faith was made tangible in a Ramadan feast and *sadaqa* funds were secured for an extensive network of charities. In the Queen Mary ISoc campaign, prayer was powerfully channeled into protest. Young people "voted with their feet" in public demonstrations of politics and piety that university administrators could not ignore. Pillared activism is effective because it harnesses the pre-existing architecture of Islamic rituals for new and creative ethical ends. Yet, as should be clear from the discussion thus far, the resulting actions are not merely spectacles staged to attract attention. Acts of prayer, fasting, or *zakat* build kinship solidarity between worshipers, endowing their causes with a sacred purpose and placing them in the dependable tides of regular Islamic practice.

Yet a significant question remains about pillared activism: while it clearly has depth, can it also have breadth? As a form of activism it tends to be restricted to a fairly narrow set of Islamic causes, such as the public accommodation of religious practices, or solidarity with the suffering of the *ummah*. It is striking that the Big IFtar organizers partnered with Islamic NGOs to distribute international aid, but relied on Christian or secular charities for their domestic outreach

---

the whole society. Those with a "church" perspective might be expected to be more trusting and optimistic about political-level change.

[27] The original definition of "secularization" refers to the differentiation, or compartmentalization, of religion into a smaller and smaller domain of authority as its previous responsibilities are absorbed by the state, the market, or particular institutions. See Casanova (2006: 7–8).

to the homeless. Indeed, pillared activism sits in some contrast with Christian activism campaigns, which have been more likely to take on broad-based issues like gun and knife crime or economic injustice.[28] Religious activism—Muslim, Christian, or otherwise—evidently bears the promise of wider social change and youth democratic renewal. But it is a potential yet to be fully realized.

---

[28] Some examples of broader-based UK Islamic activism on issues like climate change and social justice can be found in the work of charities including MADE in Europe, the City Circle, and IFEES. These charities remain at the cutting edge. For broader-based activism in Tower Hamlets, see the chapter on "British-Islamic Identity in Public Spaces" in Hoque (2015) and see DeHanas (2010a) on East End Islamic environmental activism. The most significant player in broad-based community organizing in both Brixton and Tower Hamlets has been London Citizens, which in the East End is known as TELCO (The East London Citizens Organisation). London Citizens brings mosques and churches together with other religious institutions, labor unions, schools, and community groups to campaign for common causes such as safe community spaces and the living wage. The East London Mosque, Darul Ummah, and Islamic Forum Europe are members, while the other religious organizations I profile in this book are not. London Citizens has been highly effective at public action and holding political leaders to account. However, it has less reach among young people and was never mentioned by my youth interviewees. On the potential of community organizing for Christian civic engagement see Bretherton (2010) and on its potential for Muslim civic engagement see Ali et al. (2012).

7

Believing Citizens

What kinds of citizens are London's second-generation youth becoming? The answer, in part, is "believing citizens." Most of the Bangladeshi youth I interviewed devote at least as much time and energy to religious faith as their parents do. In many cases they devote far more. Likewise for a substantial number of Jamaican youth, religion is a significant and prioritized aspect of life. Indeed religion had relevance to every one of the young people I interviewed—whether it was taken for granted, questioned, reacted against, or wholeheartedly accepted.[1]

The emphasis on religion in this book should not obscure the ordinariness of second-generation young people's lives. As 18-year-old Tariq told me, he thinks his life is quite average: "We're just Muslims, chilled out, go to college, saving up to buy a PS3." To an outsider, five daily prayers might seem like an overwhelming load, or the supernatural dimension of Pentecostalism may be hard to comprehend. But to many children of immigrants in London's East End or in Brixton, these religious elements are a regular part of life experience.

Regardless of religiosity, the youth I interviewed had strikingly similar worries and concerns. When I asked young Bangladeshis and

---

[1] I know this because all youth either ranked a religion-related item during the identity ranking exercise described in Chapter 2, or explained to me why they do not relate to religion. Young people mentioned religion in one way or another before any direct prompting from me about it. My findings stand in some contrast to those of Abby Day (2011) who has argued, following Émile Durkheim, that youth religion can be reduced to a kind of belief in the social. Day's interviews focused primarily on young White English "nominal" Christians who were able to take a more distanced approach to religion. It remains to be seen whether, as Crockett and Voas (2006) argue, subsequent generations of ethnic minorities will increasingly conform to these White English religious norms.

Table 7.1. "What is the biggest problem in your local area?"

Brixton	The East End
1. Violent crime	1. Drugs
2. Drugs	2. Lack of opportunities
3. Drunks or "mad people"	3. Identity
4. Gangs	4. Violent crime
5. Public perceptions	5. Gangs

Jamaicans about the biggest problem in their respective local areas, three of the five most commonly cited responses from *both* groups were an urban triad of drugs, "gangs," and violent crime (Table 7.1). Religious problems—such as Islamophobia, extremism, or religious discrimination—did not feature as prominently, at least not as local area issues. As we spoke further, many of the personal life concerns voiced by youth were those common to people who are coming of age in the West: getting a job or building a career, making good friends, finding a life partner, or starting a family.

The title of this chapter, "Believing Citizens," has a dual meaning. It refers not only to the religious inclinations of youth I encountered, but also to the need for listening to and "believing in" these young citizens.[2] Most young people in the second generation do not think that their voices are adequately heard by media or by the government. While British policy-making on South Asian Muslims has been uneasy and circuitous,[3] Afro-Caribbean faith institutions have simply had little political consequence.[4] I hope this book will facilitate taking young citizens more seriously and will spur investment in increasing their political participation.

In this book I have attempted to give voice to a broad segment of second-generation youth in London. The research methodology I used to recruit my interviewees—beginning by composing a broadly representative "street" sample and then complementing this with a more in-depth religious institutions sample—has been designed to help rebalance our perspective. Likewise, the comparative dimension

---

[2] On the art of listening in sociology and politics, see Back (2007).
[3] For an introduction to the changing role of Muslims in British public policy, see DeHanas et al. (2013). For a more detailed analysis of key changes, see O'Toole et al. (2013).
[4] See Muir (2010) and discussions later in this chapter.

of the book helps to expand questions of faith and civic engagement beyond the more typical exclusive focus on British Muslims.

PUTTING IT ALL TOGETHER

In my attempt to answer the "civic question" on second-generation young people in the London, I have put forward a two-part argument. I have argued, first, that second-generation young adults' levels of awareness and interest in local political issues are strikingly similar in Brixton and the East End. In these respects, many young Londoners are engaged citizens. And yet I have also argued, second, that the differing structures and cultures of political activism in the two places mean that young Muslims in the East End are on average far more politically active citizens. Contrary to accounts of Muslim separatism and "parallel lives," my data in Chapter 1 suggest that religiously active Muslims in the East End have some of the very highest levels of involvement with British civic and political institutions, even when compared with the general population.

Why are young Bangladeshis, particularly the most religious ones, becoming politically active citizens? One immediate reason could be the urgency of political issues at stake. British foreign policy (in Iraq, Afghanistan, and elsewhere) and British domestic counterterrorism policy, especially Prevent, have provided a strong impetus for seeking political change. However, to name these issues is not to provide an explanation. After all, gun and knife crime in South London have urgent consequences that have affected most Jamaican youth I met, or someone they know; yet violent crime has not prompted the same levels of political involvement. The main difference between young people in Brixton (Figure 7.1) and the East End is not the immediacy of their concerns, but rather the political opportunities available to them through local organizational networks and cultures of activism.

Over the course of this book I have built an explanation for how a young second-generation Muslim Bangladeshi may become involved in Tower Hamlets politics. In a nutshell: many second-generation youth feel ashamed of, emotionally distant from, or constrained in choices by their parents from Bangladesh, many of whom have humble origins and a limited grasp of English language and culture. Well-resourced mosques in the East End, particularly the East

Figure 7.1. Two young men on Electric Avenue, Brixton

London Mosque and Darul Ummah, promote a community-oriented, global-revivalist, and deculturated form of Islam that these young people find attractive, especially as they attempt to define themselves in distinction from the traditional cultural Islam of their parents. Islamized self-identifications have become the primary bond of "imagined citizenship" for many Bangladeshi youth in the East End, by which I mean these provide a moral orientation and a community of reference for civic activism. Coincident with these developments in self-identification is Islamic practice, which buttresses political participation. Youth activism is "pillared" by Islamic ritual, because repeated practices—especially of the Islamic Pillars of prayer, fasting, and alms giving—create in youth a sense of kinship solidarity. Islamic practices are also often political acts in and of themselves. For example *zakat* (alms giving) is an action of redistributive justice. Thus, it is the combination of the widespread local consensus of Muslim self-identification and imagined citizenship, the pillaring support of practice, and widely available political opportunities that cultivate young second-generation Bangladeshis into politically participating citizens.

There are important ways this account can oversimplify. The British Bangladeshis I interviewed in the "heartland" areas surrounding Brick Lane are distinctive, perhaps even unique, among Bangladeshis in Britain. Their parents tend to originate in particular *thanas* in rural Sylhet, rather than comparably affluent urban zones such as Dhaka or Chittagong.[5] Young Bangladeshis in other areas of London like Camden or Newham, or elsewhere in Britain such as Oldham or Birmingham, would be further removed from the strong religious institutions that have raised the temperature of religious life in Tower Hamlets. Even in Tower Hamlets there are second-generation young people like Yasmin (Chapter 2) who are exceptions to the local/global processes of superordinate Muslim identification and practice, opting instead for more Sufi or secular lifestyle alternatives.

A sizable proportion of young and religious East End Bangladeshis are highly articulate like Hamid (Chapter 1) and Rubina (Chapter 2), and they have been at the forefront of Islamic youth activism in the East End. For these young people, Islam has become a meaningful source of belonging and morality from which they proactively contribute to British life. About half of second-generation East End Bangladeshis are more like Farouq from Chapter 2, who also considers "Muslim" to be his most salient identity. Yet Farouq holds his faith tacitly, being more concerned for the moment with meeting girls and having a good time. Young people like Farouq are not activists, but many of them can be called upon to sign a petition or perhaps to

---

[5] Garbin (2008). *Thanas* are sub-districts in Bangladesh.

vote. Finally, there are youth like Khan (Chapter 2) whose hyper-Islamic identity has eliminated any allegiance to Britain or to the Bengali community. Extreme youth such as Khan are a very small minority in the East End (two or three of my thirty-six Bangladeshi interviewees).[6] However they can be a vocal minority through groups such as Hizb ut-Tahrir or al-Muhajiroon and its offshoots, and sometimes they may influence or intimidate youth like Farouq.

Today in the East End, the more constructive forms of Islamic engagement that Hamid exemplifies are having greater traction among the second generation than extremism does. Yet all of the youth I have mentioned here—Hamid, Rubina, Farouq, and Khan—have developed their views of Islam in the context of the East London Mosque, demonstrating both the broad reach of this mosque and the divergent ways in which its elastic orthodoxy can be adopted and utilized.

The elastically orthodox consensus on Islam in Tower Hamlets has not remained uncontested. Over the past ten years, various organizations and prominent figures have sought to challenge the perceived local dominance of the East London Mosque and its associated organization the Islamic Forum Europe. At various times this uneasy alliance has included Bangladeshi secularist bodies (Nirmul Committee, Swadhinata Trust), religious institutions (the Brick Lane Mosque), local political parties (sections of the Conservative and Labour groups), think tanks with an expressed interest in the East End (Quilliam, Centre for Social Cohesion), national politicians (Jim Fitzpatrick MP, Eric Pickles MP), and influential journalists (Andrew Gilligan, Ted Jeory). Considering the powerful forces arrayed against it, the continuing clout of the East London Mosque may appear highly unlikely, even miraculous. However, the perception that the Mosque's position is embattled by outside forces has only helped bolster its credibility among young people.

Moving our discussion to Brixton, second-generation Jamaican youth also show rather high levels of political literacy. Yet their participation in political activities is much lower than the average for Bangladeshis. Religiosity does not have a demonstrable impact, positive or negative, on Jamaican political participation.

---

[6] Because I sampled more than a third of my Bangladeshi interviewees from mosques, it can be expected that a sample taken entirely from street recruitment would find a lower proportion of Muslims at this extreme.

Second-generation Jamaicans have in large part left the traditional first-generation religious institutions of their parents, much as Bangladeshis have. For the Jamaican young adults who do attend church in Brixton, the most popular choice is the mega-church Ruach Ministries or one of many smaller Pentecostal or neo-Pentecostal churches. My observations at Ruach demonstrate that its youth ministry is a welcoming place for young people to come "as they are," bringing both their personal struggles and life ambitions. Ruach's youth ministry can galvanize young people to significant achievements. In some cases, such as Samuel in Chapter 3, involvement in a church like Ruach provides youth with the self-definition, mentoring, and motivation to escape delinquency and move into an entirely new lifestyle.

The individual-based ministry at Ruach, however, does not provide a strong motivation for political action. Although Youth Pastor Mark Liburd is commendable for mentioning political candidates during election seasons and for encouraging voting, his message was not taking root. In part the issue is that the individual-based ethos of the church—"where everybody is a somebody"—does not provide for much youth engagement with the community outside church doors. Local engagement is limited also because the majority of attendees do not live in the area. Likewise Mike (Chapter 1) is representative of the many Jamaican youth who do not think that British politicians or political structures serve them well, especially on moral and faith issues.

In large part, the difference between Bangladeshi and Jamaican political participation comes down to the politics of identity. The 1970s and 1980s were the height of Black identity politics in Britain, including significant activism in Brixton. The consensus around political Blackness has since faded, in part due to the rise of hybrid and mixed-race identification in Britain.[7] Indeed, among the young Jamaicans I interviewed there were various identity options that individuals might value, and these did not cohere into a clear pattern. The Brixton area is highly diverse, perhaps even ethnically fragmented. The background conditions for a strong identity-based

---

[7] Other key factors in the decline of political Blackness have been the decline of South Asian activists' willingness to identify as "Black" and the concomitant rise of religious (especially Muslim) identity politics. See Modood (1994).

politics do not exist in Brixton like they do in the East End, whether this is to be based on faith, race, or ethnicity.

WHAT IT MEANS

Today the politics of religious diversity exists in a state of flux. This book can contribute to research and policy-making in several areas that are relevant to our current times, as well as to long-standing theoretical concerns that will outlive them. Three of these broad areas of potential contribution are: the study of religion, comparative politics, and diversity and integration.

In terms of the study of religion, I hope this book will provide new opportunities to bring sociologists of religion and Islamic studies scholars into common conversation. The sociology of religion has traditionally been preoccupied with the study of (Protestant) Christianity and the much-contested processes of "secularization."[8] It has thus far paid inadequate attention to other religions such as Islam.[9] Likewise, Islamic Studies seldom builds substantially upon developments in the sociology of religion, often referring to Christianity in caricatured terms.[10] The result is that many scholars from these disciplines either talk past each other or, more frequently, are entirely unaware of each other. In Chapters 4 and 5 I have built up to a comparative discussion of "objective" and "subjective" approaches to moral authority and of experiences of "enacted community" and "imagined communion." I think these comparative terms can suggest new lines of inquiry into Muslim and Christian inter-religious differences, providing a basis for further comparative work.

Comparative research is a complex enterprise. It is easy to make either of two opposite errors of being overly ambitious or too cautious. In this book I have worked at the level that sociologist Robert

---

[8] For an authoritative overview of the sociology of religion, see Davie (2013).

[9] See Cadge et al. (2011) on current deficits of the sociology of religion, particularly as practiced in the United States. In Britain, new religious movements and alternative spiritualities have been additional areas of significant focus, but Islam and other world religions remain under-explored.

[10] For example, see Browers and Kurzman (2004) for a critique of how ideas of the Protestant Reformation have been misappropriated by scholars of Islam.

Merton called "theories of the middle range."[11] Middle-range theories contrast with macro theories that are intended to apply across all societies, and with micro theories that fit only one tightly bounded group or situation. In recent years middle-range theorizing has blossomed into a new research tradition on "social mechanisms." Social mechanisms are causal patterns in the social world that can be found in a variety of contexts, revealing the cogs and wheels of how societies work.[12] A good example is Robert Merton's own mechanism, the "self-fulfilling prophecy," in which originally false beliefs reshape reality because people have believed and acted as if they were true.[13] In Chapter 6 I delineated the social mechanisms of "solidarity through ritual," "social action through ritual," and "personal faith" as ways of motivating and sustaining political action. These social mechanisms are the building blocks of the activism campaigns I witnessed in South and East London, and could potentially also be uncovered in a range of other contexts in London and internationally. The comparative approach I advocate here and the specific mechanisms I outline can contribute to comparative politics, where they will be consonant with increasingly granular approaches used to study the dynamics of political contention.[14]

Importantly, middle-range theorizing requires humility on what we are able to know. I have not argued that all Muslims at all times and all places will be highly engaged citizens, or that all British Bangladeshi Muslims are today. Likewise, I am not making the claim often made that Islam is inherently political, with its civic and spiritual spheres inseparable. Instead, I have examined the social mechanisms that are at work in pillaring the activism of many young Muslims in certain institutions and particular streams of

---

[11] Merton (1967).

[12] This research tradition is sometimes called analytical sociology. Another frequent term for social mechanism is "causal mechanism." See Hedström and Swedberg (1998) and Hedström and Bearman (2009) for major statements on this approach and its potential applications. On mechanisms revealing the "cogs and wheels" of the social, see Elster (1983, 1998).

[13] Merton (1948). The self-fulfilling prophecy has been studied in a variety of settings from teachers' views on supposedly high achievers in school classrooms (Rosenthal and Jacobson 1968) to romantic relationships in which one partner believes the other may reject them (Downey et al. 1998).

[14] On the social mechanisms of political contention, see McAdam et al.'s (2001) modern classic *Dynamics of Contention*. For a helpful discussion of methodological developments within comparative politics, see Della Porta (2008).

Islam in the East End. Further research into these social mechanisms elsewhere would likewise need to be carefully contextualized. There appear to be many examples of Muslim pillared activism and Christian revival activism globally,[15] but work remains to be done to demonstrate that the examples I bring forward here are in fact representative of broader patterns.

One further area in which this book can contribute is to debates on diversity and integration. Various authors including Tariq Modood, Bhikhu Parekh, and Nasar Meer have advocated the positive recognition of religious and ethnic minorities as groups, often centering their work on the political claims-making of Muslims. A second school of thought is the perspective of hybrid identifications and "new ethnicities" that has developed in the work of Stuart Hall, Paul Gilroy, Les Back, Michael Keith, and others and which calls into question the validity and public usefulness of group claims. I have built from Michel de Certeau to consider young people's self-identifications in terms of the tactics of everyday life, employing an identity choice and ranking exercise in my interviews. This allows me to demonstrate that the first school of thought applies well to young Bangladeshis, who tend to tactically orient themselves around a strong sense of culturally purified Muslim self-identification. Conversely, the ideas of the second school seem to better describe young Jamaicans, who tactically draw from various sources of self-identification to suit new situations. While certainly not mutually exclusive, these two tactical orientations are somewhat at odds.

The comparative cases in this book demonstrate a paradox of integration. British Jamaicans are more likely to have ethnically diverse relationships and to fluidly adapt to new social contexts. In this sense, they could be said to be more socially integrated. Yet British Bangladeshi Muslims maintain a social distinctiveness while staying in tune with the British political system, making them more civically integrated. These two kinds of integration—social and civic—should both be valued in contemporary Britain. Yet it is worth recognizing that public policy approaches taking a strong multiculturalist stance will likely favor those who are more group-based and civically integrated, while approaches taking a strong

---

[15] For vivid examples of what I have termed "revival activism," see Miller and Yamamori's (2007) global study of Pentecostal social engagement. For examples of "pillared activism," see Satha-Anand (2004) on prayer and May (2013) on *zakat*.

assimilationist stance may favor the more individual-based and socially integrated. In other words, assimilationism and multiculturalism can have divergent effects on different ethnic populations.

Differences such as these, however, need not result in an impasse. The case studies in this book can lead to mutual insights and to the rethinking of tactics to improve one's standing in British society. Indeed, many of the issues faced by young Bangladeshis and Jamaicans boil down to a problem they share: socio-economic disadvantage. There is much to be said for the argument that social equality is fundamental to human flourishing. Sircar and Saraswati put it well when they write that equality leads to "more self-confidence to belong within a diverse patchwork of communities (cohesion), which then leads to gradual integration"—both civic and social.[16]

PRESENT REALITIES, FUTURE HOPES

This book opened with Christopher Caldwell's *Reflections on a Revolution in Europe*, as an entry point into contemporary debates.[17] Caldwell's book raises the question: "Can [Britain] be the same with different people in it?"

Britain, of course, will never return to its bygone days of Empire. As a post-colonial nation, it has transformed into a multi-ethnic one. While British investment in former colonies dissolved, migrants traveled to the "Mother Country" in search of economic opportunities. A well-known anti-discrimination slogan pithily expresses the present realities: "We are here because you were there." In somewhat different words during an interview in Brixton, 18-year-old Mabel turned Caldwell's kind of question around: "It's true, we don't come from here. It is true. But at the end of the day I am here. What are you going to do about it?"

Caldwell's concern, however, is not with immigration or religion broadly speaking, but with Islam in particular. He believes that Muslim youth are becoming adversarial separatists in European societies. However, Caldwell's analysis, as in many books on these issues,[18] is built upon reactionary news coverage of radicalization and

---

[16] Sircar and Saraswati (2012). [17] Caldwell (2009).
[18] For example, Steyn (2006); Phillips (2006); Bawer (2006).

terrorism, resulting in alarmist arguments. For example, he includes sections called "Hyper-Identities" and "Dual Loyalty" that cover the same thematic ground as Chapters 2 and 3 on identity and loyalty in this book. Most of Caldwell's quotes in these chapter sections (pages 129–35) are from British Muslims. Yet he has selected quite a skewed sample of spokespersons: Imran Waheed of the radical organization Hizb ut-Tahrir, Omar Abdullah of the banned group al-Muhajiroun, and "a Syrian trained exile from Birmingham." Inayat Bunglawala of the Muslim Council of Britain is the sole voice included who might be expected to express concerns common to a large segment of British Muslims. Because Caldwell's writing relies almost entirely on extreme voices, he amplifies the words of a small but vocal minority at the expense of presenting a balanced perspective.

Similarly, in recent years the self-made extremist spokesperson Anjem Choudary has garnered extensive media coverage, especially following any report of a domestic terrorist plot. Yet research into Choudary's organizations (al-Muhajiroun and its offshoots) finds that their following is minuscule, with events failing to draw more than forty people.[19] As sociologist Chris Bail explains in his book *Terrified*, extreme Muslim and anti-Muslim groups on the fringes that gain media attention can soon be seen as the new "normal."[20] This can have bizarre results. Terrorism "expert" Steven Emerson, speaking live on Fox News in January 2015, remarked that: "In Britain, it's not just no-go zones, there are actual cities like Birmingham that are totally Muslim where non-Muslims just simply don't go in." Birmingham, Britain's second-largest city, is in fact 21.8 percent Muslim.[21] The response to Emerson's laughable claim was swift: Twitter users lambasted him and Prime Minister David Cameron called him a "complete idiot," leading to a groveling apology. Yet this amusing example highlights a serious issue: when hearsay is posted on an extreme Muslim or anti-Muslim website today, it could easily become "expert" opinion tomorrow.[22]

Increasing media and government attention over the past few decades has given Muslims a hyper-visibility in which they are easily connected into the politics of fear. To a large extent, as Birt argues,

---

[19] Raymond (2010: 10).   [20] Bail (2015).   [21] ONS (2011).
[22] It is likely that Emerson, who had not visited Birmingham, gained his views on the city by reading about it in a fringe online source. For a critique of the terrorism "expert" industry, see Stampnitzky (2013).

"the fundamental difficulty [has been] an overemphasis upon counter-terrorism without engaging Muslims as citizens."[23] One of my central aims in this book has been to de-exceptionalize second-generation British Muslims and to re-emphasize their citizenship. I have placed young Muslims on par with others in their generation by asking a common "civic question." It is perhaps ironic that by asking this question I bring to light aspects of British Muslim politics in Tower Hamlets that are indeed exceptional: very high rates of civic engagement and activism that have made young East End Muslims *positive* outliers. Moving from the Muslim question to the broader "civic question" will mean moving from a politics of fear and towards one in which all citizens—Bangladeshi, Jamaican, Indian, White English, Christian, Muslim, or otherwise—can learn from each other and positively contribute to a common life together.

Over the past fifteen years young British Blacks have faced the equal and opposite problem of near invisibility. In religious terms, media and policy-makers have shown much less interest in Black Christians compared to South Asian Muslims. There are, however, encouraging signs that new opportunities are starting to emerge, and some of these are worth brief elaboration here. The role of London's Black churches in politics has increased in only a few years, providing potential new avenues for youth participation. A non-denominational initiative called Street Pastors, launched by Reverend Les Isaacs in Brixton in 2003, has for more than a decade sent church members on Friday and Saturday night street patrols to care for revelers and contribute to public safety. Street Pastors has been praised by the Metropolitan Police and by London Mayor Boris Johnson, and is being replicated across Britain and worldwide.[24]

Likewise, the Seventh Day Adventist LIVE March in August 2009 was an impressive sign of church civic engagement. Even if the message of the march was politically minimalist, it nonetheless brought many young people out for their first-ever public demonstration. The leadership of the Brixton Seventh Day Adventist church has since changed, and this has included bringing onto the staff the youthful and passionate Pastor Max Mackenzie-Cook. In August 2013, members of the church held a public march of their own, led

---

[23] Birt (2009: 54) is referring specifically to the counterterrorism Prevent strategy, but his words apply more broadly to "official" narratives on British Muslims.

[24] For an overview of the work of Street Pastors, see Mason (2008).

by their youth drum corps from Santley Street to the heart of Brixton at Windrush Square. In the square they sang spiritual songs and distributed leaflets about the church, its revival week services, and its new "Mission to Cities" program. The day's activities centered on a health tent in Windrush Square, where volunteers provided free blood pressure checks and medical information. Pastor E. Jones Lartey said: "We brought the church the town... we are here with the church to let everyone know that Brixton is alive, and Jesus has come to London as well." Brixton Seventh Day Adventist Church is gaining a better footing in local engagement by taking to the streets to share its talents in musical performance and knowledge of rational Adventist approaches to diet and health. As one female health tent volunteer stated: "There are a huge number of health concerns in Lambeth, and the statistics show that those health issues are significantly worse than the national average. So we're very much aware that what we're doing today is touching those key issues."[25]

While Black Majority Churches are taking positive steps, they are still in the relatively early stages of effective political engagement. Councilor Lorna Campbell, a local politician in South London, is one of a small number of Black British politicians who openly integrates her faith into politics. She notes that: "In terms of political influence in respect to policy formation, there has been little if any indication that churches with Black leadership are playing a significant role, both at national and local level."[26]

In part, this may be related to the low level of Black representation overall in significant positions of political power. According to Ashok Viswanathan of Operation Black Vote, "There is a direct link between people seeing Black faces in high places and feeling that the democratic process is something that belongs to them and something that they want to take part in."[27] Following the 2015 general election, there are now forty-one ethnic minority MPs in a House of Commons of 650 members.[28] As a more than 50 percent increase from the previous election in 2010, this represents substantial progress. However, a total of fifty-two ethnic minority MPs would be needed for representation to reach parity with the Britain's

---

[25] Brixton Seventh Day Adventist Church (2013).
[26] Quoted in Muir (2010).
[27] Quoted in Meer and Modood (2009b: 109).
[28] van Heerde-Hudson and Campbell (2015).

8 percent ethnic minority electorate.[29] Issues of representation are accentuated for Black youth, who are doubly distanced from typical British politicians by their ethnicity and age. With such issues in mind, Operation Black Vote runs a wide range of activities including civic leadership programs, MP and local councilor shadowing, informational talks, and rallies designed to inspire young people into political involvement. Other British organizations are likewise working to empower diverse young people into politics, including the Young Foundation's UpRising program and the 3 Faiths Forum's ParliaMentors initiative, in which trios from different faiths are mentored by an MP or peer to collaborate across faiths on a social action project.

The release of *Black Church Mobilisation: A Manifesto for Action* has been an especially promising development for race and faith-related political engagement.[30] Written in advance of the 2015 general election and in the style of a political party manifesto, this Black Majority Church (BMC) manifesto gathers together specific action recommendations for churches and the government drawn from consultation with a range of African and Caribbean church leaders.[31] Importantly, the manifesto does not simply offer suggestions but builds a theological case for political engagement as integral to the normal Christian life: "We do not see political engagement as optional. Rather, we see it as a mandatory part of our Christian faith as responsible citizens in accordance with biblical teaching."[32] One of the strongest elements of the manifesto is the five-point BMC-led plan for voter registration that includes appointing a voting advocate in every congregation and ensuring that sermons regularly include social and political analysis. Thoughtful recommendations are also included on a range of policy areas ranging criminal justice to the arts. While the BMC manifesto is merely one step, it is an important step that has the endorsement of some of Britain's most influential BMC leaders including co-authors of the foreword Pastor

---

[29] The size of the British ethnic minority electorate has been estimated by Heath et al. (2013: 90).

[30] Muir and Omooba (2015).

[31] Contributors to the consultation phase included Sam Davis, the Seventh Day Adventist speaker at the LIVE March that I profiled in Chapter 6. For the wide range of BMC leaders that were consulted for the manifesto see Muir and Omooba (2015: 38–9).

[32] Muir and Omooba (2015: 8).

Matthew Ashimolowo, Reverend Nezlin Stirling, Bishop Eric Brown, and Pastor Agu Irukwu.

Beyond tapping into faith-based or racial identifications, there are other ways to motivate Brixton's young people into political participation. One possibility would be to develop a greater sense of locality politics. There have been efforts towards this, including the Brixton Pound introduced in 2009 by Transition Town Brixton. The Brixton Pound is a local currency accepted by many stores that features pictures of famous former residents on the bank notes, and encourages the localization of commerce.[33] Another source of local connection is the online forum Urban75, a popular source for history, events information, and debate on Brixton life, with a special interest in built heritage and drug liberalization.[34] Perhaps most significant for young people, the innovative new Young Lambeth Cooperative is giving them direct decision power over a three-year £9 million budget for children and youth services.[35] Finally, large protests in support of the global "Black lives matter" movement and against the rapid gentrification of the area—including the arrival of upscale restaurants and gated communities—are returning a racial dimension to Brixton street politics.[36]

Brixton's potential for locality politics is to some degree limited by its political boundaries. Its four current wards slice right through the center, dividing it into three different electoral zones for Parliament. This division makes it difficult for MPs or local councilors to claim to "represent" Brixton. A recent proposal to unite Brixton into a single constituency would have divided neighboring Streatham, and was opposed by the three sitting Lambeth Labour MPs.[37] Retaining the status quo risks leaving Brixton on the political fringe. Even the symbolic act of renaming an existing parliamentary constituency to include "Brixton" would give both a stronger sense that

---

[33] The four former residents on the first edition Brixton Pound notes were Olive Morris (Brixton Black Women's Group activist), James Lovelock (environmentalist who developed Gaia Theory), C. L. R. James (Trinidadian socialist thinker), and artist Vincent Van Gogh, who lived in Brixton at age 20 and was marked by his experience of poverty there. The current notes in the Brixton Pound second edition feature Violet Szabo, Leford Kwesi Garrison, Luol Deng, and David Bowie.
[34] Urban75 (n.d.).   [35] Young Lambeth Cooperative (n.d.).
[36] In spring 2015 the group London Black Revs organized #ReclaimBrixton and #BlackLivesMatter street protests in Brixton; see Rucki (2015); Heartfield (2015).
[37] Foster (2012).

local voices are heard and impetus for MPs to speak for them in Parliament.[38]

Elections in Lambeth and Tower Hamlets in recent years bring hope that second-generation political engagement has been maturing. In the 2010 general election, the then 31-year-old Chuka Umunna successfully stood as the Labour Party candidate to become MP for Streatham. The Streatham constituency includes the wards of Brixton Hill and Tulse Hill, covering a substantial portion of central Brixton. Umunna, a former employment lawyer who grew up in his constituency, is mixed-race with a Nigerian father and an Irish/English mother. He says of his racial background: "Being mixed-race, I can operate in any environment, but I don't walk into a room and think, 'I am the only black person here.' It's not something I generally think about. When you open your mouth people tend to be interested in your ideas rather than what you look like."[39] Umunna is optimistic about young people of his generation: "I am part of a new generation which, contrary to popular myth, is not apathetic about politics but disdainful of party politics and the traditional ways of doing things."[40] Since entering Parliament in 2010, Umunna has earned his place as a rising star. He serves as Shadow Business Secretary and makes frequent media appearances. In May 2015 he made a short-lived bid for leader of the Labour Party following Ed Miliband's resignation. Umunna is now one of Labour's most recognized faces.

Looking to the East, the Bethnal Green and Bow constituency in London's East End was a fiercely contested election battleground in 2010, with the four main candidates for the seat all Bangladeshi. Rushanara Ali of the Labour Party was victorious, becoming both the first Bangladeshi MP and one of the first Muslim female MPs. Ali is an East End local who attended its well-known Mulberry School for Girls. A strong student, Ali studied at Oxford, held various positions in policy institutes and in local initiatives, and became the protégée of former local MP Oona King. Also seen as having political promise, Ali has been Shadow Minister for International Development. Her campaign for Parliament was run on the

---

[38] A good model of this kind of symbolism is the former Spitalfields electoral ward that includes Brick Lane. In 1998 the ward was renamed "Spitalfields and Banglatown" to reflect the local political and economic significance of British Bangladeshis.
[39] Quoted in Shah (2009).   [40] Quoted in Ogongo (2010).

basis of drawing together the diverse voices and strands of history in the East End:

> This is a really diverse community and, broadly speaking, people try and get along and respect each others' backgrounds. It's a community with a rich cultural heritage, as well as a proud religious heritage. That's how people see it—they're proud to be British, proud to be Bangladeshi, proud to be Muslim, proud to be east enders—and that's how I see myself.[41]

Abjol Miah, the Respect Party candidate who opposed Rushanara Ali in 2010, could hardly be more different. Miah at the time was a local councilor (introduced in Chapter 6 as a speaker at the Big IFtar rally). He grew up in the East End, where he has been a youth worker and martial arts teacher. Miah's political ambitions developed out of his reputation for activism against the US- and Britain-led wars in Afghanistan and Iraq. In the 2005 general election, Miah helped to orchestrate maverick Respect Party politician George Galloway's appeal to Muslims in the Bethnal Green and Bow constituency on a strong anti-war platform. Galloway won the Parliament seat, primarily due to the Muslim protest-vote, ousting veteran incumbent Oona King.[42] Abjol Miah is a fighter who won his own battle for a local council seat against university professor and Labour Party politician Michael Keith, going on to take a prominent place in the Tower Hamlets Council.

Abjol Miah's political ascendancy is especially interesting because it was built upon the social forces explained in this book. His family moved from Sylhet to the East End when he was six months old. He grew up in British schooling like any member of the second generation and speaks with an East End cockney accent. Miah is a key figure in the East London Mosque, and was one of the presenters of the *Easy Talk* radio show that was broadcast from the mosque's London Muslim Centre. He is also a frequent speaker at activism and charity events associated with the mosque. In his parliamentary campaign speeches, Miah connected with young Bangladeshis on the basis of all-encompassing "Muslim first" identities and by tapping into Islamic practices, like fasting and alms giving, as tools in a repertoire of activism. Yet Miah's communitarian approach to Muslim identity politics has limited cross-over appeal. To explain his bid for Parliament to a non-Muslim journalist, Miah said:

---

[41] Quoted in Brooks (2010).
[42] On George Galloway and a brief history and assessment of the Respect Party he leads, see Peace (2013) and Peace and Akhtar (2015).

We pride ourselves that we have Muslim councillors, and why not? For the last 15 years you've said we're isolationist, ghettoised, unwilling to engage and now that we engage we're fundamentalists and extremists. You can't have it both ways.[43]

Abjol Miah, who had been expected to do well, not only lost the election but came in third after Rushanara Ali of Labour and Ajmal Masroor of the Liberal Democrats. His loss was a reminder that for all the pillared strength of Islamic political activism in the East End, it is far from indomitable. Sustainable politics in Tower Hamlets and at a national level tends to require broad-based coalition building, an arena in which Rushanara Ali has proven to have greater skill. In 2015, when Mayor Lutfur Rahman of Tower Hamlets was removed from office for electoral fraud, Rushanara Ali played a highly visible role in the successful campaign to elect Labour candidate John Biggs as the sensible and "mainstream" choice for mayor.

As much as they may differ, the three parliamentary candidates I have profiled here are all exemplars of an important kind of democratic progress. Chuka Umunna, Rushanara Ali, and Abjol Miah have lived the second-generation youth story of growing up in inner city London.[44] In recent decades, ethnic minorities have participated most visibly in British politics through their actions of protest or dissent—the Brixton Riots, the Rushdie Affair, West Indian activism, and protesting the war in Iraq. Anger and critique, whether democratically channeled or not, will continue into the foreseeable future. Yet these young political candidates have been forerunners of a new phenomenon within the second generation. There has been a fundamental shift from protesting against the state of British public affairs, to becoming participants in the highest levels of political decision-making.

---

[43] Quoted in Brooks (2010). Miah is right to point to the irony that many of the same commentators who have called for more Muslims to speak out in politics have at the same time been wary of actual Muslim political participation, all too readily labeling this as "Islamist" or "extremist." It is a double standard that I hope this book will help correct. However, Miah's adversarial "us vs. them" words in this statement and in others clearly limit his political support to a narrow and almost exclusively Muslim base.

[44] Chuka Umunna is a mixed-race member of the second generation. Abjol Miah and Rushanara Ali both arrived in Britain as children (6 months old and 7 years old respectively). Although technically part of the "1.5 generation," Miah and Ali were both socialized in British schools among largely second-generation peers, giving their life histories a second-generation character.

References

Adams, Caroline. 1994. *Across Seven Seas and Thirteen Rivers*. London: THAP Books.

Ahmed, Nilufar. 2005. "Tower Hamlets: Insulation in Isolation." In *Muslim Britain: Communities Under Pressure*, ed. Tahir Abbas, 194–207. London: Zed Books.

Alexander, Claire. 1996. *The Art of Being Black: The Creation of Black British Youth Identities*. Oxford: Oxford University Press.

Alexander, Claire. 2000. *The Asian Gang: Ethnicity, Identity, Masculinity*. Oxford: Berg.

Alexander, Claire. 2011. "Making Bengali Brick Lane: Claiming and Contesting Space in East London." *British Journal of Sociology* 62, no. 2: 201–20.

Ali, Monica. 2003. *Brick Lane*. London: Doubleday.

Ali, Ruhana, Lina Jamoul, and Yusufi Vali. 2012. *A New Covenant of Virtue: Islam and Community Organising*. London: Citizens UK and Industrial Areas Foundation.

Almond, Gabriel and Sidney Verba. 1963. *The Civic Culture: Political Attitudes and Democracy in Five Nations*. Princeton, NJ: Princeton University Press.

Ammerman, Nancy Tatom. 1996. *Congregation & Community*. New Brunswick, NJ: Rutgers University Press.

Ammerman, Nancy Tatom. 2005. *Pillars of Faith: American Congregations and Their Partners*. Berkeley, CA: University of California Press.

Anderson, Benedict. 1983. *Imagined Communities: Reflections on the Origin and Spread of Nationalism*. London: Verso.

Anderson, Elijah. 1999. *Code of the Street: Decency, Violence, and the Moral Life of the Inner City*. New York: W. W. Norton.

Ansari, Humayum (ed.). 2011. *The Making of the East London Mosque, 1910–1951*. Cambridge: Cambridge University Press.

Anwar, Muhammad. 1979. *The Myth of Return: Pakistanis in Britain*. London: Heinemann.

Anwar, Muhammad. 1998a. *Between Cultures: Continuity and Change in the Lives of Young Asians*. London: Routledge.

Anwar, Muhammad. 1998b. *Ethnic Minorities and the British Electoral System*. Warwick, UK: Centre for Research on Ethnic Relations and Operation Black Vote.

Anwar, Muhammad. 2001. "The Participation of Ethnic Minorities in British Politics." *Journal of Ethnic and Migration Studies* 27, no. 3: 533–9.

References

Archbishop Cranmer. 2015. "The Undue Political Interference of 'Undue Spiritual Influence'." *Archbishop Cranmer* blog, May 15. <http://archbishopcranmer.com/the-undue-political-interference-of-undue-spiritual-influence/>, last accessed August 27, 2015.

Arnett, Jeffrey Jenson. 2000. "Emerging Adulthood: A Theory of Development from the Late Teens through the Twenties." *American Psychologist* 55, no. 5: 469–80.

Asad, Talal. 1993. *Genealogies of Religion: Discipline and Reasons of Power in Christianity and Islam.* Baltimore, MD: Johns Hopkins University Press.

Ash, Timothy Garton. 2006. "What Young British Muslims Say Can Be Shocking: Some of It Is Also True." *The Guardian*, August 10. <http://www.theguardian.com/commentisfree/2006/aug/10/comment.race>, last accessed August 13, 2015.

Aspinall, Peter and Miri Song. 2013. *Mixed Race Identities.* Basingstoke: Palgrave Macmillan.

Back, Les. 1996. *New Ethnicities and Urban Culture Racisms and Multiculture in Young Lives.* London: Routledge.

Back, Les. 2007. *The Art of Listening.* Oxford: Berg.

Back, Les, Michael Keith, Azra Khan, Kalbir Shukra, and John Solomos. 2009. "Islam and the New Political Landscape: Faith Communities, Political Participation and Social Change." *Theory, Culture & Society* 26, no. 4: 1–23.

Bail, Christopher. 2015. *Terrified: How Anti-Muslim Fringe Organizations Became Mainstream.* Princeton, NJ: Princeton University Press.

Baumann, Gerd. 1996. *Contesting Culture: Discourses of Identity in Multi-Ethnic London.* Cambridge: Cambridge University Press.

Bawer, Bruce. 2006. *While Europe Slept: How Radical Islam is Destroying the West from Within.* New York: Doubleday.

BBC News. 2008. "MPs Back Hybrid Embryo Research." <http://news.bbc.co.uk/1/hi/uk_politics/7407589.stm>, last accessed August 12, 2015.

BBC News. 2011. "England rioters 'poorer, younger, less educated'." <http://www.bbc.co.uk/news/uk-15426720>, last accessed August 15, 2015.

Birt, Yahya. 2007. "The Islamist: A Review." *Yahya Birt* blog, May 6. <https://yahyabirt1.wordpress.com/2007/05/06/the-islamist-a-review/>, last accessed August 8, 2015.

Birt, Yahya. 2009. "Promoting Virulent Envy? Reconsidering the UK's Terrorist Prevention Strategy." *The RUSI Journal* 154, no. 4: 52–8.

Blair, Tony. 1998. *The Third Way: New Politics for the New Century.* London: Fabian Society.

Blair, Tony. 2006. Speech to the "Power of One" conference at Ruach Ministries, April 3.

Bolognani, Marta and Jody Mellor. 2012. "British Pakistani Women's Use of the 'Religion versus Culture' Contrast: A Critical Analysis." *Culture and Religion* 13, no. 2: 211–26.

Bonilla-Silva, Eduardo. 2001. *White Supremacy and Racism in the Post-Civil Rights Era*. Boulder, CO: Lynne Rienner.

Bradley, Ian. 2007. *Believing in Britain: The Spiritual Identity of Britishness*. London: I. B. Tauris.

Bretherton, Luke. 2010. *Christianity and Contemporary Politics: The Conditions and Possibilities of Faithful Witness*. Chichester: Wiley-Blackwell.

Brierley, Peter. 2006. *Pulling out of the Nosedive: A Contemporary Picture of Churchgoing—What the 2005 English Church Census Reveals*. London: Christian Research.

Brierley, Peter. 2013. *London's Churches are Growing! What the London Church Census Reveals*. Tonbridge: Brierley Consultancy. <http://www.brierleyconsultancy.com/images/londonchurches.pdf>, last accessed August 16, 2015.

Brixton Seventh Day Adventist Church. 2013. "Community March 2013." Church website. <http://brixtonsdachurch.co.uk/community-march-2013/>, last accessed January 14, 2014.

Brooks, Libby. 2010. "Bethnal Green and Bow: Battle Rages in Constituency with All-Bangladeshi Field." *The Guardian*, April 19. <http://www.theguardian.com/politics/2010/apr/19/bethnal-green-bow-labour-respect>, last accessed August 27, 2015.

Browers, Michaelle and Charles Kurzman (eds). 2004. *An Islamic Reformation?* Lanham, MD: Lexington Books.

Brubaker, Rogers and Frederick Cooper. 2000. "Beyond 'Identity'." *Theory and Society* 29, no. 1: 1–47.

Bujis, Frank J. and Jan Rath. 2003. "Muslims in Europe: The State of Research." IMSCOE Working Paper.

Bunting, Madeleine. 2007. "We Were the Brothers." *The Guardian*, May 12. <http://www.theguardian.com/books/2007/may/12/religion.news>, last accessed August 11, 2015.

Burnett, Jonathan. 2004. "Community, Cohesion and the State." *Race & Class* 45, no. 3: 1–18.

Cadge, Wendy, Peggy Levitt, and David Smilde. 2011. "De-Centering and Re-Centering: Rethinking Concepts and Methods in the Sociological Study of Religion." *Journal for the Scientific Study of Religion* 50, no. 3: 437–49.

Caldwell, Christopher. 2009. *Reflections on a Revolution in Europe: Can Europe Be the Same with Different People in It?* London: Allen Lane.

Cantle, Ted. 2001. *Community Cohesion: A Report of the Independent Review Team*. London: Home Office.

Casanova, José. 2006. "Rethinking Secularization: A Global Comparative Perspective." *Hedgehog Review* 8 (Spring–Summer): 7–22.

Casanova, José. 2007. "Immigration and the New Religious Pluralism: A European Union/United States Comparison." In *Democracy and the New Religious Pluralism*, ed. Thomas Banchoff, 59–84. New York: Oxford University Press.

Certeau, Michel de. 2011 [1984]. *The Practice of Everyday Life*. Berkeley, CA: University of California Press.
Chappell, David. 2003. *A Stone of Hope: Prophetic Religion and the Death of Jim Crow*. Chapel Hill, NC: University of North Carolina Press.
Clingingsmith, David, Asim Ijaz Khwaja, and Michael Kremer. 2008. "Estimating the Impact of Hajj: Religion and Tolerance in Islam's Global Gathering." Cambridge, MA: Harvard University John F. Kennedy School of Government Working Paper.
CoDE (Centre on Dynamics of Ethnicity). 2014. "Addressing Ethnic Inequalities in Social Mobility: Research Findings from the CoDE and Cumberland Lodge Policy Workshop." <http://www.ethnicity.ac.uk/medialibrary/briefings/policy/code-social-mobility-briefing-Jun2014.pdf>, last accessed August 1, 2015.
Coleman, Simon. 2000. *The Globalisation of Charismatic Christianity*. Cambridge: Cambridge University Press.
Crick, Bernard. 1998. *Education for Citizenship and the Teaching of Democracy in Schools*. London: Qualifications and Curriculum Authority.
Crick, Bernard. 2000. *Essays on Citizenship*. London: Continuum.
Crockett, Alasdair and David Voas. 2006. "Generations of Decline: Religious Change in 20th-Century Britain." *Journal for the Scientific Study of Religion* 45, no. 4: 567–84.
Crul, Maurice and Hans Vermeulen. 2003. "The Second Generation in Europe." *International Migration Review* 37, no. 4: 965–86.
Davie, Grace. 2013. *The Sociology of Religion: A Critical Agenda*. London: Sage.
Day, Abby. 2011. *Believing in Belonging: Belief and Social Identity in the Modern World*. Oxford: Oxford University Press.
De Cordier, Bruno. 2009. "Faith-Based Aid, Globalisation and the Humanitarian Frontline: An Analysis of Western-Based Muslim Aid Organisations." *Disasters* 33, no. 4: 608–28.
DeHanas, Daniel Nilsson. 2010a. "Broadcasting Green: Grassroots Environmentalism on Muslim Women's Radio." *Sociological Review* 57, no. S2: 141–55.
DeHanas, Daniel Nilsson. 2010b. "Believing Citizens: Religion and Civic Engagement among London's Second Generation Youth." Unpublished PhD thesis. Chapel Hill, NC: University of North Carolina at Chapel Hill.
DeHanas, Daniel Nilsson. 2013a. "Keepin' It Real: London Youth Hip Hop as an Authentic Performance of Belief." *Journal of Contemporary Religion* 28, no. 2: 295–308.
DeHanas, Daniel Nilsson. 2013b. "Of Hajj and Home: Roots Visits to Mecca and Bangladesh in Everyday Belonging." *Ethnicities* 13, no. 4: 457–74.
DeHanas, Daniel Nilsson. 2013c. "Elastic Orthodoxy: The Tactics of Young Muslim Identity in the East End of London." In *Everyday Lived Islam in*

References

Europe ed. Nathal M. Dessing, Nadia Jeldtoft, Jørgen Nielsen, and Linda Woodhead, 69–84. Farnham: Ashgate.

DeHanas, Daniel Nilsson. 2014. "Immigration and Diversity in Tower Hamlets." *Public Spirit* online forum, May 6. <http://www.publicspirit.org.uk/immigration-and-diversity-in-tower-hamlets/>, last accessed August 8, 2015.

DeHanas, Daniel Nilsson, Therese O'Toole, and Nasar Meer. 2013. "Faith and Muslims in Public Policy." In *Faith with Its Sleeves Rolled Up*, ed. Daniel Singleton, 19–36. London: FaithAction.

Della Porta, Donna. 2008. "Comparative Analysis: Case-Oriented versus Variable-Oriented Research." In *Approaches and Methodologies in the Social Sciences: A Pluralist Perspective*, ed. Donna Della Porta and Michael Keating, 198–222. Cambridge: Cambridge University Press.

Dench, Geoff, Kate Gavron, and Michael Young. 2006. *The New East End: Kinship, Race, and Conflict*. London: Profile Books.

Dobbernack, Jan. 2014. *The Politics of Social Cohesion in Germany, France and the United Kingdom*. Basingstoke: Palgrave Macmillan.

Downey, Geraldine, Antonio L. Freitas, Benjamin Michaelis, and Hala Khouri. 1998. "The Self-Fulfilling Prophecy in Close Relationships: Rejection Sensitivity and Rejection by Romantic Partners." *Journal of Personality and Social Psychology* 75, no. 2: 545–60.

Eade, John. 1994a. *Routes and Beyond: Voices from Educationally Successful Bangladeshis in Tower Hamlets*. London: Centre for Bangladeshi Studies.

Eade, John. 1994b. "Identity, Nation and Religion: Educated Young Bangladeshi Muslims in London's East End." *International Sociology* 9, no. 3: 377–94.

Eade, John. 1996. "Nationalism, Community, and the Islamization of Space in London." In *Making Muslim Space in North America and Europe*, ed. Barbara Daly Metcalf, 217–33. Berkeley, CA: University of California Press.

Eade, John. 2012. "Religion, Home-Making and Migration across a Globalising City: Responding to Mobility in London." *Culture and Religion* 13, no. 4: 469–83.

Eade, John and David Garbin. 2006. "Competing Visions of Identity and Space: Bangladeshi Muslims in Britain." *Contemporary South Asia* 15, no. 2: 181–93.

Eade, John, with Ansar Ahmed Ullah, Jamil Iqbal, and Marissa Hey. 2006. *Tales of Three Generations of Bengalis in Britain: Oral History and Socio-Cultural Heritage Project*. London: Swadhinata Trust and CRONEM. <http://www.swadhinata.org.uk/document/3g-bengalis-in-uk-cover-contents-and-preface.pdf>, last accessed August 16, 2015.

East London Mosque. 2014. *East London Mosque Trust Est. 1910: Annual Review: 2013–2014*. <http://www.eastlondonmosque.org.uk/sites/default/files/documents/AnnualReview-2014_WEB.pdf>, last accessed August 16, 2015.

Ebaugh, Helen Rose. 2000. "Fictive Kin as Social Capital for New Immigrant Communities." *Sociological Perspectives* 43, no. 2: 189–209.

Economist, The. 2003. "Multicultural London: Changing Shadows: The Many Mansions in One East London House of God." December 18.

Edwards, Joel. 1993. "The British Afro-Caribbean Community." In *Britain on the Brink: Major Trends in Society Today*, ed. Martyn Eden, 107–11. Nottingham: Crossway Books.

Eickelman, Dale F. and James Piscatori. 1996. *Muslim Politics*. Princeton, NJ: Princeton University Press.

Elster, Jon. 1983. *Explaining Technical Change: A Case Study in the Philosophy of Science*. Cambridge: Cambridge University Press.

Elster, Jon. 1998. "A Plea for Mechanisms." In *Social Mechanisms: An Analytical Approach to Social Theory*, ed. Peter Hedström and Richard Swedberg, 45–73. Cambridge: Cambridge University Press.

Erlam and others v. Rahman and another. 2015. EWHC 1215 (QB). Judgment. <http://news.bbc.co.uk/1/shared/bsp/hi/pdfs/judgment.pdf>, last accessed August 28, 2015.

Fahmy, Eldin. 2006. *Young Citizens: Young People's Involvement in Politics and Decision Making*. Farnham: Ashgate.

Fazakarley, Jed. 2014. "Muslim Communities in England, 1962–92: Multiculturalism and Political Identity." Unpublished PhD thesis. Oxford: Oxford University.

Fieldhouse, Edward and David Cutts. 2007. *Electoral Participation of South Asian Communities in England and Wales*. York: Joseph Rowntree Foundation.

Flanagan, Constance A., Jennifer M. Bowes, Britta Jonsson, Beno Csapo, and Elena Sheblanova. 1998. "Ties that Bind." *Journal of Social Issues* 54: 457–75.

Flanagan, Constance A. and Erin Gallay. 2014. "Adolescents' Theories of the Commons." *Advances in Child Development and Behavior* 46: 33–55.

Foley, Michael W. and Dean R. Hoge. 2007. *Religion and the New Immigrants: How Faith Communities Form Our Newest Citizens*. Oxford: Oxford University Press.

Foner, Nancy and Richard Alba. 2008. "Immigrant Religion in the U.S. and Western Europe: Bridge or Barrier to Inclusion?" *International Migration Review* 42, no. 2: 360–92.

Foster, Alice. 2012. "New Proposed Boundary Changes Keep Streatham United." *Streatham Guardian*, October 16. <http://www.streathamguardian.co.uk/news/9987894.New_proposed_boundary_changes_keep_Streatham_united/>, last accessed August 12, 2015.

Garbin, David. 2008. "A Diasporic Sense of Place: Dynamics of Spatialization and Transnational Political Fields among Bangladeshi Muslims in Britain." In *Transnational Ties: Cities, Migrations and Identities*, ed. Michael Peter Smith and John Eade, 147–63. New Brunswick: Transaction Publishers.

References 213

Gardner, Katy. 1993. "Desh-Bidesh: Sylheti Images of Home and Away." *Man* 28: 1–15.

Gardner, Katy. 1995. *Global Migrants Local Lives: Travel and Transformation in Rural Bangladesh*. Oxford: Clarendon Press.

Gardner, Katy. 2002. *Age, Narrative and Migration: The Life Course and Life Histories of Bengali Elders in London*. Oxford: Berg.

Gardner, Katy. 2008. "Keeping Connected: Security, Place, and Social Capital in a 'Londoni' Village in Sylhet." *Journal of the Royal Anthropological Institute* 14, no. 3: 477–95.

Gardner, Katy and Abdus Shukur. 1994. "I'm Bengali, I'm Asian, and I'm Living Here: The Changing Identity of British Bengalis." In *Desh Pardesh: The South Asian Presence in Britain*, ed. Roger Ballard and Marcus Banks, 142–64. London: Hurst.

Gest, Justin. 2010. *Apart: Alienated and Engaged Muslims in the West*. London: Hurst.

Giddens, Anthony. 1991. *Modernity and Self Identity: Self and Society in the Late Modern Age*. Cambridge: Polity Press.

Giddens, Anthony. 2008. House of Lords Debate. February 2: Column 352.

Gieve, John. 2004. Letter to Sir Andrew Turnbull on "Relations with the Muslim Community." May 10. <http://www.globalsecurity.org/security/library/report/2004/muslimext-uk.htm>, last accessed August 11, 2015.

Gifford, Paul. 1998. *African Christianity: Its Public Role*. Bloomington, IN: Indiana University Press.

Gifford, Paul. 2004. *Ghana's New Christianity: Pentecostalism in a Globalizing African Economy*. Bloomington, IN: Indiana University Press.

Gilliat-Ray, Sophie. 2007. "Closed Worlds: (Not) Accessing Deobandi *dar ul-uloom* in Britain." *Fieldwork in Religion* 1, no. 1: 7–33.

Gilroy, Paul. 1987. *There Ain't No Black in the Union Jack*. London: Hutchinson.

Glynn, Sarah. 2002. "Bengali Muslims: The New East End Radicals?" *Ethnic and Racial Studies* 25, no. 6: 969–88.

Glynn, Sarah. 2005. "East End Immigrants and the Battle for Housing: A Comparative Study of Political Mobilisation in the Jewish and Bengali Communities." *Journal of Historical Geography* 31, no. 3: 528–45.

Glynn, Sarah. 2015. *Class, Ethnicity and Religion in the Bengali East End: A Political History*. Manchester: Manchester University Press.

Government Office for London. 2010. "Borough Information." <http://www.go-london.gov.uk/boroughinfo/>, last accessed April 30, 2010.

Griffin, Christine. 2005. "Challenging Assumptions about Youth Political Participation: Critical Insights from Great Britain." In *Revisiting Youth Political Participation: Challenges for Research and Democratic Practice in Europe*, ed. Joerg Forbig, 145–54. Strasbourg: Council of Europe Publishing.

Guardian, The. 1981. "How Smouldering Tension Erupted to Set Brixton Aflame." *The Guardian*, April 13. <http://www.theguardian.com/theguardian/1981/apr/13/fromthearchive>, last accessed August 1, 2015.

Hadaway, C. Kirk, Penny Long Marler, and Mark Chaves. 1993. "What the Polls Don't Show: A Closer Look at US Church Attendance." *American Sociological Review* 58, no. 6: 741–52.

Hall, Stuart. 1992. "New Ethnicities." In *"Race," Culture & Difference*, ed. James Donald and Ali Rattansi, 252–9. London: Sage.

Hamid, Sadek. 2009. "The Attraction of 'Authentic' Islam: Salafism and British Muslim Youth," in *Global Salafism: Islam's New Religious Movement*, ed. Roel Meijer, 384–403. London: Hurst.

Handlin, Oscar. 1951. *The Uprooted*. Boston: Little, Brown & Company.

Heartfield, James. 2015. "Reclaim Brixton: Gentrifiers against Gentrification. *spiked*, April 28. <http://www.spiked-online.com/newsite/article/reclaim-brixton-gentrifiers-against-gentrification/16920#.Vd8VO7xViko>, last accessed August 27, 2015.

Heath, Anthony F., Stephen D. Fisher, Gemma Rosenblatt, David Sanders, and Maria Sobolewska. 2013. *The Political Integration of Ethnic Minorities in Britain*. Oxford: Oxford University Press.

Heath, Anthony F. and Alison Park. 1997. "Thatcher's Children?" In *British Social Attitudes: The Fourteenth Report—The End of Conservative Values?*, ed. R. Jowell, J. Curtice, A. Park, L. Brook, K. Thomson, and C. Bryson, 1–22. Aldershot: Ashgate.

Hedström, Peter. 2008. "Studying Mechanisms to Strengthen Causal Inferences in Quantitative Research." In *The Oxford Handbook of Political Methodology*, ed. Janet Box-Steffensmeier, Henry E. Brady, and David Collier, 319–36. Oxford: Oxford University Press.

Hedström, Peter and Peter Bearman (eds). 2009. *The Oxford Handbook of Analytical Sociology*. Oxford: Oxford University Press.

Hedström, Peter and Richard Swedberg (eds). 1998. *Social Mechanisms: An Analytical Approach to Social Theory*. Cambridge: Cambridge University Press.

Heelas, Paul and Linda Woodhead. 2004. *The Spiritual Revolution: Why Religion is Giving Way to Spirituality*. London: Wiley-Blackwell.

Henn, Matt, Mark Weinstein, and Dominic Wring. 2002. "A Generation Apart? Youth and Political Participation in Britain." *British Journal of Politics and International Relations* 4, no. 2: 167–92.

Herberg, Will. 1955. *Protestant–Catholic–Jew: An Essay in American Religious Sociology*. New York: Doubleday.

Hill, Dave. 2015. "Tower Hamlets: The Rise and Fall of Lutfur Rahman." *The Guardian*, June 10. <http://www.theguardian.com/uk-news/davehillblog/2015/jun/10/tower-hamlets-the-rise-and-fall-lutfur-rahman>, last accessed August 27, 2015.

References 215

Hoque, Aminul. 2015. *British-Islamic Identity: Third-Generation Bangladeshis from East London*. London: Institute of Education Press, University of London.
Huntington, Samuel P. 1993. "The Clash of Civilizations?" *Foreign Affairs* 72, no. 3: 22–49.
Husain, Ed. 2007. *The Islamist: Why I Joined Radical Islam in Britain, What I Saw Inside, and Why I Left*. London: Penguin.
Husband, Charles and Yunis Alam. 2011. *Social Cohesion and Counter-Terrorism: A Policy Contradiction?* Bristol: Policy Press.
Hussain, Yasmin and Paul Bagguley. 2005. "Citizenship, Ethnicity and Identity: British Pakistanis after the 2001 'Riots'." *Sociology* 39, no. 3: 407–25.
Ipsos MORI. 1997. "How Britain Voted in 1997." IPSOS Mori website. <https://www.ipsos-mori.com/researchpublications/researcharchive/poll.aspx?oItemId=2149&view=wide>, last accessed August 11, 2015.
Ipsos MORI. 2001. "How Britain Voted in 2001." IPSOS Mori website. <https://www.ipsos-mori.com/researchpublications/researcharchive/poll.aspx?oItemId=1231&view=wide>, last accessed August 11, 2015.
Ipsos MORI. 2005. "How Britain Voted in 2005." IPSOS Mori website. <https://www.ipsos-mori.com/researchpublications/researcharchive/poll.aspx?oItemId=2252&view=wide>, last accessed August 11, 2015.
Ipsos MORI. 2010. "How Britain Voted in 2010." IPSOS Mori website. <https://www.ipsos-mori.com/researchpublications/researcharchive/2613/How-Britain-Voted-in-2010.aspx>, last accessed August 11, 2015.
Ipsos MORI. 2015. "How Britain Voted in 2015." IPSOS Mori website. <https://www.ipsos-mori.com/researchpublications/researcharchive/3575/How-Britain-voted-in-2015.aspx?view=wide>, last accessed August 11, 2015.
Izaakson, Jen. 2015. "A Review of the Judgment in the Lutfur Rahman Case." *Jen Izaakson* blog. <https://jenizaakson.wordpress.com/2015/04/24/jen-izaakson-a-review-of-the-judgement-of-the-lutfur-rahman-case/>, last accessed August 27, 2015.
Jackson, Bob and Alan Piggot. 2011. *Another Capital Idea: A Report for the Diocese of London*. London: Diocese of London. <http://www.london.anglican.org/about/another-capital-idea/>, last accessed August 16, 2015.
Jacobson, Jessica. 1998. *Islam in Transition: Religion and Identity among British Pakistani Youth*. London: Routledge.
Jenkins, Richard. 2008. *Rethinking Ethnicity*. New York: Sage.
Jeory, Ted. 2015. "Lutfur Rahman: My Part in Exposing the Mayor in the Face of Verbal Attacks and Threats." *The Independent*, April 23. <http://www.independent.co.uk/voices/my-part-in-lutfur-rahmans-downfall-in-the-face-of-verbal-attacks-and-threats-10199949.html>, last accessed August 27, 2015.

Joly, Danièle. 1988. "Making a Place for Islam in British Society: Muslims in Birmingham." In *The New Islamic Presence in Western Europe*, ed. Tomas Gerholm and Yngve Georg Lithman, 32–52. London: Mansell.

Jones, Dan. 2006. Interview. March 6. Swadhinata Trust Oral History Project. <http://www.swadhinata.org.uk/index.php?option=com_content&view=article&id=157&Itemid=189>, last accessed August 16, 2015.

Kasinitz, Philip, John H. Mollenkopf, and Mary C. Waters. 2009. *Inheriting the City: The Children of Immigrants Come of Age*. New York: Russell Sage Foundation.

Katwala, Sunder. 2008. "The Return of Enoch." *Our Kingdom*, October 28. <https://www.opendemocracy.net/article/ourkingdom-theme/the-return-of-enoch>, last accessed August 15, 2015.

Kershen, Anne. 2005. *Strangers, Aliens and Asians: Huguenots, Jews and Bangladeshis in Spitalfields, 1660–2000*. London: Routledge.

Kibria, Nazli. 2008. "The 'New Islam' and Bangladeshi Youth in Britain and the US." *Ethnic and Racial Studies* 31, no. 2: 243–66.

Klausen, Jytte. 2009. *The Cartoons That Shook the World*. New Haven, CT: Yale University Press.

Lamont, Michèle. 2000. *The Dignity of Working Men: Morality and the Boundaries of Race, Class, and Immigration*. Cambridge, MA: Harvard University Press.

Leiken, Robert S. 2012. *Europe's Angry Muslims: The Revolt of the Second Generation*. New York: Oxford University Press.

Levitt, Peggy. 2007. *God Needs No Passport: Immigrants and the Changing American Religious Landscape*. New York: New Press.

Lewis, Philip. 2007. *Young, British and Muslim*. London: Continuum.

Lindsay, D. Michael. 2007. *Faith in the Halls of Power: How Evangelicals Joined the American Elite*. New York: Oxford University Press.

McAdam, Doug. 1982. *Political Process and the Development of Black Insurgency, 1930–1970*. Chicago, IL: University of Chicago Press.

McAdam, Doug, Sidney Tarrow, and Charles Tilly. 2001. *Dynamics of Contention*. Cambridge: Cambridge University Press.

McDonald, Kevin. 1996. *Struggles for Subjectivity: Identity, Action, and Youth Experience*. Cambridge: Cambridge University Press.

McLoughlin, Seán. 2005. "The State, New Muslim Leaderships and Islam as a Resource for Public Engagement in Britain." In *European Muslims and the Secular State*, ed. Jocelyne Cesari and Seán McLoughlin, 55–69. Aldershot: Ashgate.

Macpherson, William. 1999. *The Stephen Lawrence Inquiry*. London: Home Office.

McRoberts, Omar. 2003. *Streets of Glory: Church and Community in a Black Urban Neighborhood*. Chicago, IL: University of Chicago Press.

Malik, Kenan. 2013. "In Defence of Diversity." *New Humanist*, December 11. <https://newhumanist.org.uk/articles/4477/in-defence-of-diversity>, last accessed August 15, 2015.

Marsh, David, Therese O'Toole, and Su Jones. 2007. *Young People and Politics in the UK: Apathy or Alienation?* Basingstoke: Palgrave Macmillan.

Martin, David. 2002. *Pentecostalism: The World Their Parish*. Oxford: Blackwell.

Martin, David. 2005. *On Secularization: Towards a Revised General Theory*. Aldershot: Ashgate.

Mason, Rowena. 2008. "Street Pastors Making a Difference after Hours." *The Telegraph*, June 1. <http://www.telegraph.co.uk/news/uknews/2059652/Street-pastors-help-young-revellers-on-their-way.html>, last accessed August 27, 2015.

May, Samantha. 2013. "Political Piety: The Politicization of Zakat." *Middle East Critique* 22, no. 2: 149–64.

Mead, Matthew. 2009. "Empire Windrush: The Cultural Meaning of an Imaginary Arrival." *Journal of Postcolonial Writing* 45, no. 2: 137–49.

Meer, Nasar and Tariq Modood. 2009a. "The Multicultural State We're In: Muslims, 'Multiculture' and the 'Civic Re-balancing' of British Multiculturalism." *Political Studies* 57, no. 3: 473–97.

Meer, Nasar and Tariq Modood. 2009b. *Migration, Identity and Citizenship: Approaches for Addressing Cultural Diversity in 21st Century Britain*. Bristol: University of Bristol report for the EMILIE program, European Commission.

Merton, Robert K. 1948. "The Self-Fulfilling Prophecy." *The Antioch Review* 8, no. 2: 193–210.

Merton, Robert K. 1967. *Social Theory and Social Structure*. New York: Free Press.

Miller, Donald E. and Tetsunao Yamamori. 2007. *Global Pentecostalism: The New Face of Christian Social Engagement*. Berkeley, CA: University of California Press.

Modood, Tariq. 1994. "Political Blackness and British Asians." *Sociology* 28, no. 4: 859–76.

Modood, Tariq. 2005. *Multicultural Politics: Racism, Ethnicity, and Muslims in Britain*. Minneapolis, MN: University of Minnesota Press.

Modood, Tariq. 2013. *Multiculturalism: A Civic Idea*, 2nd edition. Cambridge: Polity Press.

Mohabir, Philip. 1988. *Building Bridges*. London: Hodder & Stoughton.

Morris, Aldon. 1986. *The Origins of the Civil Rights Movement: Black Communities Organizing for Change*. New York: Free Press.

Muir, David. 2010. *The Black Majority Churches: Political and Civic Engagement*. London: SUSA. <http://www.susa.info/resources/black-majority>, last accessed August 26, 2015.

Muir, David and Ade Omooba. 2015. *Black Church Political Mobilisation: A Manifesto for Action*. London: National Church Leaders Forum. <http://www.freechurches.org.uk/Publisher/File.aspx?ID=149728>, last accessed January 11, 2016.

Murji, Karim and Sarah Neal. 2011. "Riot: Race and Politics in the 2011 Disorders." *Sociological Research Online* 16, no. 4: 24. <http://www.socresearchonline.org.uk/16/4/24.html>, last accessed April 9, 2016.

Mustafa, Asma. 2015. *Identity and Political Participation among Young British Muslims: Believing and Belonging*. Basingstoke: Palgrave Macmillan.

Nandi, Alita and Lucinda Platt. 2013. *Britishness and Identity Assimilation among the UK's Minority and Majority Ethnic Groups*. ISER Working Paper Series, no. 2013-08. <https://www.understandingsociety.ac.uk/research/publications/working-paper/understanding-society/2013-08.pdf>, last accessed August 15, 2015.

Naqvi, Ijlal. 2011. "Access to Power: Governance and Development in the Pakistani Electrical Power Sector." Unpublished PhD thesis. Chapel Hill, NC: University of North Carolina at Chapel Hill.

Norris, Pippa. 2001. "Apathetic Landslide: The 2001 British General Election." *Parliamentary Affairs* 54, no. 4: 565–89.

Norton, Anne. 2013. *On the Muslim Question*. Princeton, NJ: Princeton University Press.

Ogbu, John. 1995. "Cultural Problems in Minority Education: Their Interpretations and Consequences. Part Two: Case Studies." *The Urban Review* 27, no. 4: 271–97.

Ogongo, Stephen. 2010. "Umunna: Get Involved in Active Politics for Positive Change." *News Africa*, March 1. <http://www.africa-news.eu/component/content/article/38-africans-in-uk/361-umunna-get-involved-in-active-politics-for-positive-change-.html>, last accessed August 27, 2015.

Olofinjana, Israel Oluwole. 2010. "The History of Black Majority Churches in London." *Building on History: Religion in London* website. <http://www.open.ac.uk/Arts/religion-in-london/resource-guides/Black-Majority-Churches-in-London.pdf>, last accessed August 16, 2015.

ONS (Office for National Statistics). 2011. Census for England and Wales. <http://infuse.mimas.ac.uk>, last accessed August 27, 2015.

Osgood, Hugh. 2006. "African Neo-Pentecostal Churches and British Evangelicalism 1985–2005: Balancing Principles and Practicalities." Unpublished PhD thesis. London: SOAS, University of London.

O'Toole, Therese and Richard Gale. 2010. "Contemporary Grammars of Political Action among Ethnic Minority Young Activists." *Ethnic and Racial Studies* 33 no. 1: 126–43.

O'Toole, Therese and Richard Gale. 2013. *Political Engagement amongst Ethnic Minority Young People: Making a Difference*. Basingstoke: Palgrave Macmillan.

O'Toole, Therese, David Marsh, and Su Jones. 2003. "Political Literacy Cuts Both Ways: The Politics of Non-Participation among Young People." *Political Quarterly* 74, no. 3: 349–60.

O'Toole, Therese, Daniel Nilsson DeHanas, Tariq Modood, Nasar Meer, and Stephen Jones. 2013. *Taking Part: Muslim Participation in Contemporary Governance*. Bristol: University of Bristol. <http://www.bristol.ac.uk/media-library/sites/ethnicity/migrated/documents/mpcgreport.pdf>, last accessed August 26, 2015.

Owen, Charlie. 2007. "Statistics: The Mixed Category in Census 2001." In *Mixed Heritage: Identity, Policy and Practice*, ed. Jessica Mai Sims, 1–4. London: Runnymede Trust.

Parekh, Bhikhu. 2000. *The Future of Multi-Ethnic Britain: Report of the Commission on the Future of Multi-Ethnic Britain*. London: Runnymede Trust.

Pattie, Charles, Patrick Seyd, and Paul Whiteley. 2004. *Citizenship in Britain: Values, Participation and Democracy*. Cambridge: Cambridge University Press.

Pattillo-McCoy, Mary. 1998. "Church Culture as a Strategy of Action in the Black Community." *American Sociological Review* 63, no. 6: 767–84.

Peace, Timothy. 2013. "All I'm Asking, is for a Little Respect: Assessing the Performance of Britain's Most Successful Radical Left Party." *Parliamentary Affairs* 66, no. 2: 405–24.

Peace, Timothy and Parveen Akhtar. 2015. "Biraderi, Bloc Votes and Bradford: Investigating the Respect Party's Campaign Strategy." *British Journal of Politics and International Relations* 17, no. 2: 224–43.

Pearce, Lisa D. 2002. "Integrating Survey and Ethnographic Methods for Systematic Anomalous Case Analysis." *Sociological Methodology* 32, no. 1: 103–32.

Pew Research Center. 2006. *Spirit and Power: A 10-Country Survey of Pentecostals*. Washington, DC. <http://www.pewforum.org/files/2006/10/pentecostals-08.pdf>, last accessed August 16, 2015.

Pew Research Center. 2012. *Faith on the Move: The Religious Affiliation of International Migrants*. Washington, DC. <http://www.pewforum.org/files/2012/03/Faithonthemove.pdf>, last accessed July 24, 2015.

Phillips, Melanie. 2006. *Londonistan*. New York: Encounter Books.

Phillips, Mike and Trevor Phillips. 1998. *Windrush: The Irresistible Rise of Multi-Racial Britain*. London: HarperCollins.

Pilkington, Andrew. 2008. "From Institutional Racism to Community Cohesion: The Changing Nature of Racial Discourse in Britain." *Sociological Research Online* 13, no. 3. <http://www.socresonline.org.uk/13/3/6.html>, last accessed August 15, 2015.

Pirie, Madsen and Robert M. Worcester. 1998. *The Millennial Generation*. London: Adam Smith Research Trust/MORI.

Portes, Alejandro and Rubén G. Rumbaut. 2001. *Legacies: The Story of the Immigrant Second Generation*. New York: Russell Sage Foundation.

Portes, Alejandro and Min Zhou. 1993. "The New Second Generation: Segmented Assimilation and Its Variants." *Annals of the American Academy of Political and Social Science* 530: 74–96.

Power Inquiry. 2006. *Power to the People: The Report of Power—An Independent Inquiry into Britain's Democracy*. York: Joseph Rowntree Trust. <http://www.jrrt.org.uk/sites/jrrt.org.uk/files/documents/PowertothePeople_001.pdf>, last accessed August 11, 2015.

Purdam, Kingsley and Ed Fieldhouse with Virinder Kalra and Andrew Russell. 2002. *Voter Engagement among Black and Minority Ethnic Communities*. London: Electoral Commission.

Putnam, Robert D. 2000. *Bowling Alone: The Collapse and Revival of American Community*. New York: Simon & Schuster.

Qur'an, The. 2008. Trans. M. A. S. Abel Haleem. Oxford: Oxford University Press.

Rahman, Akikur. 2006. Interview, March 5. Swadhinata Trust Oral History Project. <http://www.swadhinata.org.uk/index.php?option=com_content&view=article&id=155&Itemid=187>, last accessed August 16, 2015.

Raymond, Catherine Zara. 2010. *Al Muhajiroun and Islam4UK: The Group behind the Ban*. London: ICSR. <http://icsr.info/wp-content/uploads/2012/10/1276697989CatherineZaraRaymondICSRPaper.pdf>, last accessed August 27, 2015.

Reddie, Richard. 2009. *Black Muslims in Britain: Why Are a Growing Number of Young Black People Converting to Islam?* London: Lion Hudson.

Riaz, Ali. 2013. *Islam and Identity Politics among British-Bangladeshis: A Leap of Faith*. Manchester: Manchester University Press.

Rogers, Andrew. 2013. *Being Built Together: A Story of New Black Majority Churches in the London Borough of Southwark*. London: University of Roehampton. <http://www.roehampton.ac.uk/uploadedFiles/Page_Content/Courses/Humanities/Being_Built_Together/Being%20Built%20Together(SB)%20web%20(D).pdf>, last accessed August 16, 2015.

Rose, Nikolas. 2000. "Community, Citizenship, and the Third Way." *American Behavioral Scientist* 43, no. 9: 1395–411.

Rosenthal, Robert and Lenore Jacobson. 1968. "Pygmalion in the Classroom." *The Urban Review* 3, no. 1: 16–20.

Roy, Olivier. 2004. *Globalized Islam: The Search for a New Ummah*. New York: Columbia University Press.

Ruach City Church. n.d. "History." Ruach City Church website. <http://ruachcitychurch.org/history/>, last accessed January 20, 2015.

Rucki, Alexandra. 2015. "Hundreds of Protesters March through Brixton to Highlight Deaths in Police Custody." *Evening Standard*, May 3. <http://www.standard.co.uk/news/london/hundreds-of-protesters-march-through-

brixton-to-show-support-for-freddie-gray-10222370.html>, last accessed August 27, 2015.
Rushdie, Salman. 1988. *The Satanic Verses*. New York: Viking.
Saggar, Shamit. 1998. *The General Election 1997: Ethnic Minorities and Electoral Politics*. London: UCL Press.
Sanders, David, Stephen D. Fisher, Anthony Heath, and Maria Sobolewska. 2014. "The Democratic Engagement of Britain's Ethnic Minorities." *Ethnic and Racial Studies* 37, no. 1: 120–39.
Satha-Anand, Chaiwat. 2004. "Praying in the Rain: The Politics of Engaged Muslims in Anti-War Protest in Thai Society," *Global Change, Peace & Security* 16, no. 2: 151–67.
Scarman, Lord Leslie George. 1981. *The Brixton Disorders, 10–12th April (1981)*. London: HMSO.
Shah, Oliver. 2009. "Chuka Umunna: 'It Would Be Spectacularly Awful If I Didn't Get Elected for Streatham'." Internet blog, February 22. <http://olivershah.wordpress.com/2009/02/22/chuka-ummuna-it-would-be-spectacularly-awful-if-i-didnt-get-elected-for-streatham/>, last accessed August 27, 2015.
Sheikh, Christine S. Forthcoming. *The American Ummah: Identity and Adaptation among Second-Generation Muslim Americans*. New Brunswick, NJ: Rutgers University Press.
Sheppard, Francis H. W. 1956. "Stockwell: Ferndale Road Area and Acre Lane." In *Survey of London. Volume 26, Lambeth: Southern Area*, ed. Francis H. W. Sheppard, 95–100. <http://www.british-history.ac.uk/survey-london/vol26/pp95-100>, last accessed August 16, 2015.
Shukur, Abdus. 2006. Interview, March 21. Swadhinata Trust Oral History Project. <http://www.swadhinata.org.uk/index.php?option=com_content&view=article&id=153&Itemid=185>, last accessed August 16, 2015.
Silver, Leon. 2014. "The Life and Legacy of the Jewish East End." *Public Spirit* online forum, May 6. <http://www.publicspirit.org.uk/the-life-and-legacy-of-the-jewish-east-end/>, last accessed August 11, 2015.
Sircar, Indraneel and Jyoti Saraswati. 2012. "From Pardesi to Desi? Cohesion, Integration, and Social Mobility amongst British-Born Asians." London: London School of Economics pilot study. <http://www.lse.ac.uk/newsAndMedia/news/archives/2012/08/FromPardesiToDesi.pdf>, last accessed 28 August 2015.
Sloam, James. 2007. "Rebooting Democracy: Youth Participation in Politics in the UK." *Parliamentary Affairs* 60, no. 4: 548–67.
Smith, Christian (ed.). 1996. *Disruptive Religion: The Force of Faith in Social Movement Activism*. New York: Routledge.
Smith, Christian with Melinda L. Denton. 2005. *Soul Searching: The Religious and Spiritual Lives of American Teenagers*. New York: Oxford University Press.

Smith, Christian with Michael Emerson, Sally Gallagher, Paul Kennedy, and David Sikkink. 1998. *American Evangelicalism: Embattled and Thriving*. Chicago, IL: University of Chicago Press.

Smith, Christian with Patricia Snell. 2009. *Souls in Transition: The Religious and Spiritual Lives of Emerging Adults*. New York: Oxford University Press.

Smith, Greg. 1996. "The Unsecular City: The Revival of Religion in East London." In *Rising in the East: Regeneration of East London*, ed. Michael Rustin and Tim Butler, 123–45. London: Lawrence & Wishart.

Solomos, John and Les Back. 1995. *Race, Politics, and Social Change*. London: Routledge.

Stampnitzky, Lisa. 2013. *Disciplining Terror: How Experts Invented "Terrorism."* Cambridge: Cambridge University Press.

Starrett, Gregory. 1998. *Putting Islam to Work: Education, Politics, and Religious Transformation in Egypt*. Berkeley, CA: University of California Press.

Steyn, Mark. 2006. *America Alone: The End of the World as We Know It*. Washington, DC: Regnery Publishing.

Swidler, Ann. 2003. *Talk of Love: How Culture Matters*. Chicago, IL: University of Chicago Press.

Talmon-Heller, Daniella. 2007. *Islamic Piety in Medieval Syria: Mosques, Cemeteries and Sermons under the Zangids and Ayyubids (1146–1260)*. Leiden: Brill.

Taylor, Charles. 1992. *The Ethics of Authenticity*. Cambridge, MA: Harvard University Press.

Taylor, Matthew. 2011. "London Riots: How a Peaceful Festival in Brixton Turned into a Looting Free-for-All." *The Guardian*, August 8. <http://www.theguardian.com/uk/2011/aug/08/london-riots-festival-brixton-looting>, last accessed August 1, 2015.

Thomas, Paul. 2010. "Failed and Friendless: The UK's 'Preventing Violent Extremism' Programme." *British Journal of Politics & International Relations* 12, no. 3: 442–58.

Thomas, Paul and Pete Sanderson. 2012. "Unwilling Citizens? Muslim Young People and National Identity." *Sociology* 45, no. 1: 1028–44.

Tilly, Charles. 1999. *Durable Inequality*. Berkeley, CA: University of California Press.

Toulis, Nicole Rodriguez. 1997. *Believing Identity: Pentecostalism and the Mediation of Jamaican Ethnicity and Gender in England*. Oxford: Berg.

Tripp, Charles. 2006. *Islam and the Moral Economy: The Challenge of Capitalism*. Cambridge: Cambridge University Press.

Turner, Bryan. 2008. "Revivalism and the Enclave Society." In *Muslim Modernities: Expressions of the Civil Imagination*, ed. Amyn B. Sajoo, 137–60. London: I. B. Tauris.

Uberoi, Varun and Tariq Modood. 2013. "Inclusive Britishness: A Multiculturalist Advance." *Political Studies* 61, no. 1: 23–41.

Urban75. n.d. <http://www.urban75.com/>, last accessed August 12, 2015.
van Heerde-Hudson, Jennifer and Rosie Campbell. 2015. "Parliamentary Candidates UK Dataset (v. 1)." <http://www.parliamentarycandidates.org>, last accessed August 27, 2015.
Vine, Jeremy and Richard Watson (presenters). 2009. "Muslim First, British Second." *Panorama* television program episode. BBC. Broadcast February 16.
Walzer, Michael. 1982. *The Revolution of the Saints: A Study in the Origins of Radical Politics*. Cambridge, MA: Harvard University Press.
Walzer, Michael. 1989. "Citizenship." In *Political Innovation and Conceptual Change*, ed. Terence Ball, James Farr, and Russell L. Hanson, 211–19. Cambridge: Cambridge University Press.
Walzer, Michael. 2015. "Islamism and the Left." *Dissent* (Winter). <https://www.dissentmagazine.org/article/islamism-and-the-left>, last accessed July 24, 2015.
Ware, John. 2015. "The Rotten Borough that Lutfur Rahman Built." *Standpoint* (June). <http://standpointmag.co.uk/node/6072/full>, last accessed August 27, 2015.
Warikoo, Natasha Kumar. 2011. *Balancing Acts: Youth Culture in the Global City*. Berkeley, CA: University of California Press.
Waters, Mary C. 1990. *Ethnic Options: Choosing Identities in America*. Berkeley, CA: University of California Press.
Waters, Mary C. 1999. *Black Identities: West Indian Immigrant Dreams and American Realities*. New York: Russell Sage Foundation.
Waters, Mary C. 2003. "Optional Ethnicities: For Whites Only?" In *Race, Class, and Gender: An Anthology*, ed. Margaret L. Anderson and Patricia Hill Collins, 444–54. New York: Wadsworth Publishing.
Watson, James L. (ed.). 1977. *Between Two Cultures: Migrants and Minorities in Britain*. Oxford: Blackwell.
Weller, Paul. 2009. *Mirror for Our Times: The Rushdie Affair and the Future of Multiculturalism*. London: Continuum.
Werbner, Pnina. 2002. *Imagined Diasporas among Manchester Muslims*. Oxford: James Currey.
Wesley, John. 2013 [1739]. *The Journal of John Wesley*. Charleston, SC: CreateSpace.
Whiteley, Paul. 2003. "The State of Participation in Britain." *Parliamentary Affairs* 56: 610–15.
Wong, Joon Ian. 2014. "The 'Canary Wharf-isation' of Shoreditch." *Londonist*, February 4. <http://londonist.com/2014/02/the-canary-wharf-isation-of-shoreditch.php>, last accessed August 8, 2015.
Wood, Richard. 2002. *Faith in Action: Religion, Race, and Democratic Organizing in America*. Chicago, IL: University of Chicago Press.
Woodhead, Linda. 2013. "Tactical and Strategic Religion." In *Everyday Lived Islam in Europe*, ed. Nathal M. Dessing, Nadia Jeldtoft, Jørgen Nielsen, and Linda Woodhead, 9–22. Farnham: Ashgate.

Woods, David, Chris Husbands, and Chris Brown. 2013. *Transforming Education for All: The Tower Hamlets Story*. London: Tower Hamlets Council. <http://www.towerhamlets.gov.uk/idoc.ashx?docid=97c33ccb-15f7-44d4-91a9-7352903051f5&version=-1>, last accessed August 13, 2015.

Worley, Claire. 2005. "'It's Not about Race: It's about the Community': New Labour and 'Community Cohesion'." *Critical Social Policy* 25, no. 4: 483–96.

Wuthnow, Robert. 2000. *After Heaven: Spirituality in America Since the 1950s*. Berkeley, CA: University of California Press.

Young Lambeth Cooperative. n.d. "What Is the YLC?" <http://www.younglambethcoop.co.uk/content/what-ylc>, last accessed August 12, 2015.

Index

Acre Lane 111, 121
activism 10, 171, 185-7, 190, 200, 206; see also pillared activism; revival activism
adhan 149
adolescents, see youth
Adventist Youth Service (AYS) 122, 123, 124, 127-8
Adventist, see Seventh Day Adventism
Afghanistan War 190, 205
African 10, 25, 90-1, 139-41; see also Pan-Africanism
Ahmed, Syed 176
Al-Aqsa Mosque 156-7
Al-Muhajiroun 193, 199
alcohol 23, 46, 104, 126, 134
Alexander, Claire 58, 87, 101
Ali, Altab 13, 132-3
Ali, Monica 13
Ali, Rushanara 204-6
alienation 27, 28, 42, 48-50
Aliens Act (1905) 82
Altab Ali Park 13, 132-3, 176, 182
ambassador (for Christ) 142, 148-9
Ammerman, Nancy 118
analytical sociology, see social mechanisms
Anansi the spider 90
Anderson, Elijah 97, 110
Angell Town 148
Anglican 121, 140
Anwar, Muhammad 57
apathy 24-5, 26-7, 28, 42, 52, 204
Arabic 155
arranged marriage 69-70, 75-6
Ash, Timothy Garton 54-5, 105
Ashimolowo, Matthew 140, 202-3
Asian 4, 5-6, 25-6, 56-7, 75, 105-6, 117, 189
  East Asia (China and Japan) 101
  prejudice against 82, 104
assimilation 11, 129-30, 197-8
atheism 2, 31, 146
Atlantic Road 94

atomism 28-9, 42-3, 48, 53, 173
authenticity 29, 61-2, 89, 93

Back, Les 58, 197
Bagguley, Paul 113
Bail, Christopher 199
Baishakhi Mela 68
Balfour, Arthur 82
Bangladesh 12, 73, 131, 134, 192
Bangladeshi Youth Association (BYA) 132
Bangladeshi:
  in British history 12-15, 130-3
  mosques 67-8
  culture 57-8, 67-76, 134, 153-4
  identity 67-8, 72-4, 134, 152-4
  political participation 38-48, 53, 132-3, 190-3
  prejudice against 132-3
  in this research study 4, 15, 30
  values 72-5, 134
Banglatown 12-13
Barelwi Islam 57, 67, 134-5
Battle of Cable Street 132
Baumann, Gerd 58
bee (Surah 16) 23-4
Bengali, see Bangladeshi
Bethnal Green and Bow 204-6
between cultures 57-8, 60, 87, 91-2, 100
Bible:
  David and Goliath 145-7
  Last Supper 126-7
  Parable of the Wheat and Tares 168-9
  Proverbs 95-6, 127-8
  Psalms 95-6
Big IFtar 175-83, 186-7
Biggs, John 206
Birmingham 57, 112, 199
Birt, Yahya 199-200
Black (racial identification) 4
  culture and achievements 9, 86
  identities 9-10, 20-1, 58, 85-8, 91-2, 93, 101-2

Black (racial identification) (*cont.*)
  problems faced by 4–5, 10, 85, 91–2, 116–17, 200
  race-based politics 14, 108, 132, 194–5, 201–2
  racism faced by 9–10, 81–3, 85, 86–8, 91–2, 104
  voting 4–5, 25, 201–2
  see also Black Majority Church; mixed race
Black Church Mobilisation: A Manifesto for Action 202–3
Black lives matter movement 203
Black Majority Churches (BMCs) 115–17, 118–21
  growth of 140
  history of 139–40
  political involvement of 138, 170–1, 200–3
Blair, Tony 83, 138, 164
Bolognani, Marta 76
boycotting products 43–8
Brem-Wilson, Thomas Kwame 139
Brick Lane 12–13, 121, 128–30, 132, 133, 192
Brick Lane (Ali) 13
Brick Lane Mosque 67, 112, 128–37
  and Bengali culture 67–8, 134, 153–4
  and Brixton Seventh Day Adventist Church compared 133–4, 136–7, 158–9
  and East London Mosque compared 67–8, 134–6, 153–4
  history of 128–32
  leadership 131–4
  as a research site 16, 118, 121, 135–6
  and youth numbers 135–7, 158–9
Brick Lane Youth Development Association (BLYDA) 152
Brierley, Peter 119, 140
British 102–7
  citizenship 6, 21, 34, 103–4, 106–7, 113, 141–3
  empire 7–8, 12, 198
  identity 21–2, 58, 82, 83–4, 102–7, 143
  nostalgia 104–5
  patriotism 21, 26, 103, 142
  political system 48–9
  see also Britishness; English
British Nationality Act (1948) 7–8
Britishness 23–4, 34, 52, 68, 102–7, 142

Brixton 9–10, 109–11, 189, 194–5
  constituencies 203–4
  as a research site 16, 109–11
Brixton Hill 143, 204
Brixton Market 9, 11
Brixton Mosque 10, 110
Brixton Pound 203
Brixton riots 9, 85
Brixton Road 89
Brixton Seventh Day Adventist Church 120–8
  and Brick Lane Mosque compared 133–4, 136–7, 158–9
  history of 121–2
  leadership of 123–4, 126–7, 200–1
  as a research site 16, 118, 120–1
  and Ruach Ministries compared 158–9
  and social change 167, 172, 200–1
  and youth numbers 123, 127–8, 158–9
brown (skin color) 88, 92, 93
Brown, Gordon 48, 146
Bunglawala, Inayat 199

Cable Street 132
Caldwell, Christopher 1, 198–9
call to prayer 149
Cameron, David 199
Camilla, Duchess of Cornwall 138
campaign badge 38, 41, 89
Campbell, Lorna 201
cannabis, *see* drugs
Cantle, Ted 5, 25–6, 84
Caribbean 4–5, 10, 25, 88, 139–41, 144–5
Casanova, José 158
Catholic 11, 129, 130
causal mechanisms, *see* social mechanisms
CD Bar (Brixton) 109–10, 114–17
Certeau, Michel de 56, 197
  strategies 56, 61, 66–8
  tactics 56–7, 60–1, 68–80, 92, 197, 198
champion (in Christ) 145–7, 148–9
change, social 165–87
Chappell, David 170
charitable giving 28–9, 40, 51, 157, 175–6, 178, 181–6
Charles, Prince of Wales 138
Choudary, Anjem 77, 199

Index 227

Christ Church Spitalfields 112
Christian:
  identities 21, 93, 95–102, 112, 161
  immigration in Europe 2, 3
  theology 126, 146–7, 202
Christianity, subjectified 159–61
Christian Street Mosque 118
church:
  architecture 121–2, 128–30, 143–4
  attendance 31, 36–7, 119, 140
  case study selection 115–17, 118–21
  culture 115–17, 170
  see also Black Majority Churches; Brixton Seventh Day Adventist Church; Ruach Ministries
Church of England 121, 140
Citizen of the United Kingdom and Colonies (CUKC) 8
citizenship:
  active 26, 84, 124, 190
  believing 189
  British 6, 21, 34, 103–4, 106–7, 113, 141–3
  "denied or delayed" 79
  dutiful 124–8, 134, 137, 158–9
  ethnic 125–6, 128, 134, 137, 158–9
  global 145
  in heaven 142–3, 145, 148–9, 153, 163–4
  imagined 113, 121, 156, 164, 190–2
  Islamized 152–8, 190–2
  nation 106–7
  responsibilities 106, 113, 159
  rights 34, 106, 113
  skills 124
  spiritual 112, 142–3, 145, 148–9, 153, 163–4
Citizenship in Britain (Pattie, Seyd, and Whiteley) 28–9, 32–6, 38–9, 43, 48, 50
civic engagement 4–5, 26, 24–30, 32, 113, 158, 163, 200; *see also* civic identification; political literacy; political participation
civic identification 28, 32, 34; *see also* citizenship
civic question 3–4, 18, 190, 200
civil disturbances (2001) 5, 25–6, 84–5
Civil Rights Movement 170–1
class, social 36–7, 69–70, 147–8, 152–3
code-switching 60, 97, 100

Commonwealth Immigrants Act (1962) 12
Communion (Eucharist) 126
community cohesion 66, 67, 83–5, 198
community organizing 187
comparative politics 195–7
Conservative Party 39, 48, 193
continuity 56–7, 60, 134–5
Crick, Bernard 26
culture versus religion 67–72, 74–6, 152–4; *see also* deculturation
Cypriot 20–1

Danish Cartoons affair 43, 44–6
Darul Ummah 56, 68, 71, 79–80, 190–1
David and Goliath 145–7
Davis, Sam 168–72, 183
de-territorialization 164
deculturation 18, 59–61, 67–72, 75–9, 107, 191
deen (Islamic way of life) 156, 157, 160
deliverance 147
democracy 185, 201, 206
demons 147
Denmark (boycotting) 43–6
devil 95–6, 169
diaspora 162
discipline 90, 105, 125–8, 172, 174
discrimination 9, 13, 87, 189; *see also* racism
diversity 10, 62, 106, 144–5, 197–8, 205
drugs 10, 14, 65, 96, 127, 189
  liberal views on 10, 203
  tackling 67, 141, 152, 159
dua (petitionary prayer) 157

Eade, John 58
East End, *see* Tower Hamlets
East London Mosque (ELM) 67–8, 138–9, 149–58
  and Bengali culture 67–8, 79–80, 107, 134–5, 152–4
  and Brick Lane Mosque compared 67–8, 134–6, 153–4
  facilities and offerings 67, 71, 149–51, 152, 159
  internal diversity of 192–3
  leadership of 71, 151–8
  London Muslim Centre (LMC) 149–52
  and Muslim identity 14, 67–8, 192–3, 152–8

East London Mosque (ELM) (*cont.*)
  opponents of 193
  as a research site 16, 118–19, 151
  and Ruach Ministries
    compared 159–64
  women's facilities 67, 150–1
education:
  achievements in 75–6, 147–8, 153
  Catholic 11
  civic 26, 113
  Islamic 134, 136
Edwards, Joel 139
elastic orthodoxy 78–80, 193
elections 4–5, 25, 39–40
  1978 Tower Hamlets election 132
  1997 general election 25
  2001 general election 25, 28
  2005 general election 25, 205
  2008 Mayor of London
    election 39–40
  2010 general election 25, 201, 204–6
  2015 general election 25, 201–2
  2015 Mayor of Tower Hamlets
    election 206
  see also voting
Electric Avenue 11, 191
embryo bill 48–50
emerging adulthood 6
Emerson, Steven 199
Empire Windrush (ocean liner) 7–9
enacted community 163–4
End Times 124, 126
Engagement, *see* civic engagement
English 103–5
  being different from 21–2, 23–4, 62, 82, 104–5
  identity 21–2, 23–4, 103–6
  language 23–4, 72–3, 135, 155, 190–1
  nostalgia 104–5
English riots of 2011 81–2, 85
Enlightenment 2
ethics of authenticity 29, 61–2, 89, 93
ethnic:
  diversity 8, 83, 197–202
  hub institutions 126, 128, 158–9
  minorities 4, 25, 105–6
  options 87, 102
  rivalry 90–1, 108
  see also new ethnicities
Eucharist 126
Europe 1–3, 198–9
evangelicalism 185–6

extremism 1, 5, 54, 56, 66, 76–7, 189, 193, 198–200, 206

Facebook 45, 66, 93, 123, 184
faith gospel 146–7
FAME (Families Against Murders
  Escalating) 174, 178
family 90, 127–8, 167; *see also* marriage
fasting 147, 162, 175, 178, 180, 182, 186, 192
50 Cent (rapper) 116–17
first generation 56–7, 67, 68, 111–13, 115–16, 118, 131–7, 158–9
Flanagan, Constance 113
foreign policy 23–4, 27, 190
FOSIS (Federation of Student Islamic
  Societies) 50
Fournier Street 11, 128–9, 130
Francis, John 140, 143, 148
Francis, Penny 140
Franklin, Kirk 115

Gale, Richard 113
Galloway, George 205
gangs 14, 91, 189
Gardner, Katy 58, 59
gathered church 163–4
Gaza War (2008–9) 156
gender 47, 69–72, 75–6, 115, 136–7
generation gap 69–72, 123, 134
gentrification 10, 14–15, 163–4, 203
Gest, Justin 27
Giddens, Anthony 29, 106
Gieve, John 26
Gilliat-Ray, Sophie 120
Gilroy, Paul 59, 82, 197
Gittens, Jamie 123–4, 128
globalization 60, 79, 140, 145, 163–4
God:
  as creator 169
  faith in 173
  honor of 155–7
  power of 21, 148, 156–7, 170
  relationship with 21, 65, 93, 96–9, 164
"God culture" 142–3, 164
Golding, Bruce 122
gospel music 93, 96–7, 115
government, trust in 27, 48–50, 189
gun and knife crime 89, 91, 98, 165–75, 187, 189, 190

Index

hadith 155, 156
hajj 178, 180
Hall, Stuart 9–10, 59, 102, 197
Handlin, Oscar 158
Hannan, Ehsan Abdullah 151–4, 157
health and wealth 147
Heath, Anthony 26
Herberg, Will 158
Hillsong Church London 119, 139–40
hip hop 14, 94–6, 98–9, 116–17, 144–5
Hizb ut-Tahrir 77, 193, 199
homelessness 175–8, 182, 186–7
Huguenot 11, 128–30
Huntington, Samuel 1
Husain, Ed 14
Hussain, Yasmin 113
hybridity 10, 58–9, 60, 79, 87, 88, 94, 100–2, 107–8, 194, 197; *see also* situational identity

identity 55–6
 between cultures 57–8, 60, 87, 91–2, 100
 continuity 56–7, 60, 134–5
 crisis 57–8, 67–8, 152–3
 deculturated 18, 59–61, 67–72, 75–9, 107, 191
 hybrid 10, 58–9, 60, 79, 87, 88, 94, 100–2, 107–8, 194, 197
 politics 83, 194–5, 205–6
 ranking exercise 55–6, 62–6, 85–8, 100–2, 134
 situational 58, 60, 79, 99–102, 107–8, 197
IF Charity 175–6, 177–8, 181, 183
iftar 175–6, 178, 180, 182, 186
imagined communion 164
immigration:
 in British history 7–15, 82, 128–31, 139, 198
 of Christians into Europe 2, 3
 fears of 9, 82
 of Muslims into Europe 1–3, 198–9
 and religion 10–12, 128–31, 139–40, 158–9, 163–4
 see also first generation
individuality 61–2, 93, 164, 194; *see also* atomism
inequality 14–15, 147–8, 198; *see also* poverty; social class
information and communication technologies (ICTs) 45–6

integration 1–4, 6–7, 26, 54–5, 79, 129–30, 197–8
Internet 45; *see also* social media
Iraq War 190, 205, 206
Irish 11
Isaacs, Les 200
Islam:
 Barelwi 57, 67, 134–5
 deculturated 18, 59–61, 67–72, 75–9, 107, 191
 as objective truth 160–2
 revivalist 14, 78–9, 107, 190–2
 Salafi 20, 60, 67
 Sufi 57, 67, 74–5, 134–5
 as a way of life 22, 156
 see also Muslim
Islam Channel 150, 176
Islam4UK 77; *see also* al-Muhajiroun
Islamic etiquette (*adab*) 155
Islamic Forum Europe (IFE) 150, 159, 193
Islamic NGOs 50, 150, 178, 181, 186–7; *see also* IF Charity
Islamic Society, *see* ISoc
Islamic Studies 195–7
Islamism 14, 205–6
Islamist, The (Husain) 14
Islamization 149–58, 160, 190–2
Islamophobia 66–7, 189, 199
ISoc (university Islamic Society) 50–2, 177, 183–6
Israel 43–8, 145–6, 156–7

Jacobson, Jessica 57, 59
Jamaat-e-Islami 67, 68
Jamaica, visit to 89
Jamaican:
 in British history 7–10
 churches 115, 120–1
 culture 81–2, 89–90, 105
 identity 62, 89–92, 103
 political participation 38–48, 53, 194–5
 prejudice against 81–2
 proverbs 90
 in this research study 4, 15, 30
 values 89–90, 105
Jamme Masjid (Brick Lane), *see* Brick Lane Mosque
Jerusalem 130, 156–7
Jesus Christ 126–7, 172
Jesus House 119, 138

Index

Jewish question 2
Jews:
   in East End history 11–12, 129–30, 132
   and Mosaic Law 126
   prejudice against 2, 82
   see also Israel
Johnson, Boris 39
Joly, Danièle 57
Jones, Su 27
Judgment Day 124, 126
justice (economic) 181, 187, 192

Keith, Michael 181, 197, 205
Kennedy, Helena 27
Kennington Park 165–9, 175
Kensington Temple 119, 139–40
Kershen, Anne 12, 158
khutba, *see* sermon
Kibria, Nazli 59
King Jr, Martin Luther 170
King, Oona 204, 205
Kingsway International Christian Centre (KICC) 119, 140
kinship 162, 180–2, 186, 192
knife crime, *see* gun and knife crime

Labour Party 39, 48–9, 83–4, 133, 181, 204–6
Lambeth 15, 140, 203–4
Lartey, E. Jones 201
lascars 12
Levitt, Peggy 112–13
Liberal Democrats 133, 206
Liburd, Mark 39–40, 141–3, 145–9, 153, 155, 164, 194
LIVE march and rally 165–75, 178, 183, 200
Livingstone, Ken 39
London bombings (2005) 5, 54, 66, 84
London Mosque Fund 149
London Muslim Centre (LMC) 67, 149–52; *see also* East London Mosque
Londoner 62
loyalty, civic 34, 54–5, 105–7, 142–3, 199

Mackenzie-Cook, Max 200
Macpherson Report (1999) 83
Madani, Abdur Rahman 71
marriage 69–70, 75–6
Marsh, David 27
Martin, David 185

Masroor, Ajmal 206
mawlid (birthday of the Prophet) 135
McAdam, Douglas 170
McDonald, Kevin 29
McRoberts, Omar 110, 148
Mecca 130, 180
mechanisms, *see* social mechanisms
media 22–3, 26, 50–1, 66–7, 85, 189, 199
Meer, Nasar 197
mega-church 119, 139–40, 163
Mellor, Jody 76
Merton, Robert 195–6
Methodist 130
methods, research 2–4, 6–7, 15–17, 20, 29–34, 55–6, 118–21, 189–90
Miah, Abjol 181–3, 205–6
Miah, Sajjad 131–4, 153–4
middle-range theory 195–7
migration, *see* immigration
Miliband, Ed 204
minaret 131, 149
mixed race 10, 20–1, 86, 88, 101, 103, 194, 204
modesty (in clothing) 115–16, 123, 127, 156
Modood, Tariq 197
moral authority 159–62
Morris, Aldon 170
Mosley, Oswald 132
mosque:
   architecture 130–1, 149
   case study selection 118–19, 121
   community role 134, 163
   see also Brick Lane Mosque; Darul Ummah; East London Mosque
Muhammad (Prophet of Islam) 70, 135
Mulberry School for Girls 204
multi-faith 51, 183–4
multiculturalism 62, 83–4, 128–9, 145, 197–8; *see also* diversity
Murji, Karim 85
music:
   gospel 93, 96–7, 115
   and identity 92–102
   industry 93, 116
   nasheeds (Muslim music) 176–7, 178
   rap 14, 94–6, 98–9, 116–17, 144–5
   R&B 96, 99, 176
   see also CD Bar
Muslim:
   as "first" identity 14, 54–6, 64–72, 75–80, 190–2, 205–6

Index

focus of public policy 82–5, 189, 197–8
immigration to Europe 1–3, 198–9
Muslim Aid 150, 178
Muslim Community Radio (MCR) 150, 162, 181–2, 205
Muslim Council of Britain (MCB) 83, 199
Muslim question 2–4, 200
Muslims Against Crusades 77, *see also* al-Muhajiroun
MySpace 93, 94
myth of return 57, 131

Naseeha (musician) 176–7, 178
nasheed 176–8
National Front 13, 132
national identity, *see* civic identity
Neal, Sarah 85
neo-Pentecostalism 120, 140–1, 163–4, 194
new ethnicities 9–10, 102, 107–8, 197
New Testament Church of God (NTCG) 112, 118
NGO 50, 178, 181, 186–7
Nigerian 90–1, 108, 138, 204
9/11, *see* September 11, 2001
"no-go" zones 199
non-religious 2, 3, 31, 65
Norris, Pippa 26
Norton, Anne 2

objectified Islam 160–2
Operation Black Vote 4, 201–2
O'Toole, Therese 27, 113

Pakistan 55
Pakistanis 57, 59, 76, 113, 180
Palestine 43–8, 156–7, 164
Pan-Africanism 10, 104, 127–8
Panorama 54, 105
"parallel lives" 5, 25–6, 84–5, 190
Parekh Report (2000) 83–4
Parekh, Bhikhu 83, 197
parish 163
Park, Alison 26
Parliament 48–9, 165–6, 201–6
participation, political 24–9, 33–4, 38–48, 49–53, 163–4, 166, 190–2, 193–5
patois (Jamaican) 81, 82, 89
patriotism 21, 26, 103, 142
Pattie, Charles, see *Citizenship in Britain*

Pattillo, Mary 170
Paul, St 142
Pentecostalism 2, 139, 160, 185, 194
differences with Seventh Day Adventism 125, 159
neo-Pentecostalism 120, 140–1, 163–4
persecution 11, 129–30
personal faith (social mechanism) 164, 172–5, 178, 185–6
Phillips, Trevor 5
picketing, *see* political demonstration
pillared activism 178–87, 192, 196–7, 205–6
Pillars of Islam 178–9, 180, 192
Pirie, Madsen 26
police 9, 81, 83, 85, 200
political alienation 27, 28, 42, 48–50
political alternatives 52–3
political apathy 24–5, 26–7, 28, 42, 52, 204
political atomism 28–9, 42–3, 48, 53, 173
political blackness 83, 194
political demonstration 38, 77, 132–3, 157, 165–7, 175, 184, 200–1
political literacy 26–8, 32–3, 35–8, 50, 193
political opportunities 179–80, 190–2
political participation 24–9, 33–4, 38–48, 49–53, 163–4, 166, 190–2, 193–5
political representation 133, 183, 201–2, 203–6
politics of fear 199–200
poverty 10, 12, 15, 37, 70, 181–3
Powell, Enoch 82
prayer (Christian) 117, 127, 168
prayer (Muslim) 22, 30–1, 51–2, 74, 130–1, 151, 154, 156–7, 160–1, 175, 179–80
prayer room controversy 51–2, 183–5, 186
preaching, *see* sermon
Prevent (counter-terrorism strategy) 5, 66, 84, 190
prosperity gospel 147
protest, *see* political demonstration
Protestant 11, 129, 130, 195
pub 21–2, 24, 104
Purdam, Kingsley 40

Qayyum, Abdul 71, 154–7, 160
Queen Mary University of London (QMUL) 22, 51–2, 183–5, 186
Qur'an 23–4, 62, 76, 155, 156

R&B music 96, 99, 176
race 9–10, 81–4, 85–8, 91–2, 108, 194–5, 203
racism 9–10, 13–14, 44, 47–8, 82, 83, 88, 104, 132
radicalization, *see* extremism
radio 150, 162, 181–2, 205
Rahman, Lutfur 181, 206
Ramadan 23, 149, 162–3, 175–6, 180, 178, 182
rap 14, 94–6, 98–9, 116–17, 144–5
Rastafarianism 10, 110, 127–8
religion versus culture 67–72, 74–6, 152–4; *see also* deculturation
religiosity 29–32, 35–6, 38, 40–2, 64–5, 188, 193
religious architecture 121–2, 128–31, 143–4, 149
religious district 110–11
remittances 56–7, 181
research methods 2–4, 6–7, 15–17, 20, 29–34, 55–6, 118–21, 189–90
Respect Party 181, 183, 205
revival activism 173–5, 178, 185–6, 196–7
revivalism (Christian) 169–71
revivalism (Muslim) 14, 78–9, 107, 190–2
Rigby, Lee (murder) 5, 54
riots (2001), *see* civil disturbances (2001)
riots (2011), *see* English riots of 2011
ritual 178–81, 186, 192
Rocky 146
Roy, Olivier 60, 78, 164
Royal Albert Hall 142
Ruach Ministries 20–1, 138–49, 194
and Brixton Seventh Day Adventist Church compared 158–9
and East London Mosque compared 159–64
history 140–1
leadership 40–1, 138, 140–1, 194
name change to Ruach City Church 141
as a research site 16, 20–1, 115–16, 118–19, 143–4
Tony Blair's speech at 152, 164
Rushdie Affair 5, 75, 83
Rushdie, Salman 13

Sabbath 122, 126, 165
Sabbath school 123–5
sadaqa 181, 186
Salafism 20, 60, 67
salat, *see* prayer (Muslim)
Santley Street 121, 122, 159, 200–1
Saraswati, Jyoti 198
Satanic Verses, The (Rushdie) 13; *see also* Rushdie affair
Scarman Report (1981) 9
second generation 2, 6–7, 206
secular 2, 185–6
   contexts 16–17, 30, 100–1
   see also atheist; non-religious
secularization 185–6, 195
segregation 5, 84, 152–3, 199
September 11, 2001 terrorist attacks 1, 66
sermon 126, 134, 135, 145–7, 154–7, 168–72
7/7, *see* London bombings (2005)
Seventh Day Adventism 120–1, 122, 126, 128, 165, 201
   see also Brixton Seventh Day Adventist Church
Seyd, Patrick, *see Citizenship in Britain*
Shadwell (as a research site) 16, 110
shahada 178
sharia law 77
Sheikh, Christine 58
Shukur, Abdus 58, 59, 133
Shuttlesworth, Fred 170
Sircar, Indraneel 198
situational identity 58, 60, 79, 99–102, 107–8, 197
Smith, Christian 160
social change 165–87
social change through ritual (social mechanism) 181, 192
social class 36–7, 69–70, 147–8, 152–3
social mechanisms 172–3, 195–7
   personal faith 164, 172–5, 178, 185–6
   social change through ritual 181, 192
   solidarity through ritual 157, 179–80, 181–3, 186, 192
social media 45, 66, 81, 93, 94, 123, 184, 199
social movements 170–1, 196
sociology of religion 195–7
solidarity through ritual (social mechanism) 157, 179–80, 181–3, 186, 192
Southwark 140
Spitalfields (as a research site) 16, 110
Starkey, David 81–2

Index

strategies (Michel de Certeau) 56, 61, 66–8
Streatham 203–4
Street Pastors 200
structural change 174, 185
subjectified Christianity 159–61
Sufism 57, 67, 74–5, 134–5
Sumner Road Chapel 139
Sunday school, *see* Sabbath school
Swadhinata Trust 132–3, 193
Swidler, Anne 100
Sylhet 12, 65, 135, 192
synagogue 130, 132

tactics (Michel de Certeau) 56–7, 60–1, 68–80, 92, 197, 198
Taylor, Charles 29
teenagers, *see* youth
TELCO (The East London Citizens Organisation) 187
territory 164
terrorism 5, 66, 84, 190, 198–200
text messages (SMS) 45–6, 81
There Ain't No Black in the Union Jack (Gilroy) 82
3 Faiths Forum 202
tolerance 62, 112–13, 180
tongues, speaking in 125, 160
Toulis, Nichole 112–13, 158
Tower Hamlets 7, 10–15
  council (local government) 66, 132–3, 181
  distinctiveness of 192, 200
  elections in 132–3, 181, 204–6
  Muslims in 7, 190–3
  schools in 11, 76
  social deprivation in 15
Transition Town Brixton 203
Tulse Hill 204
Turner, Bryan 79
Twitter 199

Uddin, Pola 176
Umbra Summus 129
ummah 46, 156–8, 162, 164, 186
Umunna, Chuka 204, 206
Universal Church of the Kingdom of God (UCKG) 118, 120
Universal Pentecostal Church-Brixton 111
Urban 75 (online forum) 203

violent crime 89, 91, 98, 165–75, 187, 189, 190
Viswanathan, Ashok 201
voting:
  low turnout 4–5, 25, 26, 39–40, 41–2, 52–3, 194
  potential solutions 201–4

Walzer, Michael 1, 113, 171
Warikoo, Natasha 99
Waters, Mary 87, 91, 102
Watson, James L. 57
weed, *see* drugs
Werbner, Pnina 162
West Indian:
  civic values 121–8, 136–7
  identity 9–10, 102
  subject to racism 82
White (racial identification):
  as different from youth identities 58, 62, 63, 86, 91–2, 104, 153
  as having ethnic options 87, 102, 105–6
  as part of youth identities 20–1, 58, 86, 88
  racism and exclusion 9, 13, 81–2, 132, 139
White, Ellen 126
Whitechapel:
  as a research site 16, 110
  St Mary's Church 132–3
  Whitechapel Road 13, 45, 67, 149, 162–3, 175
Whiteley, Paul, see *Citizenship in Britain*
Williams, Hamilton 126
Windrush, Empire (ocean liner) 7–9
Windrush generation 7–10, 139
Windrush Square 109, 201
Wood, Richard 171
Worcester, Robert 26
worship 122, 129–31, 134, 151, 165, 184

xenophobia 9, 82

Yasin, Sheikh Khalid 23
Young Foundation 202
Young Lambeth Cooperative 203
Young Muslim Organisation (YMO) 78, 159, 177

youth:
  delinquency 117, 127, 134, 152-3
  leaving religious institutions 123, 127-8, 134-6, 158-9
  low voter turnout 4-5, 25, 26
  mentoring and role models 97-8, 109-10, 116, 153, 194, 201-2
  in this research study 2, 6-7
  YouTube 184

zakat 40, 178, 181-6, 192

Printed and bound by CPI Group (UK) Ltd, Croydon, CR0 4YY